# Rebel of the Regency

# Rebel of the Regency

## The Scandalous Saga of Caroline of Brunswick, Britain's Queen Without a Crown

Ann Foster

ISBN-13: 978-1-335-00063-7

Rebel of the Regency



Hanover Square Press
22 Adelaide St. West, 41st Floor
Toronto, Ontario M5H 4E3, Canada
HanoverSqPress.com

HarperCollins Publishers
Macken House, 39/40 Mayor Street Upper,
Dublin 1, D01 C9W8, Ireland
www.HarperCollins.com

Printed in U.S.A.

For Caroline of Brunswick
and anyone else who has ever been
made to feel like you are too much

"Is it me? Am I the drama?
I don't think I'm the drama. Maybe I am.
Am I the villain? I don't think I'm the villain."

—SCARLET ENVY,
*RUPAUL'S DRAG RACE ALL STARS*,
SEASON 6

# CONTENTS

## PART THREE:
## QUEEN CAROLINE
## 187

# A NOTE ON NAMES

Because this story is about a very large family who reused the same names, there are a *lot* of people with similar names. Many of these people also have titles (like Duke, Marquess, Lady, etc.). *Burke's Peerage* is a reference invented during this book's events, and it lists the correct way to refer to people with these titles. However, to make this easier for you to read than it was for me to research, I have made the following choices, which *Burke's* would not approve:

› Royals will almost always be referred to by their title and first name (Queen Charlotte, Prince Augustus). Many of these people have secondary titles (like Prince Frederick, Duke of York and Albany). I will use only their royal title (Prince, Princess) as these additional titles change over time. Exceptions: Caroline of Brunswick is called "Caroline," and her daughter Princess Charlotte is called "Charlotte."

› Nonroyals are referred to initially by their first and last name; subsequently, they are referred to by their surname (Bartolomeo Pergami is "Pergami," Louise Demont is "Demont"). Exception: Napoleon Bonaparte will be usually referred to as "Napoleon," as that's how he is best known.

- People with titles are referred to by their title and first name (Lady Charlotte, Lady Anne), except in situations where multiple people have the same first name (Lady Charlotte Bury, Lady Charlotte Campbell) or if they are widely known by their surname (Lord Byron).

- An exception to all of the above is when a person was known by a nickname during their life, in which case, I will refer to them by the nickname.

I am using the local spellings for place names, including Braunschweig. However, as Caroline is widely known by the Anglicized name Caroline of Brunswick, I will use that spelling when referring to her or other people's English-language titles.

The monarchy discussed throughout this book was known as the Kingdom of Great Britain from 1707 to 1800, then as the United Kingdom of Great Britain and Ireland from 1801 to 1922. For ease of reading, we will most often refer to this kingdom as simply "Britain."

# Rebel of the Regency

# INTRODUCTION

May 1821. More than three hundred thousand British soldiers have died in the Napoleonic Wars, which have been going on for two decades. Napoleon was forced into exile by a coalition of nations, including Britain. Widely hated throughout Europe, news of his death is greeted joyfully by world leaders. Except for one.

Admiral Sir Edmund Nagle, an army officer serving as groom of the bedchamber to Britain's King George IV, rushes to inform him of the news.

"Sire, your bitterest enemy is dead," Nagle reports.

"Is she, by God!" replies the King.

The "she" in question was, in fact, not dead. Despite the years of war and crisis instigated by Napoleon, he was not George's most hated foe. That distinction went to his long-estranged wife, Caroline of Brunswick. By May 1821, George had publicly (and unsuccessfully) attempted to divorce her twice. She consistently refused to end the marriage, but not because she loved him. Rather, she refused to agree to his condition: that she admit to adultery. She refused to besmirch her name, and held steadfast she'd never cheated on him. And besides, as long as she remained his wife, she was Queen. Which was interesting, as by this point, she had become the face of anti-monarchist revolutionaries.

Caroline herself wasn't opposed to the concept of monarchy. She opposed George and his family, who had treated her cruelly, and appreciated the support of people who happened to hate her in-laws for their own reasons. Their marital discord and the anti-monarchist climate had delayed George's coronation. He became King in January 1820, but he still had not had his official coronation by July. Having a crown placed on his head would mark the formal investiture of a monarch, and traditionally, his spouse would also receive a crown as Queen.

George may not have been able to end their marriage, but he refused to allow her to be crowned Queen. Caroline, rumor had it, was planning to crash the crowning event. And their subjects, primed for years on tabloid coverage of their toxic relationship, were living for the drama.

Who was this woman, and how had her bad marriage gotten so tangled up in the fomenting revolution? Why was George more eager for news of her death than that of Napoleon?

The story of Caroline of Brunswick is fascinating. She was incredibly famous in her own time, yet effectively unknown in ours. The era in which she lived, the Regency, is the setting for countless novels, films, TV series, and live-action role-play settings. This era is named after its unusual ruling structure, where Caroline's husband, George, stepped in as Regent due to his father's ongoing illness. Caroline was one of the most talked-about figures of this era, with contemporaries such as Mary Shelley, Jane Austen, and Lord Byron compelled to make statements for or against her. Yet while the Regency continues to be popular today, her story is barely known.

The 2023 Netflix series *Queen Charlotte: A Bridgerton Story* tells the story of Caroline's parents-in-law, Queen Charlotte and George III. A major plot point in the first episode is the death of their only legitimate granddaughter, Princess Charlotte. Her death in childbirth leaves the British monarchy without an heir to the throne, as the dead princess had no siblings nor legitimate cousins. Left unmentioned in this episode and the rest of the series are the questions: If having heirs was so important, why didn't Princess Charlotte have any siblings? Who was this young princess's mother? Why wasn't she present in this story?

We can answer these questions by looking at the life of Caroline of Brunswick, the absent mother of this dead young princess. Much like Princess Diana a century and a half later, Caroline was selected as Princess of Wales for her seeming naïveté, youth, and fertility. Those who hoped to use her as a baby-making machine were unprepared for the ferocity of this woman, how much she loved to make a scene and refused to be ignored.

While it took several years for Diana's strong-willed personality to become known to the royal family and the general public, Caroline came out swinging immediately. She gave birth to Princess Charlotte nine months after her wedding. By that point, she was already living separately from her husband, and the monarchy-hating public had begun cheering her on at public appearances specifically because they knew the royals hated her.

The British public knew about Caroline's outsider status within the royal family because the tabloid press had just begun to wield its power. Sped up by the extremely unpopular royal family, the tabloids made Caroline a sympathetic heroine, easy for the anti-monarchists to celebrate. The royals hated her; the public hated the royals. Therefore, she became a star.

Unlike Diana, who famously stated her desire to be the "Queen of People's Hearts," Caroline took the public's love as her due and felt no need to give back in any way. Though her title as Princess of Wales and her unhappy marriage share similarities with Diana's story, Caroline's contemporary parallels are closest to the wildest members of Bravo's *Real Housewives* franchise.

Showing up uninvited at a formal event? Causing a scene? Forcing people to listen to her untalented musical performances? Consistently showing up in outfits many felt were inappropriate for a woman of her age? Caroline would have fit right into any of these shows. Without reality TV, her scandalous adventures were rapturously outlined in tabloid papers, thrilling the readers on their way to the latest antimonarchical protest.

Though people on the streets cheered for her, the monarchy loathed Caroline. And so when biographers in subsequent decades deigned to mention her, it was with a promonarchical stance making her the villain, rather than victim of the story. This bias continued through to twentieth-century biographies of her, sidestepping George's well-documented lifetime of misbehavior to portray *her* as the problem in their relationship. Were George the bad guy, then many of Caroline's "eccentric" actions would become much more reasonable: separating from him immediately, fleeing the country to stay away from him and his toxic family. To suggest that George IV is at all a sympathetic character necessitates turning Caroline into a strange blend of duplicity and chaos. After all, what other sort of woman would reject a life among the British royal family, which is still widely believed to be a fairy-tale ending to this day? For starters, a foreign-born woman with powerful relatives in another country.

Caroline of Brunswick was German; it's right there in her name. *Brunswick* is the Anglicized spelling of her hometown, the German city Braunschweig. While her cousins had culturally amalgamated themselves into English culture as the Hanover dynasty, Caroline was always an outsider. It's not ours to say whether she proudly wore this difference, but the cultural differences add a fascinating element to her story.

Eighteenth-century Britain was struggling to define its national identity following the recent loss of the American colonies. This nationalism often manifested as xenophobia against other Europeans, such as widespread hatred of the George III's Scottish-born adviser, Lord Bute. Yet this foreign-born, German-speaking woman was for a time more popular than the English-speaking family she'd married into.

Caroline also lived during a time of social change for upper-class women. She could travel independently, make her opinions known by writing letters to newspapers, and, most importantly, chart her own course. Previous royal wives like Henry VIII's abandoned Katherine of Aragon and executed Anne Boleyn could only dream of her ability to fight back.

The twenty-five years of Caroline and George's marriage were filled with social change and near-revolution. They were betrothed the year after Marie Antoinette's beheading as part of the French Revolution. London was filled with unemployed former soldiers who had recently fought on the losing side of the Haitian Revolution, and the American Revolution. Women's rights were being discussed publicly for the first time in British history, spurred on by Mary Wollstonecraft's incendiary feminist tract *A Vindication of the Rights of Women* (published two years before Caroline's betrothal). Abolitionists were advocating for the rights of Britain's Black population, and working-class men were fighting for the right to vote. With social change and revolution in the air, this was one of the only eras in British history where a story like hers could unfurl.

Despite her tabloid fame and status as a revolutionary heroine, Caroline's name faded quickly from the headlines following her death. Her strange, scandalous saga was efficiently stomped out by the legacy of her husband's reign and that of his niece, Queen Victoria, whose ruthlessly moralistic reign created the reputation of British royals as inherently ethical and respectable that we still see today. Caroline of Brunswick was, to the Victorians, simply too vulgar to fit neatly into the official historical record of the Regency era, so she was removed from it.

Until now.

# PART ONE

# CAROLINE BEGINS

CHAPTER ONE

# Once upon a Time

Once upon a time, in a fairy-tale-looking castle* in what is now Northern Germany, a teenage princess cried out in pain. Servants rushed to her side and found her writhing in agony, her face a disturbing crimson, clutching at her swollen stomach.

Caroline Amelia Elizabeth, Princess of Brunswick, had a history of illness. This was an era before people knew about germs, so diseases weren't thought of as having separate names and symptoms but were all combinations of swelling, heat, redness, and pain brought about by excessive blood. Therefore, the primary treatment for most symptoms was bloodletting. During Caroline's childhood, this would be done by lancing, using a small blade to cut into the inflamed area and letting the blood drip out into a small bowl until a sufficient amount had been removed.†

Caroline's issues were often based in her stomach, and led to her being confined to bed for long periods of time. However, that wasn't too different from her regular life, as she was

* The Grimm Brothers, whose versions of most fairy tales are still the best known, were from this region and so I mean this literally. The sorts of castles in *Grimm's Fairy Tales* would look just like the ones Caroline grew up in.

† Leeches were occasionally used, but weren't as popular yet as they would be in a few decades' time.

usually confined if not to her bedroom, then to the castle. Her mother, Princess Augusta of Great Britain, claimed that Caroline was prone to acting out when permitted in company. One might ask Augusta, "how do you know when you never let her try?" Caroline would watch from the upper windows as guests entered their palace, peering through upstairs bannisters at the parties below. She was forbidden to dance, forced to play cards with her governesses on the rare chance she had to attend a ball.

Caroline was the fourth of five children. Her older brothers Karl Georg and Georg William both had cognitive difficulties. Karl Georg was also blind. Her sister, Auguste, had been betrothed four years earlier, sent away to an unhappy marriage. Her younger brother Friedrich Wilhelm was unofficially the heir to the duchy as the only boy deemed capable of handling the responsibility. Caroline's value was entirely that of an asset to be married off strategically.

That value would be lost entirely if Caroline's reputation suffered the scandal of a premarital affair. Which is what seemed to have occurred.

"I am in labor," she told her shocked attendant, "and entreat you, Madam, to send for an accoucheur* immediately."

Instead, the attendant went downstairs† to find Caroline's mother, who was attending the ball being held in their palace. Caroline's mother, Augusta, was a popular society hostess. She was English, the sister of the current King George III, and had been sent to Braunschweig to solidify the alliance between the two regions. Upon her arrival, Augusta had quickly found that she hated German people, her husband in particular. She

* A kind of obstetrician/midwife.

† It is not known where the ball was happening when this incident occurred. I am guessing that the whole family was likely in their palace in Wolfenbüttel, where they spent most of their time.

commissioned Schloss Richmond, a summer palace for herself, in the English style. Surrounded by gardens inspired by the landscape she'd grown up with, she spent much of her time there, imagining she was back home.

One reason she was unhappy in Braunschweig was due to a habit of her husband's, Karl Wilhelm Ferdinand,* who elevated his mistresses publicly into the wifely role that Augusta wanted herself. A royal man taking mistresses was not uncommon in this era, nor in all of Western European history. Some wives were cool with this, and some were not. Augusta was among the latter. She had been raised in a strictly religious household, and she absorbed this conservative way of life as the direct route to Heaven. To her horror, Braunschweig was not like that, from her husband's casual adultery to the laissez-faire vibes of the courtiers. Perhaps this is why Augusta kept Caroline sequestered. She wanted to ensure her daughter did not stray from the morally superior way Augusta lived her life and wanted to keep her from the racy Braunschweig court.

So imagine her shock when she arrived in her teenage daughter's room in time for Caroline's reveal of the cause of her medical distress: she was pregnant and in labor.

"How is this possible?" one imagines Augusta either yelling or thinking, her mind whirling to figure out how her daughter-prisoner had gotten into this state, let alone how nobody had noticed for nine months.†

The only outings Caroline was permitted was paying charitable visits to their poverty-stricken subjects, but Augusta was at a loss as to how this could have led to pregnancy. Caroline

* Karl Wilhelm Ferdinand was consistently referred to by all three names by the historians I spoke with in Braunschweig, and therefore we will refer to him by all three names in this book.

† If you want to make a drinking game, I suggest taking a shot every time it seems like Caroline might be pregnant and/or has a secret baby. It is going to happen a lot more.

had a big heart and wanted to help every unfortunate she encountered, especially children, so could she have had a relationship with a boy during one of these charity visits? Or had one of the household staff taken advantage of her romantic nature and seduced her? However it had happened, her mother would both have realized with horror that this would ruin her daughter's chances on the marriage market entirely. Virginity was a nonnegotiable part of any marriage contract; a teenager who had given birth illegitimately could surely never be taken as the wife of anyone suitably important.

Unlike the Featherington sisters in Season 3 of *Bridgerton* (who reached adulthood and get married before learning how babies are made), young women like Caroline likely would have had some knowledge about sex acts and pregnancy. Isolated though she was, Caroline was fond of reading, and likely could have gotten her hands on spicy reads of the time, such as *Pamela* by Samuel Richardson, *Moll Flanders* by Daniel Defoe, and *Dangerous Liaisons* by Pierre Choderlos de Laclos. If her parents wouldn't let her leave her room, at least she could escape through her imagination.

But back to the crisis at hand. Once her mother was on the scene and had witnessed Caroline's performance, the girl stopped shrieking and instead, a smile formed on her face. She started to laugh. Perhaps even more shocking than the reveal of her pregnancy was the way Caroline pulled a cushion out from under her dress and rubbed makeup off her face. She was not pregnant at all!

"Now Madam, will you keep me another time from a ball?" Caroline challenged her bemused mother.

Reader, would it surprise you to know that this stunt did not change her situation at all? For it did not. If anything, this proved to Augusta that she was warranted in keeping Caroline locked up.* The amount of work she put into this scheme is also notable. Where had she procured the makeup to make her look so ill? When had she witnessed a woman giving birth in order to pantomime it so accurately? Did she have a cover story ready to explain how she had become pregnant?

While this performance did not affect her parents' willingness to allow Caroline to attend social events, word did spread of her alleged pregnancy. When Caroline later fell ill for real and had to leave town for treatment, rumors spread that she had been taken away to secretly give birth.† Pregnancy rumors would follow her throughout the rest of her life and, yes, did come to affect her marriage prospects. Upon hearing stories of her labour prank, some contemporaries spread rumors that she was insane.

Insane? Or was she just an extremely bored teenage girl with a flair for the dramatic who had far too much time on her hands? Caroline's education had never been a priority to her mother (who oversaw it, as much as it was), and she was left mostly free-range to entertain herself. The more she was left to herself, the more her imagination seemed to soar.

Aside from novels, Caroline would also have grown up hearing the stories of her scandalous relatives. Her maternal aunt, Caroline Matilda, died in exile after attempting to take over Denmark with her physician lover when Caroline was seven years old. From this tragic example, Augusta would have confirmed her idea that women should stay in an unhappy marriage, as to stray is far too dangerous, and after all, life isn't meant to be enjoyable. On the other hand, Caroline may have

---

* Did Caroline really think this would improve her situation? Unclear. She often felt the solution to her problems was a dramatic stunt, but this one may have been more to ruin her mother's evening rather than to convince her to allow Caroline more freedom.

† Drink!

learned from her aunt's example that if you're going to pursue a life of sensuality, you better do it outside the royal court.

Still, young Caroline dreamed of the day she could get married to a man who would sweep her off her feet, rescue her from her unbearably small town, and open up her life to one of travel and adventure. More specifically, she imagined leaving the oppressive isolation overseen by her dominating mother.

Braunschweig was a bustling merchant town, founded seven hundred years prior by Caroline's medieval ancestor Henry the Lion. Henry was part of the Guelph dynasty, a powerful family that ruled much of Central Europe and Italy. He married Princess Matilda of England, which meant that Caroline was also descended from previous English monarchs. Henry had chosen Braunschweig as the capital of his kingdom, and his descendants oversaw this region as Dukes for centuries. None of them had married English royals until Caroline's father married her mother.

Caroline's uncle, George III, also took a German bride: Queen Charlotte. Charlotte felt very firmly that women should stay modest and out of the way; as conservative as Augusta was, Charlotte was even more so. Augusta was also known to state a desire to involve herself in politics; Charlotte, who firmly believed women should be seen and not heard, disapproved. When handsome Karl Wilhelm Ferdinand arrived in London in 1764 to marry Augusta, the public enthusiastically welcomed the swashbuckling war hero. Both Charlotte and George disapproved of his flashy ways.

A few days after the wedding, all four royals went to the opera at Covent Garden. The public, aware from newspapers and pamphlets that George and Charlotte hadn't treated their new brother-in-law warmly, loudly cheered for the newlyweds and were silent at the entry of the King and Queen. Horace Walpole, a prolific writer of the era, recorded that "In the middle of the play, [Karl Wilhelm Ferdinand] went to be elected a member of the Royal Society, and returned to the theatre, when the applause was renewed."

Despite the public's adoration, Karl Wilhelm Ferdinand was so disgusted by the way he was treated by the royals that he never again returned to Britain. Augusta also stayed away until she was summoned in 1772 by her dying mother (also named Augusta). Even though the elder Augusta had specifically requested her presence, George and Charlotte continued to ice her out. The younger Augusta was not permitted to stay in a royal residence, and George refused her request to be chief mourner at their mother's funeral. Moral of the story: British royals hold a grudge.

Sometimes, a shared enemy brings a couple closer; such was not the case for Augusta and Karl Wilhelm Ferdinand. Caroline recalled being a "shuttle-cock" between her warring parents: "when I was civil to the one, I was scolded by the other."

Caroline doesn't seem to have found respite among her siblings, none of whom she was close to in childhood. Her sister Auguste was four years older than her, and of an entirely different disposition. Each girl inherited a different part of their mother's personality. While their mother was conservative, she could be overly talkative and fond of gossip, like Caroline. Auguste took after their mother's better behaved aspects, doing what was expected of her and staying out of trouble. After being sent away at age fifteen to marry twenty-six-year-old Duke Frederick of Württemberg, the sisters do not seem to have corresponded (though Auguste kept in touch with their mother).*

---

* Auguste's marriage was unhappy, and she attempted to divorce her abusive husband several times before successfully leaving him. She had issues with menstruation, and died at age twenty-three from blood loss.

Caroline, by now nineteen, continued to live with her parents, witnessing daily the results of an unhappy arranged marriage between two people who hated each other. Her mother and father lived mostly separate lives, with Caroline and her remaining siblings treated as afterthoughts. She spent most of her time with elderly governesses, only able to experience the mini-Versailles atmosphere of Braunschweig royal court when she snuck away.

An important part of her education and interest was learning the history of her famous ancestor, Henry the Lion. He had commissioned a bronze lion statue, in the style of Italian sculpture, whose silhouette became the heraldic symbol of himself and the city. The lion (which looks more like a dog than a lion to modern eyes) was everywhere as Caroline grew up there: on statues, decorated door-knockers, and most commonly of all, in Braunschweiger Dom, the immense cathedral he had commissioned centuries earlier. When one of Caroline's tutors quizzed her on where lions lived in the world, she replied, "In the heart of a Brunswicker."

Caroline was a curious, intelligent, and incredibly bored young girl who entertained herself by instigating arguments with her tutors and governesses. Her religious education was vague, as her mother wanted to keep her options for marriage open to either a Catholic or a Protestant, and so she settled on neither. Of her lessons, Caroline most enjoyed music and was skilled at the harpsichord. Like all German princesses, she had a working knowledge of English in case she wound up marrying one of her English relatives. She was also fluent in French and German. Her English grammar and spelling were never excellent, and she relied on servants and secretaries to write most of her correspondence from dictation.

Descriptions of young wealthy girls are often flattering, as are their portraits. So it is with young Caroline, described by a visitor named Sir Jon Thomas Stanley as "the lively, pretty Caroline, the girl my eyes had so often rested on, with light and powdered hair hanging in curls on her neck, the lips from which only sweet words seemed as if they could flow, with looks animated, and always simply and modestly dressed." She was certainly pale, with blond hair, brows, and lashes like most members on both sides of her family.

She also had a spirited and indomitable personality. Her mother noted, "Caroline is born for adversity; nothing would destroy her." Like her mother, she was often overly casual in formal situations and tended to talk more than most people wanted to listen as well as to gossip and overshare, perhaps in her attention-starved way.

She also had, from a young age, a devotion to charity, especially involving children. While in Braunschweig, she spent time with young protégés from the local community, children she had met during her aforementioned charitable visits to local homes. Above all else, she looked forward to one day raising children of her own.

There were virtually no happy marriages in Caroline's family tree, nor were there stories of women contentedly living independently. She knew that her fate was to marry someone arranged for her and to make the best of it. Yet as the years passed, Caroline continued on as a single woman. Her parents had been approached by some candidates for her hand, but either they or Caroline had turned each down. One candidate she turned down was Prince George of Darmstadt, as she found him "false," which in this context meant she suspected he was not being genuine with her about his personality or intentions. She also believed the rumors that he had previously been a lover of Marie Antoinette, which rather than making him seem glamorous by association rather hinted at some level of depravity. She wanted to marry, but she wanted it to be someone whose company she could enjoy.

Caroline was alleged to have had a chaste affair with a low-born German soldier, Major von Tobingen, who wore a large amethyst brooch widely believed to have been given to him by Caroline. There were also rumors that she had been involved with an Irish soldier.* Nonetheless, by age twenty-six, she was still living in an extended infancy, kept away from society by her mother.

Yet everywhere she looked were reminders of the wider world she longed to visit. She hated being stuck in Braunschweig, telling a friend later, "I was sick, tired of it." The dining room of her mother's English-style summer palace, Schloss Richmond, was decorated in the style of the recently discovered remains of the destroyed ancient town of Pompeii. Edward Gibbon's multivolume work *The History of the Decline and Fall of the Roman Empire* so affected popular culture of this era that people named Mary changed their name to Maria to lean into the classic vibes. Women's fashion was influenced by the ancient statues and artwork being discovered, as dresses moved toward filmy, thin fabrics and hairstyles changed to natural colors styled atop the head in curls. While this style was most flattering on slender women, Caroline was fond of how the silhouette fit her voluptuous figure and sizable chest. If she couldn't visit the Mediterranean, she would dress as though she were there.

When she attended church services in Braunschweiger Dom, she would be surrounded by stunning decor commissioned centuries earlier by her famous ancestor, Henry the Lion. His travels around the Mediterranean and the Levant were referenced in the art and architectural choices of the building. Yet Caroline grew to age twenty-six, still stuck in

---

* As we will continue to see, Caroline was especially drawn to men in uniform.

her hometown, unable to live out her dreams of travel and romance.

Until one day, a marriage proposal arrived. Unfortunately for her, it came from her first cousin, George Augustus Frederick, the Prince of Wales.

CHAPTER TWO

# We Need to Talk About Prinny

George Augustus Frederick, Prince of Wales, was the eldest child of George III and Queen Charlotte of Great Britain and Ireland. Luckily for us, he was known by the nickname "Prinny," which we will use for the rest of this book, thus avoiding having one more person named George to contend with.

At around the same time his teenage cousin Caroline was feigning pregnancy to teach her parents a lesson, twenty-two-year-old Prinny was applying face paint for his own manipulative purposes. To understand why he was doing this, we need to look at what kind of guy he was, specifically his dating history.*

When you're the Prince of Wales, you don't just date. You take mistresses. And when you're Prinny, you take a lot of them. His friend Richard Brinsley Sheridan remarked that Prinny "was too much a ladies' man ever to become the man of one lady." Prinny was always emotionally demonstrative, as young men were encouraged to be in this era. He felt things

---

* According to *Royal Mistresses and Bastards* by Anthony Camp, thirty-six women were rumored to have been involved with Prinny by the time he was betrothed to Caroline. We won't talk about all of them, just the most notable ones.

deeply, was quick to laugh and quick to cry. He lived in the manner advocated by his acquaintance, the poet Lord Byron, who wrote:

"The great object of life is sensation—to feel that we exist, even though in pain. It is this 'craving void' which drives us to gaming—to battle—to travel—to intemperate but keenly felt pursuits of every description, whose principal attraction is the agitation inseparable from their accomplishment."

This passage is equally true of Byron himself, Prinny, and what became known as the Byronic Hero, a young man prone to dramatics, who claimed to feel everything very deeply and yet was really quite shallow. The nearest contemporary comparison is early 2000s emo culture, in which the most important thing was to seem like you were feeling things very deeply, in a performative manner. Like Byron, Prinny's allegedly deeply felt personal emotions did not extend to any sort of empathy for the way he treated the women in his life.

Walpole reported that by age eighteen, Prinny, along with his younger brother Frederick, "drank hard, swore, and passed every night in brothels . . . He passed the nights in the lowest debaucheries, at the same time bragging of intrigues with women of quality, who he named publicly."

Prinny enjoyed beautiful and luxurious things: fashion, food, art, wine, and decor, especially anything gold-plated. This contrast with his frugal, prim parents was a frequent topic of political cartoons from his teenage years onward. His parents were so austere they wouldn't even add sugar to their tea; Prinny oversaw great feasts, and his preferred beverage was cherry brandy.

One of his greatest passions was beautiful, voluptuous, older women who would dote upon him. As he was the Prince of Wales, they were often powerless to resist his advances, though, according to his friend the Duke of Wellington, "No woman was ever really attached to him . . . he was too selfish."

Prinny first fell in love at age sixteen. The object of his affection was Lady Mary Hamilton, his younger sisters' twenty-three-year-old governess. He sent her a love letter every day for seventy-five days, and although she did not respond, his method of seduction was established. For the rest of his life, his go-to move would always be to inundate his crush with the intensity of his emotions via letter, hoping to eventually break down her defenses.

Moving beyond the women he encountered around the royal palaces, the teenage Prinny's next major crush was twenty-four-year-old actress Mary Robinson, known as Perdita. This nickname came from her iconic performance as said character in an adaptation of Shakespeare's *A Winter's Tale.* After seeing one of her performances, Prinny began his usual deluge of letters, this time including sending her a lock of his hair and a miniature painting of himself. He begged her for an in-person meeting, where he suggested she arrive dressed as she had in the play, in boy's clothes.

As he had not yet come of age, Prinny did not have access to his own money so he couldn't offer her any. He therefore promised to give her £20,000 in four years, or around $4 million today, if she became his mistress. Perdita agreed, leaving her husband and retiring from acting to be with him. After only a few months, Prinny grew bored with her and ended things. She demanded payment, and Prinny was forced to plead with his father for a loan.

His next affair was with the Scottish courtesan Grace Dalrymple Elliott, who was seeing other men at the same time. She became pregnant during their affair and claimed Prinny was her child's father. She named the girl Georgiana in his honor. Prinny denied this claim, stating baby Georgiana's complexion was too dark for her to be his descendant.* Another potential illegitimate child was born in 1784, when Elizabeth Lamb, Viscountess Melbourne, had a son named George. Prinny was named his godfather but never acknowledged him as his son.

When he turned twenty-one, Prinny finally acquired access to his own funds. George III was shocked when Prinny requested £100,000 per year, around $19 million today, to cover his extravagant lifestyle. Parliament eventually gave him half this amount, along with the revenues of the Duchy of Cornwall—a lump sum of £60,000, or $12 million today—and his late grandmother's former residence, Carlton House in Westminster. Prinny quickly spent the lump sum and blew through the rest of his money on household renovations, gambling, horses, women, art, and food. Two years after being given this money, he was nearly £270,000, or $52 million today in debt, most of which Parliament agreed to pay off.†

Though he had more independence from his parents, Prinny's life was still heavily controlled by his role as Prince of Wales. He desperately wanted to travel to continental Europe as other young men did, to experience different cultures (and voluptuous, older women). As heir to the throne, he was forbidden from leaving the country, which also put a stop to his other dream of taking an active role in the military. Not able to join an actual brigade, Prinny instead dressed as though he were a soldier, wearing tasseled boots, tight-fitting pantaloons, and decorated coats. While he may not be able to step onto a battlefield, he merged his longing for military service

* In his very slight defense, Prinny's family was startlingly blond and pale and Dalrymple had other dark-haired lovers at the same time she was with him.

† Within ten years, he owed a further £630,000, $127 million in today's money.

with his love of aesthetics and designed new stylish uniforms for his regiment.*

Like Caroline dreaming of traveling to far-off lands, Prinny decorated the interiors of Carlton House to resemble what he'd heard about palaces in other countries. He covered nearly all visible surfaces in gold, including furniture, bookshelves, sculptures, and the pedestals the sculptures stood upon.

Within this pleasure dome, Prinny led a life of constant partying. He lounged in bed much of the day, inviting guests to visit him as he rested, and then partied with them into the night. He continued to seduce women who had three main things in common: they were independent-minded, several years older than him, and had the curvaceous figure he clearly preferred.†

Prinny was by now living with the health concerns that would affect him for the rest of his life. He gained a large amount of weight in his early twenties, about which he was self-conscious and forbade portrait painters from accurately portraying. His friends knew his sensitivity to his size and never mentioned it, though while on the outs with Prinny, one man stung him by referring to him as their "fat friend."

Like Caroline, Prinny had chronic stomach pains, which he dealt with by consuming large amounts of alcohol‡ as well as up to two hundred drops of laudanum per day. A popular all-purpose treatment during this era, laudanum was a tincture combining opium with alcohol and other proprietary ingredients various physicians chose to include, like honey,

* Later in her life, Caroline would note that Prinny "understands how a shoe should be made or a coat cut. . . and would make an excellent tailor, or shoemaker or hairdresser but nothing else."

† Sigmund Freud would want me to note here that his mother, Queen Charlotte, was very thin, felt that being demure was the most important trait in a woman, and had always been emotionally withholding toward him.

‡ Which some doctors at the time advised could help improve one's health.

camphor, or cloves. As with all opiates, this worked as a painkiller, relaxant, and sleep aid. It was also used to help babies with teething pain, people with PMS and menopause pain, and even as a cough suppressant. Perhaps unsurprisingly, this led to widespread addiction issues for its many users, including Prinny.

Prinny soon found another addiction: twenty-six-year-old Catholic widow Maria Fitzherbert.* Prinny spotted her at the opera and, as Fitzherbert was leaving, Prinny approached her escort and demanded, "Who the devil is that pretty girl on your arm?" And thus was Prinny introduced to the love of his life.

Five years older than him, Fitzherbert had only recently returned to town after losing her second husband. She was a very devout Catholic and refused to become his mistress or to have sex with him without marriage. In this way, she was emulating the actions of Anne Boleyn, who refused to have sex with Prinny's predecessor, Henry VIII, unless they married. Henry VIII was stymied in his pursuit of Boleyn because he was already married to Katherine of Aragon whereas Prinny wasn't able to marry Fitzherbert because he was not yet twenty-five and required his father's permission to marry. And George III would never permit him to marry a commoner, let alone a Catholic,† especially as the King was at the time very angry with Prinny. His ongoing debts to clothiers, jewelers, and wine merchants had meant the King had to approach Parliament to forgive Prinny's debts and increase his royal allowance. This money would ultimately come from

---

* Born Mary Anne Smythe, she was one of the many women who adjusted their names to Maria due to the late eighteenth-century Ancient Roman trend.

† The 1701 Act of Settlement forbade the heir to the throne from marrying a Catholic. If Prinny did so, he would be removed from the line of succession and would never be King.

the taxpayers, another reason for the public to hate the shopaholic Prince of Wales.

Prinny, of course, didn't care about any of this. He wanted Maria Fitzherbert, and if he needed to fake a marriage, he was willing to do so. When his usual love bombing didn't work, he channeled his inner Romantic poet and elevated matters to a series of alleged suicide attempts, which leads us to the beginning of this chapter, with Prinny putting on stage makeup.*

As Caroline had done in her fake labor scheme, Prinny applied pale makeup to his face to add a deathly pallor. Having been bled by his doctor for his anxiety, Prinny wrapped these bleeding wounds in cloth as evidence that he had stabbed himself. He lay in bed, looking as tragic as he could, and Fitzherbert was summoned to his bedside. He croaked out that he might die from the wounds and could only recover if she agreed to marry him. Fitzherbert, displaying extremely good instinct, demanded to have an unbiased doctor examine the wounds to confirm that they were the result of a suicide attempt. Prinny evaded this request with his usual dramatic gaslighting, claiming it would be inappropriate for him to be seen by an unfamiliar doctor, and maybe just to get out of there, Fitzherbert finally capitulated and agreed to marry him.

The marriage ceremony was held in secret on December 15, 1785, in her drawing room. In the eyes of the Catholic church, the marriage was valid. But according to English law,† it was not. Following a short honeymoon outside the city, the couple returned and were rarely apart. Fitzherbert was often illustrated alongside Prinny in the cartoons that mocked him in broadsheets and newspapers sold on the streets. All

* Perhaps he had learned how to use this makeup from his time with Perdita.

† The aforementioned laws forbidding Prinny from marrying without his father's permission, and forbidding him from marrying a Catholic.

of society assumed she was his mistress, and rumors spread that they planned to marry or had already. Only the few witnesses to their secret ceremony knew that the marriage had already occurred.

They did not cohabitate, but Fitzherbert attended all soirees at his home as the de facto mistress of Carlton House. Prinny paid for her to maintain her own town house nearby, meaning that he was now paying for the ongoing remodeling and running of two houses, hiking his debts up even more. In 1786, he was forced, again, to turn to his father for help as his debts now amounted to £269,878 ($53 million in today's money) as reported on an incomplete spreadsheet that didn't explain where much of it had gone.* George III refused to pay this debt, and Prinny, enraged, decided to move to the countryside to live a more frugal lifestyle.

He paused all work on his home and Fitzherbert's, sold many of his possessions, fired many of his servants and reduced the wages of those who remained. His new residence would be in the seaside town of Brighton, which was just making its name as a holiday destination for London's wealthy. People like Prinny, who lived with chronic illness, had been drawn to the seaside town ever since a book was published in 1750 extolling the health-giving properties of Brighton's seawater both for bathing in and for consuming. After Prinny relocated, other nobles and aristocrats flocked there. Between 1789 and 1801, the population of the town quadrupled and continued to grow for the next three decades.

Many people came to Brighton hoping for face time with the Prince. Despite his frugal aspirations, Prinny quickly began renovating the small house he had rented into a mansion

* Likely because Prinny did not get itemized receipts from the racetrack bookies and brothel owners whose businesses he frequented.

and, ultimately, into what is now known as the Royal Pavilion. Demonstrating his love of non-English architecture, the building today is an Asian-influenced domed pleasure palace, like the tackier sibling of the Taj Mahal. The interiors were inspired by Chinese design, along with Prinny's beloved gold-plated everything, and can be seen today as a case study in cultural appropriation.

The time at Brighton, with Fitzherbert's calming presence, seems to have been among the happiest eras of his life. Certainly, he had fewer flare-ups of his health concerns at this time. Yet, as ever, his debts continued to mount. Years of bad credit meant that no moneylender in the country would offer him even a small loan. Nor would any outside the country, after he and his brother Prince Frederick ruined a Jewish banking firm in the Hague by refusing to repay their loan. Prinny persuaded a friend to bring a motion to Parliament that the King must pay off Prinny's debts. Some members hesitated to pass this bill due to the rumors of Prinny's secret marriage. Desperate for money, Prinny officially denied his marriage to Fitzherbert to convince them to push through his motion. Fitzherbert was privately devastated but remained devoted to him even as he continued to pursue other women.

Other lovers of George's came and went, but Frances Villiers, Countess of Jersey, was the first real threat to Fitzherbert's influence. Lady Jersey, who we'll shorten to just Jersey for ease, was a married grandmother in her forties, just one year older than Fitzherbert. Her husband had held various posts in Prinny's household, and she was well-known around the royal court. Some historians suggest that Queen Charlotte wanted to separate Prinny and Fitzherbert (who she still thought was merely a mistress) in order to free him for marriage to a foreign royal. To that end, the Queen may have encouraged or hired Jersey to pursue Prinny, placing the Queen's ally in place as mistress. Whatever the Queen's involvement in these relationships truly was, Jersey did quickly supplant Fitzherbert.

Jersey convinced Prinny that his unpopularity with the public was due to Fitzherbert's religion. Without her, he could be as widely beloved as his father. All he needed to do was marry an appropriate princess. His debts would be cleared and his life would become much less challenging. Her arguments were appealing to the vain, cash-strapped Prince.

George III had also made it clear that he wouldn't encourage Parliament to clear Prinny's debts until he was married.* His marriage to an acceptable bride was the only way that Parliament would agree to pay his enormous debts. This wife had to be Protestant and royal, which meant in the current landscape of mostly Catholic continental Europe, she must be a German princess. Rumor has it that Jersey was the one who suggested Caroline of Brunswick, a sheltered girl who would not threaten Jersey's domination over Prinny. Or perhaps Prinny chose Caroline, knowing that his father would quickly agree to the match as she was his sister's daughter. The quicker the marriage, the sooner Prinny's debts could be repaid.

Usually, royal marriages were carefully considered, with the potential brides vetted by diplomats who visited to learn about their personalities. But Prinny didn't give much thought to who he would marry, feeling that "one damn frow† was as good as another." He was impatient to have his debts paid, and

* Which was becoming more important because Prinny's younger brother, Prince Frederick, and his wife, Frederica, had not had any children and it did not seem like that was in the cards. So it was up to Prinny to father an heir to the throne.

† He meant "frau," the German word for woman; he knew he had to marry a German princess.

so he informed his parents of his choice of bride one month after breaking up with Fitzherbert.

George III wrote that he heartily approved of the match, provided that Prinny planned "to lead a life that would make him appear respectable, and consequently render the Princess happy." Prinny lied that he would, and the King sent word to Caroline's parents in Braunschweig to gain their approval and blessing.

Queen Charlotte, however, did not approve. She wanted Prinny to marry her niece Princess Louise of Mecklenberg-Strelitz, who was younger and more beautiful than Caroline.* Charlotte also had secret information about Caroline's bad reputation, as she had once been considered as a potential wife to one of Charlotte's brothers. Charlotte had learned enough at that point to inform her brother Caroline was "a woman I do not recommend at all," due to her rumored teenage pregnancy and alleged insanity. But she did not raise these doubts to George or Prinny, as Charlotte had long ago pledged to remain uninvolved in political matters.

And so a delegation was sent to Braunschweig to escort Caroline back to London for her marriage to Prinny.

---

* Which could be another reason Jersey lobbied hard for the plainer Caroline, who she saw as less of a potential rival.

CHAPTER THREE

# Princess Lessons

Caroline was thrilled at her future as Princess of Wales, wife of Prinny. She hadn't met him, but had heard good things and was excited to begin her new life. She wrote at this time:

> *His generosity I regard, and his letters bespeak a mind well cultivated and refined. [George III] is a good man, and I love him very much, but I feel that I shall never be inexpressibly happy. Estranged from my connections, my associations, my friends, all that I hold dear and valuable . . . I fear for the consequences. Yet I esteem and respect my intended husband, and I hope for great kindness and attention. But, ah me! I say sometimes, I cannot now love him with ardour. I am indifferent to my marriage, but not averse to it; I think I shall be happy, but I fear my joy will not be enthusiastic. The man of my choice I am debarred from possessing,* and I resign myself to my destiny . . . I shall strive to render my husband happy, and to interest him in my favour.*

Thomas LeMesurier, a British lawyer sent to assess Caroline, reported that she was "a very handsome woman, at least

* One of her lowborn soldier suitors, presumably.

as far as we could judge through a very thick layer of rouge* which was on her cheeks. Her eyes have much fire, but there is a sharpness in them which was not pleasant." He also reported that she was carefully monitored by chaperones.

As Caroline intensified her English language lessons, officials in Braunschweig and London made preparations for her journey. Even with careful planning, she would be journeying near many battlegrounds of the ongoing wars of the French revolutionary period, and the trip needed someone trustworthy and knowledgeable as a leader. English diplomat James Harris, Baron Malmesbury,† was chosen.

Malmesbury was a trustworthy man who had been involved in several fraught diplomatic negotiations throughout Europe. For this mission, George III directed him solely to request Caroline's hand on Prinny's behalf and escort her safely back to England. He was not to assess her suitability as Princess of Wales nor to report on her behavior. It was hoped this task would be completed in a few weeks.

Malmesbury arrived in Braunschweig on November 20, where he was warmly greeted by Caroline's parents. He maintained a detailed diary of this experience, and his first impression of Caroline sounds similar to a man inspecting a new farm animal:

> *Pretty face—not expressive of softness—her figure not graceful—fine eyes—good hand—tolerable teeth, but going—fair hair and light eye-brows—good bust—short, with what the French call*

---

* Caroline preferred bold blush on her cheeks as a signature look. The beauty standard of this time was one of "rosy-cheeked" youth, which shows how on-trend she was.

† Later, he was named Earl of Malmesbury and is mostly written about by that title. So, we will call him Malmsbury in this book.

*les epaules impertinentes.* Vastly happy with her future expectations.*

As we will often see in this story, spending time with Caroline changed his initial impressions as she won him over. A few days after this first meeting, he noted, "Princess Caroline improves on acquaintance, is gay and cheerful, with good sense."

Caroline was presented with a portrait of Prinny, which, in his family's long tradition of catfishing foreign fiancées,† made him look much slimmer and more handsome than he really was. Prinny, impatient for the increase in cash flow his marriage to Caroline would bring, sent a letter pressuring Malmesbury to take every shortcut possible to return to England quickly, despite the ongoing wars they would be traveling near. This suggestion was ignored.

During these early days in Braunschweig, Malmesbury recorded being taken aside by Caroline's father, who was concerned about the impending marriage. Karl Wilhelm Ferdinand knew the viper's nest Caroline would be entering and also suspected that her high-spirited personality may not fit in well. He had heard about Prinny's personality and habits and wanted Malmesbury to coach Caroline to help her succeed, noting that his daughter was not a fool but "has no judgment." He advised Malmesbury to warn her not to ask questions and to refrain from giving her opinions out loud. Caroline, her father noted, tended to forget to modify her behavior based on her audience. He also wanted Malmesbury to advise her

---

* "Impertinent shoulders," perhaps meaning that she expressed herself with her arms and shoulders in a way that Malmesbury found immodest or audacious. Her later affection for cold-shouldered gowns could mean that she enjoyed showing off this area.

† See also: Henry VIII and Anne of Cleves.

to never show any jealousy of Prinny's other relationships, and to never insult his appearance.

As her father predicted, Caroline took this advice more seriously coming from Malmesbury than she would have coming from her parents. She was eager to learn all he had to advise, which included the suggestion she remain silent on all subjects for six months after her arrival, to avoid giving any opinions on anything, not to trust anyone, and to be attentive to and respectful of Queen Charlotte. He also noted that court ladies would take the hint from her on how they should behave together, and suggested she should not be too familiar or easy with them, always bearing in mind she was Princess of Wales.*

Both of Caroline's parents, as well as other courtiers, all of whom were looking out for her, begged Malmesbury to be very strict with her and to train her to speak with more tact. She tended to talk before thinking, which could lead to misunderstandings and hurt feelings. Augusta had this same habit, and had been bad-mouthing Queen Charlotte in Caroline's presence for so long it was inevitable Caroline had absorbed some of this opinion.

But remember the free-spirited young woman we met in Chapter One? For all of Caroline's desires to improve herself, her personality was too strong to be easily tamed. Think of her like Rapunzel in *Tangled*: She grew up with mainly her imagination as a friend, was prevented from socializing with people her age, and spent her days daydreaming about what she thought the world was like. We can't know how her personality may have developed in a more nurturing environment where she was able to socialize with anyone other than

---

* He also cautioned her not to allow them to manipulate her. The vibes were a bit like Cady Heron getting ready to attend high school for the first time in *Mean Girls*.

her servants and absentee parents. The refrain from those who knew her was that she was well-intentioned and charming, but acted without thinking.

"I tell you," warned Malmesbury's acquaintance Mademoiselle Hertzfeldt, "she has never done anything bad, but she is without judgment."

Malmesbury continued to record his impressions of Caroline, writing that she had a "light and flighty mind" but was "meaning well." When she spoke to him of her hope to be loved by her subjects, he attempted to explain that shouldn't be her goal. He noted that a "nation at large can only respect and honor a great princess," not love her.

In terms of love, Malmesbury thought that Caroline's impulsive nature would benefit from a partnership with a dependable man, writing, "in the hands of a steady and sensible man [Caroline] would probably turn out well, but where it is likely she will find faults perfectly analogous to her own, she will fail." Notably, he added that she had "her father's courage," which he knew would be necessary to survive marriage to the decidedly mercurial Prinny.

And then an anonymous letter arrived from England, addressed to Caroline's mother and warning of Lady Jersey's influence over Prinny.* In her usual indiscreet manner, Augusta shared the letter with Caroline, who demanded Malmesbury explain what was going on. Malmesbury deduced the letter was meant to warn Caroline not to trust Jersey, who the letter made out to sound like "the worst and most dangerous of profligate women." The letter did not out her as Prinny's mistress but more as the queen bee of royal court mean girls. Malmesbury emphasized to Caroline that, as Princess of Wales, she must not fall into traps set by other

---

* This is the first of numerous anonymous letters that will show up in this story. Get ready for *Pretty Little Liars*: 1790s version!

women, particularly those who could put her reputation into question.

Additionally, he warned, as Princess of Wales, it would be death for any man to approach her inappropriately. Malmesbury emphasized that it was British law that "anybody who presumed to *love* her was guilty of *high treason*, and punished with *death* if she was weak enough to listen to him: so also would *she*." What he meant was that if Caroline had an affair with a British subject, both she and the man would be guilty of treason because Prinny represented the Crown, and to betray him was to betray the nation. Caroline was startled by this information, but had no reason to presume she'd ever stray from her husband.

Caroline, Malmesbury, and their entourage headed off on December 30, but ran into difficulties right away due to unusually cold weather. There were a number of extreme weather events throughout the late eighteenth century, and the winter of 1794 saw one of them as extreme cold weather descended upon the region. Augusta had to be coerced by Malmesbury to join them as Caroline's chaperone, and it was soon clear why she'd rather have avoided this journey (other than her general disinterest in spending time with Caroline). As trains had not yet been invented, Caroline, Malmesbury, and her unwilling mother huddled under furs and blankets in carriages as footmen braved the freezing temperatures outside. The situation quickly became untenable, and Malmesbury arranged for the whole entourage to stay in Bishop's Palace at Hanover until the weather improved.

Prinny continued to write to Malmesbury, despairing at how much he needed the cash infusion Caroline would provide. Malmesbury stood firm, like Hector Elizondo in *The Princess Diaries*, loyal above all to the oddball princess he was charged with protecting. The snowbound extension to their commute provided more time for further English language and princess lessons. Malmesbury continued to at least try to teach her to be a conventional princess, despite Caroline's clear unwillingness and/or inability to change anything about herself. It was at this time that he addressed the delicate topic of her personal hygiene.

Frequent bathing was not a widespread practice in Western Europe at this time, but Prinny was fastidious about it. Caroline, having been raised free-range and kept away from polite society, had never been taught the importance of regular bathing or changing her undergarments frequently. Malmesbury was shocked at how her education on this topic had been neglected "and how much her mother, although an Englishwoman, was inattentive to it."

Caroline, in fact, was proud of how quickly she was able to complete her toilette; Malmesbury pressed on about the importance of taking much more time. The critique of a German princess's hygiene echoes that of three centuries earlier, when Henry VIII claimed to have been revolted by the hygiene of his fourth wife, Anne of Cleves. It also echoes a criticism lobbied against Marie Antoinette fifteen years earlier when she arrived in France to marry the future Louis XIV. Perhaps all three women did have more prominent body odor than other women around them. Perhaps this was anti-German xenophobia. In the cases of Caroline and Anne, tales of poor hygiene overrode most other facts of their lives to be one of the few things many people know about either of them. But clearly Malmesbury's intervention was successful, as there were no reports of Caroline being unclean after this.

Caroline's first English lady-in-waiting arrived to meet her in Hanover. The woman, Mrs. Harcourt, was immediately charmed by her, noting that "she is so affectionate . . . and her desire to please is very engaging . . . She is all openness of heart, and has not a shadow of pride . . . She seems of a cheerful temper, perfectly void of art or design." She also noted, as Malmesbury had already found, that "the more you see of [Caroline] the more you will like her, as I do."

The party was able to leave Hanover on March 24, heading to the coast to board a ship to England. Augusta bid farewell to her daughter at this point, and Caroline was without parental presence for the first time in her life. Other than the small barges Caroline may have used to commute between homes in Braunschweig, this was her first time on the open waters.

Despite being in the proximity of French privateer vessels, Caroline was all joy. Harcourt noted that the "English captains are enchanted with her. Her sweet temper and affability of manners has charmed and delighted every one . . . She is always contented and always in good humour, and shows such pleasant, unaffected joy at the idea of her prospect in life that it does one's heart good to see any one so happy."

Malmesbury echoed this impression of Caroline's "perfect happiness" as they set sail. She suffered a toothache* while en route and had to have a tooth removed. She sent the tooth along with a note to Malmesbury, similar to the way that a cat will sometimes bring a dead mouse to its owner. *See what I have done? Isn't this interesting?* her act seemed to say.

Their party landed at Greenwich, then a town on the outskirts of London, at noon on Easter Sunday, April 5. Caro-

* To put this in context, dental problems were very common in this era among people of all levels of society due to dietary reasons such as scurvy (from a lack of vegetables) as well as from a lack of knowledge of dental hygiene. We know Caroline lost this tooth, but likely most people in this book also had a less than complete set of teeth.

line had anticipated an official royal greeting, as had been arranged, but no one was waiting to greet them. This was the first, but far from the last time that Caroline's idealistic vision of her life in England would be utterly ruined by Prinny and others scheming against her.

CHAPTER FOUR

# "What an Odd Wedding"

Caroline and her entourage waited for nearly an hour, during which many churchgoers from a nearby service left early to catch sight of the new Princess of Wales. These included veterans with amputated limbs, leading Caroline to jokingly inquire if all Englishmen were missing an arm or a leg. Some who overheard her statement later used it as an example of either her insanity or her poor manners.

When the welcoming committee arrived, it was led by none other than Lady Jersey, Caroline's new lady of the bedchamber. This appointment was orchestrated by Queen Charlotte, using Jersey to spy on Caroline. The group's late arrival was entirely Jersey's doing, as she had intentionally dawdled in order to show disrespect to Caroline right away.

Paving the way for later villainesses like Meredith in the 1998 *The Parent Trap* or Lana in *The Princess Diaries*, Jersey was glamorously intent on making the naive young woman feel immediately unwelcome. You might think, *but wasn't it Lady Jersey who pressured Prinny to choose Caroline as his bride?* Yes, she was. And that choice seems to have been the first step in her multistage scheme to remain queen bee by choosing a simpleton to become Princess of Wales. This was a similar error that Prinny made when he neglected to consider Caroline more than a personified line of credit. Jersey assumed Caroline would be a wallflower she could easily trample. Caroline, as you are likely now becoming familiar with, was nothing of the sort.

Caroline had always been a fashion girlie, carefully choosing the fabric and style of her dresses to make a style moment wherever she went. For this important outfit, she arrived beautifully dressed in a white muslin dress with a blue satin petticoat and a black beaver hat with blue and black feathers.* Jersey, in full Baroness Schroeder from *The Sound of Music* mode, criticized this ensemble so extremely that Malmesbury was offended on Caroline's behalf. Jersey then presented Caroline with an unfashionably white satin gown that she lied was all the rage in the British royal court. Caroline graciously agreed to change, but refused to switch out her beaver hat for a white one Jersey was offering; nobody came between Caroline and her hats.

Having tricked Caroline into this unflattering new gown, Lady Jersey then made a production of her tendency to motion sickness, demanding that she sit next to Caroline, facing frontward in the carriage ride into London, a more prestigious seat than facing backward. Malmesbury again transformed into Hector Elizondo from *The Princess Diaries*, suggesting that if Jersey was so incapable of sitting backward, she should take a ride in a separate carriage. Sulking, Jersey sat backward in the carriage with Caroline.

These mean girl antics left Caroline's mind as they began the procession toward London. The lonely girl who'd dreamed of being adored suddenly found her wish had come true as crowds cheered her along the route. She cheer-

* As we will see throughout this book, Caroline was a big fan of feathers on hats.

fully waved and greeted them as Jersey sat opposite her, pouting.

At 3:00 p.m., they arrived in London at St. James's Palace, where a set of empty apartments had been prepared for her. At this time, St. James's was the primary residence for the monarch, while Buckingham House (not yet a palace) served as a smaller family residence for the Queen and children. Caroline stood at an upper-floor window to wave at the crowd, who greeted her with hearty huzzahs that lasted for several minutes. And then Prinny arrived.

Prinny, drunk, entered the room where Caroline was waiting along with Malmesbury. Caroline began to kneel when Prinny entered, but he reached out to embrace her before she could. He then walked away from her across the room, not saying anything. Finally, he said to Malmesbury, "I am not very well, pray get me a glass of brandy."

Malmesbury replied, "Sir, had you not better have a glass of water?"

Prinny swore, then said, "No, I will go directly to the Queen," and left.

It was an incredibly impolite greeting for his fiancée, let alone a foreign princess, let alone his cousin, and Caroline, stunned, turned to Malmesbury and said, "My God! Is he always like that? I find him very fat, and not as handsome as in his portrait."

Truly, no introduction between a royal couple had been so disastrous since Henry VIII surprised Anne of Cleves by showing up in disguise, and she shuddered at his age and appearance. In this instance, Prinny's reaction was not caused by his disappointment in Caroline's looks. Despite the unflattering outfit Jersey dressed her in, Caroline was consistently described as being pretty at this time. It is more likely that Prinny, impatient for the allowance increase her arrival would bring, hadn't fully thought about the fact that he would have to marry an actual woman. He was also likely upset at how the crowd had cheered for her as they never did for him.

Caroline was too proud and full of Brunswick spirit to let anyone dismiss her like this. Where another woman may have sat quietly in sadness or confusion, she headed to her welcoming dinner party that evening, ready for a fight.

All of Malmesbury's warnings forgotten, Caroline's worst habits manifested that night in front of Prinny, his parents, Malmesbury, and other notable guests. She was overly talkative, spoke with inappropriate casualness, and made a spectacle of herself. When Prinny, the fashion snob that he was, criticized Caroline's shoes, she retorted that he should make her a better pair and bring them to her. Her behavior at this dinner cemented Prinny's hatred of her, which would never waver. But she found a champion in his father (and her uncle), George III, who found her charming.

It was too late to cancel the wedding without causing an international incident, so the ceremony went ahead three days later in the Chapel Royal at St. James's Palace.* Much as in today's royal coverage, details of Caroline's ensemble were shared with the press. The gown, captured in paintings by both Gainsborough Dupont and John Graham, was described as: "A royal robe; silver tissue petticoat, covered with silver Venetian net and silver tassels; body and train of silver tissue, festooned on each side with large cord and tassels." The press noted the width of her skirt as ushering in a new, slimmed silhouette that was "very small, such as is used for morning dress."

Caroline was walked down the aisle by Prinny's brother, Prince William, the Duke of Clarence, and she chatted hap-

* Later royal events in this chapel include the marriage ceremony of Queen Victoria and Prince Albert in 1840, and the 2013 christening of Prince George.

pily with him along the way. Up at the altar, Prinny was a gruesome combination of profoundly drunk and profoundly hungover and "looked like death," having to be held up in a standing position by two of his groomsmen. One attendee recalled him being practically carried up the aisle, blubbering.

The Archbishop of Canterbury oversaw the ceremony. He paused significantly when he reached the part of the vows about anyone knowing a reason why these two could not be wed, looking meaningfully at Prinny (who the archbishop and others in the room suspected was already married to Maria Fitzherbert, making this marriage bigamous). Prinny burst into tears, but did not voice an objection, nor did anyone else. The archbishop, truly doing the most, twice read out the part about living in fidelity as though to telekinetically force Prinny to actually listen to him. Throughout the ceremony, Prinny kept his eyes fixed on Jersey rather than Caroline.

"What an odd wedding," Lady Maria Stuart, one of the guests, wrote to her friend. Though Prinny was a drunken mess, Stuart noted that Caroline "appeared in the highest spirits . . . smiling and nodding to every one."

The wedding party progressed to a reception in the council chambers of St. James's, where Caroline stood at a window for the public to view her and her sparkling gown. One servant who went to see her recalled that Caroline seemed "Beautifull (sic) . . . very lively and pleasing in her manner."

Caroline and Prinny left the festivities at midnight, by which time he was blackout drunk, and she was more than aware of what a terrible situation she had landed in. She later described their wedding and wedding night as follows:

"Judge what it was to have a drunken husband on one's wedding day, and one who passed the greatest part of his bridal night under the grate,* where he fell, and where I left him!"

---

* The fireplace.

The days that followed carried on as though this was any normal royal wedding. Caroline joined the rest of the family at Windsor Castle for the weekend, where Prinny avoided her entirely. George III stepped up in his place, serving as Caroline's escort to church services and on a walkabout to greet the locals. The King continued to adore Caroline as much the subjects did when they met her. Prinny's absence did nothing to improve his own popularity.

Three weeks after the wedding, Malmesbury joined the family for dinner. Prinny took him aside, challenging him as to why he hadn't sent advance warning of Caroline's unsuitability for this role. Malmesbury reminded Prinny that his task had been merely to escort her back. And if he'd had any concerns, he would have raised them to the King, not to Prinny.

The newlyweds progressed to a rented home in the South of England near Basingstoke, where the only other woman present was Jersey, as Caroline's lady of the bedchamber. Prinny did not lack for male companionship, surrounding himself with men who would drink, swear, sleep on the sofas and behave in such a way that Caroline described the setting as resembling "a bad brothel more than a palace."

Despite their mutual hatred, Caroline became pregnant at some point during this honeymoon period. She joined Prinny in Brighton in June, at which point her pregnancy was confirmed. She was surprised to find herself in this condition, as she and Prinny had lived as man and wife for only a few weeks, and she'd thought him incapable of fathering children. Still, the sea air at Brighton agreed with her, and the pregnancy increased her importance to the royal family. After all, this child would be a future monarch.

To Prinny, the marriage was a disaster. Not only did he detest Caroline, but he hadn't acquired the raise in allowance he'd expected upon taking a bride. Funds weren't available for him due to the government's spending on wars, combating widespread political unrest, and dealing with an economic crisis. None of that mattered to Prinny, who had never been able to live within his means. Unable to curb his spending, he fired more members of his household staff to cut costs.

Speaking of household staff, Caroline had one demand: to dismiss Lady Jersey as her lady. This plea was ignored by Prinny and by Queen Charlotte (who, remember, had placed Jersey in that role as her personal spy on Caroline). Prinny knew Caroline hated having Jersey around and delighted in tormenting her. For instance, he had given Caroline pearl bracelets as wedding gifts; later, he took them back and re-gifted them to Jersey, who wore them in public in front of her.

Jersey was a capable spy, intercepting Caroline's correspondence so the Queen could keep tabs on her private thoughts. In June, Jersey obtained a packet of letters Caroline had written to her family in Braunschweig and instead rerouted them to the Queen. Palace sources revealed this interception to popular newspapers, who supported Caroline entirely. Soon, Jersey was hated by the public as much as she was by Caroline. Isolated and treated cruelly by her in-laws, Caroline found strength in the support of the public. She wrote, "When I appear in public, nothing can be more flattering than the reception which I meet with."

While dealing with all of this, Caroline was in the later stages of pregnancy. Childbirth was dangerous and frequently deadly in this era. Caroline, as the mother of the future monarch, was provided with the best care available for the child, if not for herself. Queen Charlotte, who had given birth fifteen times and knew about this part of life, took charge of hiring nurses, doctors, governesses, decorating the child's room and even picking out a crib. Caroline had yearned to be a mother for years; Queen Charlotte removed any of the happy preparations Caroline could have made for herself.

Caroline gave birth to a baby girl on January 7, 1796, almost exactly nine months after the day of their wedding. Her labor lasted twelve hours. Diarist Ann Michelson reported that there was no more celebration among the royal family "than if the Royal Cat had kittened." Despite the lack of fanfare, the infant Princess Charlotte Augusta (named for her grandmothers)* was destined to be Britain's first female monarch in a century.

At the same time his daughter was born, Prinny had a sudden mental collapse, convinced he was dying, and wrote himself a new will. In it, he swore to leave all his money† to Maria Fitzherbert, the true wife of his heart; he left Caroline a single shilling. The will further stated that Princess Charlotte should be left in the care of the King and Queen and not in any circumstances to be taken care of by "the mother of this child, called the Princess of Wales."

The will was not made public, and ultimately was not needed as he quickly recovered. But even without this document, palace insiders shared details to the press of Prinny's cruelty toward Caroline and Caroline's ostracism. By the date of Princess Charlotte's christening, it was widely known that Caroline and Prinny's marriage was unhappy.

Caroline later remembered this as one of the darkest periods of her life. Her postpartum depression was exacerbated by her isolation, the cruel treatment of her in-laws, and her time with Princess Charlotte being limited. Later, Caroline recoiled at the thought of living this experience over again:

---

* One of whom actively hated Caroline, the other of whom actively ignored Caroline.

† lol

"If anybody [said] to me at this moment will you pass your life over again, or be killed, I would choose death, for you know, a little sooner or later, we must all die; but to live a life of wretchedness twice over,—oh! mine God, no!"

The acrimony between Caroline and Prinny continued to be shared in the popular press. Gossip spread that Prinny had been physically abusive to her and/or that he had infected her with a sexually transmitted infection. Caroline's mission to have Jersey removed as her lady continued with her writing letters to Prinny, then to the King. George III supported Caroline's proposal, and Jersey was told to resign or be dismissed; she chose to resign. Not one to go without having a final word, Jersey wrote Caroline a letter of such startling rudeness that *The Times* called it "one of the most disrespectful" they had ever read.

With Jersey finally expunged from Caroline's home, she presented herself open to a reconciliation with Prinny. But Prinny would have none of it. He was privately grateful to have gotten rid of Jersey, as his romantic thoughts had turned back to Maria Fitzherbert. This also colored his desire to officially separate from Caroline, as Fitzherbert would never take up with him again if he was living with his other wife.

Fitzherbert had by now moved to a new home on Park Lane in Mayfair. He had been inundating her with love letters, and she agreed to a reunion only if the Pope would confirm they were truly man and wife. In late 1799, the Pope came through via private correspondence, pronouncing her Prinny's wife in the eyes of Catholic church law. And so, starting in early 1800, Prinny and Fitzherbert began appearing together in public again. And swiftly, she was just as unpopular with the public as Lady Jersey had been before her.

Caroline responded privately with a snide remark, hoping that "*her husband* would not feel *her* any impediment to the reconciliation he was so desirous for." However, she bore no ill will toward Fitzherbert, who she respected as Prinny's wife. She referred to Fitzherbert as "the Prince's true wife; she is an excellent woman; it was a great pity for him he ever broke [with] her."

In May, Caroline was rapturously applauded upon her arrival at the opera. She noted, "I suppose the public has been acquainted with what is only *too true.*" By which she meant, how cruelly Prinny had treated her and that she was entirely blameless. She also took her baby daughter out for walks in public parks, which the public loved to see and made them love her more. The more they loved her, the angrier Prinny became.

The pair continued to live separately: Caroline at Carlton House and Prinny at Windsor and Brighton. Similarly to her adolescence, Caroline was again under the control of other people who dictated who she could see. She could only have visitors personally approved by Queen Charlotte and was not permitted to go anywhere without a chaperone, with her outings limited to carriage rides in nearby Hyde Park or occasional visits to the theater or opera.

George III, ever the optimist, attempted to reconcile the couple. But eventually he relented to Caroline's pleas to allow her to establish her own household away from Prinny. Caroline got this permission in writing and ensured that the paperwork noted under no circumstances would she ever again be expected to cohabit with her husband. Prinny agreed, writing: "I shall now finally close this disagreeable correspondence, trusting that as we have completely explained ourselves to each other, the rest of our lives will be passed in uninterrupted tranquillity."

This separation should not be mistaken for a divorce or an annulment. Divorce was technically permitted for the heir to the throne, as evidenced by Prinny's ancestor George I having divorced his first wife prior to becoming King of Great Britain. But Prinny's father, George III, was a firm believer in the importance of the royal family as role models for their subjects. Divorce proceedings would be costly and were likely to bring more attention to Prinny's rumored marriage to Fitzherbert. Were that to become common knowledge, he could be forced to step down as heir to the throne for marrying a Catholic.

What this settlement meant was an amicable separation. Prinny and Caroline were permitted to live entirely separate lives, still technically married.

Caroline told a friend, "Oh! how happy I was . . . Oh! mine God, what I have suffered! Luckily, I had a spirit, or I never should have outlived it."

And so, two years after her unhappy wedding day, she took up residence in Shrewsbury House in the village of Charlton, near Blackheath, to begin the next chapter of her life.

CHAPTER FIVE

# Blackheath

Today, Blackheath is an area in Southeast London you can reach via train in around one hour from King's Cross station. In Caroline's time, Blackheath was part of County Kent, a two-hour carriage ride from central London. This distance was what Caroline needed to remove herself from Prinny and his toxic family, and the locals were delighted to have her there.

The opportunity to live so far from Prinny delighted Caroline, who said of him at around this time: "I cannot say I positively hate the Prince of Wales, but I have a positive horror of him. Nothing shall shake the determination I have taken to live in no other way than the state of separation we are now in."

The matter of Charlotte's custody had never been up for discussion. As per British law until the twentieth century, a father's rights overrode those of the mother regardless of circumstances. If a couple lived separately, the mother had no rights over their children. Caroline was permitted to visit her daughter at Carlton House, which she did regularly. Prinny avoided the nursery wing entirely to avoid even accidentally encountering his wife.

Charlotte, by now an energetic toddler, seemed unconcerned by the family strife she had been born into. She had a similar personality as her mother: high-spirited and capable of charming most people she met. Her governess, Miss Hayman, described the young princess as being "the merriest thing I ever saw—pepper-hot too." Given the powerful characters of both her parents, it comes as no surprise that the heir to the throne was a force to be reckoned with. Caroline's friend Lord Minto noted the child was perhaps overly fond of "romp and play" but otherwise excelled with her vivacity and clear intelligence.

Caroline was hands-on with her daughter in a way her own mother never was with her. Minto described how she "romped about with [Charlotte] on the carpet on her knees." He further reported that the toddler princess was "really one of the finest and pleasantest children I ever saw." Caroline's engaged parenting style was unexpected for a noblewoman, let alone a member of the royal family.* Caroline was also fond of Hayman, glomming on to her as a close friend without concern for the social rules dictating friendships between a royal and a servant. She gossiped with her about novels, played music with her, and gave her tours of Prinny's silly home renovation projects, mocking him. Word of their friendship reached the Prince, who fired Hayman on November 7. Caroline hired her back straightaway to join her household as her bookkeeper/accountant.

In addition to Caroline's visits to the nursery at Carlton House, Princess Charlotte came to Blackheath every summer for extended visits with her mother. The first visit occurred in 1799, by which time Caroline had leased Montague House.† Prinny leased her former home, Shrewsbury House, for Charlotte and her entourage. These houses were only

---

* To her haters, this was another example some share of Caroline's alleged insanity; having fun playing with her own toddler-aged daughter.

† Fifty years earlier, notable Black writer Charles Ignatius Sancho lived in this house when he worked as butler for the Montagu family. His time there is commemorated today on the site by a plaque at the house's former site, as well as a nearby café named for him.

three miles apart, allowing for frequent visits between mother and daughter.

Caroline took to country living right away. Unlike Prinny's gilded rooms in Carlton House, here she could be close to nature in a way she had been back in her Braunschweig days. Having taken a lengthy lease on her new property, Caroline set about making various improvements. Her choices were practical and made the place feel more like home. Caroline joked she "endeavoured to acquire the honourable name of a farmer," and sold her produce in local markets to supplement the income she received as an allowance from the Crown.

In the spring of 1801, Caroline fell ill. She was visited by a local physician, Dr. Mills, who provided her usual course of bloodletting and supplied her with laudanum for the pain. Like all opiates, laudanum was addicting and caused constipation; likely, for this latter reason, Caroline was not a fan of it at this time as her symptoms were often gastrointestinal. Her London physician, Dr. Baillie, provided her with some sort of pills that allowed her to stop taking laudanum, much to her relief. Still, Caroline's illness continued such that Queen Charlotte was concerned enough to refer her physician, Sir Francis Millman, to consult.

Caroline eventually recovered and returned to her various hobbies. In addition to gardening, she also took on the project of writing a humorous book describing all of the notable British people she had met.* She was still a huge fan of reading, with some favorites from this time including Voltaire's French satire *Candide* and the novels of Madame de Genlis.†

"She reads a great deal and buys all the new books," wrote

---

* This book has never been located, but her friend Lady Charlotte Bury noted that it made for "most piquant reading."

† A Frenchwoman who also wrote encouraging hands-on parenting and the importance of spending time in nature; clearly an influence on Caroline's parenting style.

her friend Monk Lewis, author of Gothic novels that Caroline presumably also devoured.

Caroline took lessons in English, music, and painting from luminaries of the time. She was keen to learn new art styles, including learning to model clay busts of her daughter, father, and friends. Whatever she did, she committed herself entirely to, as evidenced by this description by her visitor Joachim Heinrich Campe, who wrote about her in his travel memoir *Travels Through England*:

> [Caroline] had the condescension to conduct me to a garden at some distance, which she had principally laid out herself, and which she superintended in such a complete sense of the word that no person presumed to do anything in it but what she herself directed . . . I was charmed with the neat borders of flowers between which we passed, and was doubly rejoiced to find them so small; because, as the Princess remarked, too much room ought not be taken from the useful vegetables, merely for the purpose of pleasing the eye.
>
> I was transported with the elegance, taste, and convenience displayed in the Pavilion, in which the dignified owner, who furnished the plan and the directions for every part of it, had solved the problem, how a building of but two floors, on a surface of about eighteen feet square, could be constructed and arranged in such a manner that a small family, capable of limiting its desires, might find in it a habitation equally beautiful, tasteful, and commodious. The manner in which this has been effected deserves, in my opinion, the notice and admiration of professed architects.

She showed Campe another one of her art projects, a table that seemed at first to be mosaic work. Campe reported it was something different, quoting Caroline's description:

"It is nothing more than a square of ground glass, on which I have fastened with gum different kinds of natural flowers, which were first carefully dried and pressed, and then turned the glass with the smooth side upper-most."

She continued to delight in expressing herself through fashion, both in her accessory-laden daily wear and complex ensembles for costume parties. At one of the latter, she was seen "in a gorgeous dress, which was looped up to show her petticoat, covered with stars, with silver wings on her shoulders."*

Perhaps in reaction to the isolation experienced in her youth as well as during her postpartum period, she now kept herself constantly surrounded by friends and company. She hosted dinner parties, inviting anyone she had heard about and was curious to meet. These included luminaries of the worlds of science, literature, the arts, and law. Some notable repeat guests include notorious poet Lord Byron and portrait artist Sir Thomas Lawrence. Her residence was far enough from London that the usual rigid etiquette was not required, lending the gatherings a laid-back vibe. Minto wrote how Caroline "made herself extremely agreeable, seemed delighted herself, and contrived to satisfy all her guests. Nothing can be more unexceptional than her conduct."

While Prinny was annoyed these guests enjoyed visiting Caroline, high society was otherwise on friendly terms with her. She also continued to be popular with the general public, who sympathized with her as the cruelly ill-treated and abandoned wife.

The royal family did nothing to dissuade this truth. Prinny and his mother refused all of Caroline's requests, keeping them from the King, who might have granted them. She was not

* Caroline took every opportunity to show off those impertinent shoulders as well as her feet and ankles, which she knew were especially pretty.

allowed to maintain a home in London. Her request to hire a friend as her lady-in-waiting was refused; in her place, they suggested one of her enemies.

George III was the only family member to regularly visit her in Blackheath, delighting in her company and that of his only legitimate granddaughter. Following his 1801 illness, his first trip outside the home was to visit them. He arrived so early in the morning that Caroline had to greet him in her nightgown and nightcap.

George appointed Caroline as the Ranger of Greenwich Park in order to provide some public recognition of his favor. Minto reported, "The King is as fond of her as ever and has at last given her the rangership of Greenwich Park, which I am very glad of. They used to be very shabby and blackguard in refusing her half-roods of green under her windows; now the whole is at her own disposal."

This unpaid position was similar to the head of a home-owner's association and allowed Caroline to decide who could live in the houses on the estate.* She also got to oversee the park itself, a task suited to her interest in plants and gardening. Once she took on this role, she approved her own renovations to Montague House, extending the garden and adding an outdoor bathing area with a recessed bathtub for her daily soaks.

While other women of this era assembled literary salons of intellectual conversation, Caroline was more interested in having a good time and chatting with as many interesting people as she could. She was an extrovert, gaining energy from being in a crowd. Minto recorded that "When her subject engages her, her eyes and countenance speak louder than many people . . . could bawl at the top of their voices." She delighted in staying up all night chatting with guests, forc-

* Remember this, it will become important in a few chapters.

ing them to stay even as they tired of the party. Anecdotes about her parties were exaggerated and shared with Prinny, who was paying off some of her servants to spy for him. His hope was to gather evidence of her debauchery that he could use as grounds for a divorce.

One habit that spies reported on was the way Caroline would occasionally disappear, sometimes for long periods of time, with male visitors. Hayman attempted to explain to her, as Malmesbury had before, what this might suggest to others and how it may impugn her reputation. But Caroline, finally freed of the gilded cage she'd been in her whole life, did not take kindly to advice or suggestions and continued to escape the hustle and bustle of the party with her men in tow. This was the most independence she'd ever had, and she was determined to enjoy herself.

Some of the men singled out as her favorites for one-on-one dates included up-and-coming politician George Canning, a constant visitor to Montague House in the late spring and early summer of 1799. The artist Sir Thomas Lawrence was another rumored lover, who raised eyebrows when he stayed overnight at Montague House during the process of painting a portrait of Caroline with Charlotte.

If she was having as much sex with men as gossip suggested, she was either infertile, perpetually pregnant, or knowledgeable about contraception. Having conceived Charlotte quickly, infertility is unlikely in this situation. If she had been pregnant, what would have become of the children?* Could she, or her lovers, have known about contraception? What kinds of contraception were even available in England in the early 1800s?

Condoms would have been an option. These were made of lambskin or dried animal guts and had become popular among

* We'll get to that shortly.

men wanting to avoid sexually transmitted infections (which they weren't especially useful for; they did help prevent pregnancy, though). Caroline would likely not have learned about condoms during her isolated childhood or young adulthood in Braunschweig, but by the time she was living in England, she may have learned about condoms (and other sexual matters) from the 1790 pornographic German novel *The Candid Confessions and Wanton Pleasures of Lina.**

If she was having sex, it was also likely that her experienced lovers would have arrived prepared. Condoms were straightforward to acquire in London, where they could be purchased from brothels or specialized shops that advertised via discreet leaflets.

Caroline may also have considered the use of sponges or tampons followed by douching, a method known to be used in France at this time for sexually active women looking to avoid pregnancy. She may also have had luck using a more popular contraceptive strategy in England at the time: the withdrawal method. This method was free and available to all, making it prevalent among servants and others without the disposable income to purchase condoms (or those who didn't enjoy the sensations of animal guts on their genitalia). What is notable about this method would be the physical evidence that could be visible afterward on sheets or clothing; no such evidence was ever mentioned by those gossiping about Caroline's sexual behavior. Given that her sheets were regularly examined and changed by household servants, this may provide a clue as to what she was or wasn't doing.

The rumors that spread about Caroline were not that she was having consequence-free sex. Rather, word spread that she was, in fact, frequently pregnant and hiding the babies with her

* Caroline was known to be an avid reader of novels, and was fluent in German, so it is possible she came across this book.

in Blackheath. The basis for this was her long-held fondness for children. Unable to be with her own daughter as much as she wanted, she turned her maternal instincts toward helping poor children. She took in eight or nine wards, boarding them in a nearby house called The Pagoda,* and arranging their education and instruction. Her visitor Campe recorded what he saw of these interactions:

"She herself not only directed everything relative to their education and instruction, but went every day to converse with them, and thus contribute towards the formation of their infant minds. Never while I live shall I forget the charming, the affecting scene which I had the happiness of witnessing when the Princess was pleased to introduce me to her little foster-children . . . [Caroline] conversed with them in a lively, jocose, and truly maternal manner."

He quoted Caroline's plans for these children as:

"People find fault with me for not doing more for these children after I have taken them into my care. I ought, in their opinion, to provide them with more elegant and costly clothes, and to keep masters of every kind for them, that they may later make a figure as persons of refined education. However . . . It is not my intention to raise these children into a rank superior to that in which they are placed; in that rank I mean them to remain, and to become useful, virtuous, and happy members of society. The boys are destined to become expert seamen; and the girls skilful, sensible, industrious housewives—nothing more."

Caroline's defense was aimed at those who assumed she was raising these children as adopted royals. In a strict class-based system, for her to elevate poor children in this way was

* Built in 1760 as a summer house for then-residents of Montague House, it was built in a "Chinese" style similar to Prinny's Brighton pavilion. It's currently a private home, across the street from present-day Greenwich Park in London.

seen as inappropriate. However, as Caroline explained, she was schooling them in preparation for careers within their social class.

For a warmhearted woman like Caroline, there was no lack of children in need for her to help. The population in Great Britain had been increasing as the cost of living went up, leaving young children as the most vulnerable. This was the reason that London's Foundling Hospital had been founded decades earlier, but the high demand meant that not all children in need were taken in. Children left with poor parents might have starved, as would children who were sold into service or left on the streets. Parents could pay for insurance on young children such that they'd receive a payout upon their death; this led to parents intentionally abstaining from calling for medical help during periods of illness.

One of Caroline's wards was a young girl she named Edwardina Kent.* She claimed Edwardina had been abandoned by her Irish parents to a peasant woman in Blackheath. The peasant woman spent the money they had left for the child's care, and the parents did not return. This woman came to Caroline for help, and Caroline agreed to take the infant into her care.

Caroline knew about the rumors that these were her illegitimate children and did nothing to dissuade them, as she found the scandal funny. In her characteristic manner, she intentionally shocked visitors by claiming that some of these children were biologically hers.

As Malmesbury had warned her back in Braunschweig, Caroline's tendency to speak without thinking could get her in trouble in England's high society. Other habits he'd warned

---

* Named for Caroline's brother-in-law Prince Edward, with whom she was on good terms. "Kent" was chosen as surname based on the county in which the infant had been found.

her against included that of becoming overly fond of new friends in a short time and trusting too easily.

As long as rumors were spreading of her unconventional manners, Prinny and the palace could turn the other cheek. But in short order, these allegations became unavoidable when specific accusations were submitted to the royal palace.

CHAPTER SIX

# Willikin

In late 1801, Lady Charlotte and Sir John Douglas moved near Caroline in Blackheath along with their infant daughter. Sir Douglas had fought in the recent wars, and had been awarded the position of equerry to Prince Augustus, one of Prinny's younger brothers.* This position meant he was responsible for Augustus's horses, which increased the Douglas's social prestige, but did not help with their financial difficulties. What did help was when Sir John's army friend, Admiral Sir Sidney Smith, was in need of a place to stay and agreed to pay them for the use of their guest room. Lady Douglas was soon rumored to be providing more than room and board; she was said to have taken him as a lover.

The Douglases hadn't yet been invited to Caroline's house parties, but Smith quickly found himself on her guest list and, like many eligible men, was widely assumed to be her lover.

Lady Douglas would have heard much about Caroline, both as her neighbor, as well as from Smith's tales of her parties. On a cold November day, Lady Douglas noticed Caroline and Hayman loitering outside her home, walking up to the

---

* Augustus, like Prinny, had secretly married without the King's permission. His marriage to Lady Augusta resulted in two children. The couple separated in 1801, at the time that Sir Douglas was taken on as his equerry.

gate and pausing as though they were considering coming in. Caroline was dressed in her usual colorful garb, in a "lilac satin pelisse, primrose-coloured half-boots, and a small lilac-satin travelling-cap, faced with sable." Lady Douglas went outside to welcome the Princess in. Caroline greeted her warmly, asking to be introduced to her young daughter.

The girl and her father were both spending the winter in London, Lady Douglas apologized, and she was only in Blackheath for a short visit. Caroline and Hayman came in and spent an hour of pleasant conversation. One week later, Caroline sent a formal invitation for Lady Douglas to visit her at Montague House.

As Malmesbury had noted after spending time with Caroline, she had a habit of becoming very close friends with other women extremely quickly. Such was the case with Lady Douglas, who later claimed to have been overwhelmed by Caroline's enthusiasm to spend time with her.

In March 1802, four months after their first meeting, Caroline invited Lady Douglas to spend two weeks at Montague House to fill in as a temporary lady-in-waiting. Lady Douglas was provided with apartments and her own staff, with permission for her daughter to stay and Sir John allowed regular visits. She accompanied Caroline to the theater, out to dinners, and enjoyed the luxurious lifestyle of a princess.

Their close friendship continued after Lady Douglas, pregnant again, moved back to her own home. Caroline was a frequently visitor. On one occasion in May or June, Caroline revealed that she, too, was pregnant.* She outlined the circumstances of the conception in near-magical explanations, claiming:

"I am with child and the child came to life when I was breakfasting with Lady Willoughby. The milk flowed up into

* Drink!

my breast so fast that it came through my muslin gown, and I was obliged to pretend that I had spilt something and go upstairs to wipe my gown with a napkin."

Caroline further intimated she hoped the child would be a boy and, "if it was discovered, she would give the Prince of Wales the credit of being the father, for she had slept two nights at Carlton House within the year."

Lady Douglas, knowing of Caroline's habit of telling tall tales along with her irreverent sense of humor, wasn't sure whether or not to take her seriously. Caroline claimed that, as she was already known for her kindness in taking in abandoned infants left in baskets at her home, she would whisk this new child away in the same manner so that nobody would know she'd ever had another child. She was already a full-figured woman, which would disguise the telltale bump, and she had plans to cleverly pad her gowns when visiting the royal family so they would not suspect her condition.

This all sounds like classic Caroline silliness, with the telltale clue being her claim that she had sex with Prinny, a situation neither of them would have ever desired. Caroline promised to sit with Lady Douglas during her birth and play a tambourine to keep her merry. And in fact, Caroline did attend the birth, where she elbowed a nurse aside, and took the newborn in her arms from the doctor.* Lady Douglas named her new daughter Caroline in honor of her friend, who was also named godmother.

As the summer progressed, Caroline continued to allude to her secret pregnancy when Lady Douglas was present. She also invited Lady Douglas over numerous times, encouraging her to breastfeed in front of her. Caroline likewise came to visit Lady Douglas at her home, spending hours caring for the young children.

---

* She didn't seem to have brought a tambourine, though.

That autumn, Caroline had a falling out with Smith. He was still living with the Douglases, causing Caroline to avoid the household to steer clear of him. Lady Douglas did not see her for several months other than one occasion when she saw Caroline emerge from church dressed in a huge coat that hid her figure, and looking "very morose." Perhaps, Lady Douglas assumed, Caroline had miscarried her child. Or perhaps she had never been pregnant at all.

Shortly after this sighting, Caroline sent a note to her friends requesting they stay away from her home as one of her wards had contracted measles. Lady Douglas was out of town anyway, visiting friends for for Christmas. In her absence, Caroline received an anonymous letter* claiming that Lady Douglas had been bad-mouthing Caroline and had such a poor reputation that Caroline should steer clear of her. Caroline sent her staff out to investigate these claims, which she learned were true: Lady Douglas had been trashing her to other people.

When Lady Douglas returned in January, she paid a call on Caroline. Permitted inside despite what Caroline had heard about her, Lady Douglas found Caroline on a sofa, asleep with an infant around four months old in her arms. Perhaps setting up Lady Douglas with false gossip, Caroline claimed this was her child and introduced him as William, nicknamed Willikin. He was cared for by the same nursemaid she was paying to care for Edwardina.

Caroline's lady-in-waiting, Mrs. Fitzgerald, clarified that Willikin was another child who had been left with Caroline as his parents couldn't afford to keep him. Caroline was determined to perform all of the diaper changing, which Lady Douglas found scandalous and an indication of Caroline's insanity.

---

* *Pretty Little Liars*: 1800s!

With Caroline's attention now focused on Willikin, her friendship with Lady Douglas receded. Sir John was invited to take a new position in Portsmouth, and both Douglases were pleased to move on from what had become a perplexing situation in Blackheath. Caroline went to their home to bid a warm farewell to Sir John. When Lady Douglas went to Montague House with her daughters to say goodbye to Caroline, she was met with a brief reception and was given a gold necklace as a parting gift.

A few months later, Prince Augustus returned to England,* meaning his equerry Sir John and family would return to Greenwich as well. Lady Douglas stopped by Montague House to let Caroline know she was back in town, but was dismissed with a note from a lady-in-waiting indicating Caroline did not want to see her.

Now, as you may recall, it was at this time that George III had appointed Caroline as Greenwich Park Ranger. She was quick to wield this power to evict the Douglases from their Greenwich property. Sir John took this very personally, threatening to appeal to the King.

Lady Douglas also turned on her friend, writing a venomous letter all but threatening to blackmail her over the secret of Willikin's parentage. Lady Douglas then received insulting anonymous letters,† including one with a crude drawing of Lady Douglas having sex with Smith. The handwriting on these letters resembled Caroline's, and one was affixed with her royal seal. Lady Douglas insinuated the letters were from Caroline, but it was equally likely someone was trying to frame her for writing them.

The Douglases, who knew that Prinny was eager to hear anything about Caroline that could allow him to divorce her,

---

* Due to his financial difficulties; a habit that ran in the family.

† *Pretty Little Liars* alert.

called for an official audience with him. Caroline turned to her cousin, Prinny's brother Prince Edward (namesake of her ward Edwardina), for help. Edward pressured the Douglases to forget their grievances for the sake of George III, who was known to be ill and would be negatively affected if word of this scandal got to him. Edward promised to remind Caroline to behave herself, and seemingly, the Douglases acquiesced.

But too many people had heard about all of this for the tale of Caroline's secret love child to die down. During the spring and summer of 1805, rumors about Caroline's illegitimate son spread around drawing rooms and clubs among the haut ton. Caroline claimed it was the Douglases spreading these stories; the Douglases claimed that Caroline herself had fanned these flames. Sir John approached his employer, Prince Augustus, with all the juicy details and requested he intervene.

Prince Augustus passed the information on to his brother, Prinny, who demanded a full written account from the Douglases of the entire affair. Prinny wanted this to become a larger scandal, one that would ruin Caroline's popularity and—he hoped—provide evidence of adultery.

The final document was damning, not only concerning Caroline's alleged infidelity, but also about her character. Lady Douglas accused Caroline of having a lesbian attraction to her, of publicly mocking Prinny and other members of the royal family, of flagrantly having affairs and bragging about them, and otherwise being an appalling woman unfit for the role of Princess of Wales. The document was passed along to the prime minister, William Grenville, who insisted that the affair be passed along to the King for consideration.

George III had no choice but to investigate further. If the document had merely outlined infidelity, it would have been problematic. But the claim that Caroline potentially had a son that could contest Princess Charlotte's rights as heir meant a more serious investigation must be held. And so George III called for a commission to investigate the truthfulness of the Douglases' account. This affair would become known as the Delicate Investigation.

CHAPTER SEVEN

# A Not-So-Delicate Investigation

At this time, the government of the United Kingdom of Great Britain and Ireland was comprised of three parts: the King, the House of Lords, and the House of Commons. The House of Commons was an elected group of landowning men (elected by other landowning men) to represent the population. All men in this house belonged to one of the following political groups: Whigs, Tories, Radicals, and Independents.

Whigs and Tories weren't formal parties like in twenty-first-century politics, and people could easily switch from one faction to the other. In each election, a majority of one group or the other would be elected to the House of Commons. The Monarch would then appoint one of them to be the prime minister based on who he felt was most capable of running the government.

The majority of members of the House of Commons belonged to one of these two groups. Broadly speaking, the Whigs were more progressive and the Tories were more conservative. At this point in the story, Prinny sided with the Tories, which made Caroline defiantly side with the Whigs.

Caroline often invited Whig politicians to her parties and was able to leverage these friendships by hiring several as her advisers. The Whigs, understanding her continued popularity among the population, leaned into this support, hoping this would translate to more votes for them in the next election. This political maneuvering was equally important to the whole drama as Caroline's actual behavior had been. She and Prinny were proxies for a political battle between Whigs and Tories.

At the time that Lady Douglas's written statement was handed over to the prime minister, the British government was being overseen by a Whig/Tory coalition self-described as The Ministry of All the Talents.* Prime Minister Grenville selected a small group to look into allegations of Caroline's love-child, including Lord Chancellor Erskine, Lord Chief Justice of England and Wales Ellenborough, and the Home Secretary Lord Spencer.

These men, arguably the most prestigious lords in the country, set about secretly interviewing Caroline's household staff. The information that they gathered was contradictory and often second- or third-hand gossip. Some claimed to have seen Caroline having sex with Smith; others claimed never to have seen her alone with him. All agreed that Smith had spent considerable amounts of time in Caroline's home. Other alleged lovers were also named. No one could confirm she'd had sexual relations with any of them, and she seemed primarily guilty of being a flirtatious person. Perhaps Caroline's lady-in-waiting, Mrs. Lisle, phrased it best, that Caroline behaved toward these men "only as any woman would who enjoys flirting."

More pressing was the question of Willikin's parentage. Household staff was divided between those who believed (or claimed to believe) Caroline had given birth to him and those who knew firsthand he had been a foundling delivered by his

* British government officials really liked naming their committees; this is the first of several very catchy names coming up in this book.

struggling parents. Caroline's full figure, one claimed, made it hard to tell if she was pregnant or not. One laundress noted that she had found Caroline's sheets particularly bloody at one point, hinting perhaps at a miscarriage.

Most persuasively, those more equipped to know the truth all agreed she had not been pregnant. Her dresser, who saw her unclothed daily, denied the pregnancy, as did the ladies-in-waiting who spent time with her every day, the housemaid who changed her sheets, and most notably, the doctors who attended to her throughout the period in question.* Caroline herself would also have denied the charge, but she still hadn't been asked for a statement.

And then, like the most dramatic *Law & Order: SVU* episode, a surprise witness arrived. This was Sophia Austin, Willikin's biological mother. She came to see the committee on June 7 and made a sworn statement that she had delivered Willikin on Sunday, July 11, 1802. Baptized William Austin, he had been born at the Brownlow Street Lying-In Hospital. Her husband, having lost his job due to a lack of demand for dockworkers during a brief period of peace between France and England, was unable to financially care for the child. They hoped to appeal to Caroline's famous charity to intervene and have him reappointed to his job at the dockyard. Sophia walked to Blackheath, Willikin in her arms, with a petition asking for her help. Caroline was not home when she first arrived, so she returned on November 6.

This time, Caroline met with her and was charmed by the infant. Caroline offered to take in the boy and treat him like a prince. Sophia agreed and took a week to begin weaning him from her breast milk. She then returned to leave Willikin at Montague House.

"I swear it is my child," she stated.

---

* Reminder: Caroline had been living with a chronic illness since her teenage years.

Her recollection of the date of birth and baptism was correlated with the records of the Brownlow Hospital. The Delicate Investigators were convinced by this testimony, stating that it was their "perfect conviction that there is no foundation whatever for believing that the child now with the Princess of Wales is the child of her Royal Highness, or that she was delivered of any child in the year 1802."

However, Caroline continued to treat Willikin differently than her other wards. While the other children were boarded out to working families to learn trades, Willikin remained by her side, being raised as though he were her own. She often brought him with her on her social calls, paying care that he was having a good time. She nursed him through an attack of the measles, infecting herself in doing so. On another occasion, she went with him to the theater despite feeling under the weather so as not to disappoint him on his birthday.

Caroline's acquaintance, Lady Hester Stanhope, criticized the maternal way Caroline interacted with Willikin, writing: "It was unpardonable in the Princess to lavish her love upon such a little urchin of a boy, a little beggar, really no better." She referred to him as being "a nasty, vulgar brat" who was "spoilt and mischievous."

When questioned about her affection for him, Caroline claimed that "Everybody needed something to love," and as she detested most pets, that left only children.

It is important to note at this point that, though Caroline had been permitted regular visitation with her daughter, Charlotte (who was ten years old at the time of the Delicate Investigation), Caroline had often been apart from her. It would be understandable that Caroline, who had always wanted to be a mother and had strong maternal instincts, would be devoted to this boy who no one could take away from her.

Charlotte, for her part, later claimed to have always implicitly understood Willikin and Caroline's other favorite ward, Edwardina, were her half-siblings via Caroline's affairs.

As we have seen and will see many times throughout this saga, nobody in this era was capable of keeping a secret. The first public mention of the investigation was in the June 20 edition of the *Morning Post.* Supporters of the Douglas side fanned the flames by publishing vaguely fictionalized versions of the saga in novels such as *The Royal Eclipse.* In the absence of legitimate news sources sharing the actual documents, rumors swirled. All of these vilified Caroline, treating the accusations as true. In her time of need, she found an unexpected champion in Spencer Perceval, a Tory with a grudge against the Ministry of the Talents.

Perceval was a short man, pale, who always dressed in black. In opposition to the vainglorious Prinny, Perceval was so averse to vanity that no portraits were ever made of him during his lifetime. He was also an enemy of Prinny, who he had once referred to as a bankrupt liar, causing Prinny to swear "with most offensive personal abuse, and an oath which cannot be recited, that he felt he could jump on him and stamp out his life with his feet." Perceval made for an odd pairing with the flamboyant Caroline. But they both knew their unexpected team up would be lucrative for them both: she was using him to help craft her message; he was using her to restore his position within the government.

In mid-July, the investigators submitted their report to the King. While Caroline's name was cleared of having given birth to an illegitimate child, they formally questioned her morality and behavior. Prinny was furious with this result, as he had hoped she would be found guilty of treason and supply him with grounds for a divorce. It was still up to the King to decide if Caroline would be reinstated with the privileges of her role as Princess of Wales, primarily an invitation back to the royal court.

Perceval requested authenticated copies of all the evidence given during the inquiry. Upon receiving these, he wrote a 156-page formal letter in her defense. When this did not provoke the King to reinstate her privileges, Perceval wrote a follow-up protest. In January, Parliament advised George III that it was unnecessary to continue the princess's exclusion from the court, although she was warned that she must "be more circumspect in her future behaviour."

Prinny then intervened, persuading his father that the case should be reexamined by Prinny's own lawyers. Caroline was determined to win this battle. She wrote to her friend Lady Townshend:

> *[A] Brunswicker never has been conquered yet,* and that my honour is more dear to me than all my jewels, that I am ready to pawn them all, to defend my own honour, and to discover all my accusers.*

But during this battle, two sudden tragedies affected her. In October 1806, she was riding in a carriage with her companion, Miss Cholmondeley, and encouraging their coachman to drive faster. He overturned on a corner, and Miss Cholmondeley was killed.† Returning home from this traumatic situation, she was informed via letter that her eldest brother, Karl Georg, had died of an illness. This grief on top of the stressful investigation and Caroline's chronic illness led her to take to her bed for several weeks.

---

* Caroline, always tying her fighting spirit back to her homeland and her father's reputation for winning battles.

† Death in carriage accidents was tragic, but not uncommon, in this era. One of Jane Austen's cousins, for instance, died when a carriage overturned.

More heartbreak was to come for her. That past August, King Frederick William III of Prussia had declared war against Napoleon and his army. Caroline's beloved father, Karl Wilhelm Ferdinand,* now aged 71, was appointed Commander of the Prussian forces. As she waited for word from King George about her position at court, Caroline was also kept up-to-date with news of her father's actions in battle.

On October 14, the Prussian forces were defeated at Auerstädt, where her father was badly wounded and left nearly blind in one eye. Karl Wilhelm Ferdinand reached out to Napoleon, requesting that Braunschweig remain neutral in the battle. Napoleon agreed, but only if Karl Wilhelm Ferdinand retired from the Prussian army. Caroline's father, a lifelong soldier, refused. Ever proud of her father's legacy, Caroline recounted in a letter to the Reverend George Locke: "As long as he could use his limbs and vital air was in him, he would defend his King and Country."

But his age, and the gravity of his wounds meant that his condition worsened. Needing extra care, and family nearby in case of his death, Caroline's mother, Augusta, left Braunschweig with the rest of the family to be with him in Altona. This entourage included Caroline's two disabled brothers, Georg and Augustus; her late brother Karl Georg's widow, Princess Louise of Orange-Nassau; her younger brother Friedrich Wilhelm's wife, Maria of Baden, and their two sons. They brought with them as many treasures as they could carry from Wolfenbüttel. Her youngest brother Friedrich Wilhelm remained behind to lead the army.

Word soon reached Caroline that her father was too ill to travel with them to safety, and the family traveled farther on

* Karl Wilhelm Ferdinand and Caroline's mother, Augusta, had both written in support of her this same month, pleading with George III to treat her more considerately.

without him. On November 27, she learned that he had died in Ottensen. Caroline was devastated. Her illness triggered again; she fell ill with "nervous headaches."

By December, she still had not heard from the King, not even with condolences for the death of her father.* And so, with Perceval's approval, she took things one step further by threatening to publish all of the papers dealing with the investigation in the newspapers. Caroline wrote to the King:

> *As far as myself am concerned, I am aware of the observations to which this publication will expose me . . . [but] my silence, under such circumstances, must lead inevitably to my utter infamy and ruin. The publication, on the other hand, will expose to the world nothing which is spoken to by any witness . . . which can, in the slightest degree, affect my character for honour, virtue, and delicacy.*
>
> *"If I am judged of as Princess of Wales, with reference to the high rank of that station, I must be judged as Princess of Wales, banished from the Prince, unprotected by the support of the countenance which belong to that station; and if I am judged of in my private character, as a married woman, I must be judged of as a wife banished from her husband, and living in a widowed seclusion from him, and retirement from the world.*

This threat of publication affected Prinny such that he could "neither sit nor stand." Others worried that the stress might exacerbate the King's ongoing health issues. Caroline persisted, writing once more to the King: "Your Majesty . . . will not be surprised to find that the publication of the proceedings alluded to will not be withheld beyond Monday next."

Five thousand copies of Delicate Investigation documents were printed and secretly stored in Perceval's house. This book was given the vague yet iconic title of *The Book*.

---

* Also his brother-in-law.

In the weeks leading up to its planned publication, chaos behind the scenes in the House of Commons stalled Perceval. The coalition government, overseen by Grenville, had fallen. They would soon be replaced by Tories, who at this time counted among their numbers many of Caroline's friends and advisers, with Perceval installed as Chancellor of the Exchequer. Therefore, the publication was no longer needed for her to win this battle, as the new government would restore her royal privileges. Perceval and the new government did not want to be associated with the controversial *The Book*.

Unfortunately, there was the matter of the five thousand printed copies. Perceval arranged to have these books burned, though some had already been distributed to a) every Cabinet minister, b) several of Perceval's friends and c) friends of the printer, Richard Edwards. One copy was known to have been acquired by pamphleteer William Cobbett, who shipped it off to New York City for safekeeping. The government paid over £10,000, $1 million today, to procure six more copies from the eBay sellers of the era.*

The following notice appeared in the March 27, 1807, edition of *The Times:*

> **Any person having in their possession a CERTAIN BOOK, printed by Mr. Edwards in 1807, but never published, with W. Lindsell's name as the seller of the same on the title page, and will bring it to W. Lindsell, Bookseller, Wimpole Street, will receive a handsome gratuity.**

Political affiliations were much more casual then as now, and Prinny changed his affiliations several times depending on his mood. As he switched sides, Caroline did too, so that

* *The Book* still lives today, and can be easily found in digital format online.

she was always supporting whichever party was opposed to Prinny. So at this point, she supported the Tories, and he supported the Whigs. Delighted by the new government, she hosted a dinner party for the new Speaker and members of Parliament at her home. She traveled from Blackheath to London to attend the parliamentary session in which Perceval delivered his first speech as Chancellor of the Exchequer. She and Perceval remained on good terms; he named her godmother to his youngest son.

Most importantly, one of the new pro-Caroline government's first actions was to draft a document acquitting Caroline on all charges and recommending the King receive her back at court with "as little delay as possible." They also noted Caroline's request for a London residence. George III agreed, finally inviting Caroline to appear at court and assigning her apartments at Kensington Palace.

A relieved Caroline wrote to Hayman:

> *At last the comedy has ended and the curtain drops: 'Much ado about nothing.' I only think my grandchildren will look upon it as being indeed a parody to Shakespeare!*

She made her return to royal court on May 7, 1807, where she was warmly received by the King and ignored by the Queen and her sisters-in-law/cousins. She had never expected anything different from the women, writing later to Lady Charlotte Campbell: "I cannot say, treating me as they do, that I feel that affection for them I should otherwise feel, except for my dear old uncle."*

Privately, she was in a state of hesitant joy, not confident

* Interesting this is how she describes the King, a man who was both her uncle and father-in-law. She was defining him in context as her mother's brother, rather than as her estranged husband's father.

that things would take another turn against her. As ever, she found solace in support from the public, who adored her as much as they ever had. When she made her reappearance into society, attending the opera, Caroline was greeted by tumultuous applause. As she made her way to the royal court to appear at the King's birthday, crowds cheered for her on the street.

Perhaps she thought of the goal she'd spoken aloud to Malmesbury while en route to London years before: she wanted to be loved by the people. Despite Prinny's constant attacks, at least this was still true.

CHAPTER EIGHT

# Family Reunion

Following the death of Karl Wilhelm Ferdinand, Caroline's mother, Augusta, was a Princess without a home. She had no need to remain in the German territories and sought a reason she could return to her homeland of England. Her status as the King's sister, mother of the Queen-to-be, and grandmother of the future Queen was reason enough. By May 1807, she had convinced Caroline to let her move in with her in Blackheath, or at least so she claimed in a letter to her brother George III. Of course, she needed his permission to visit, which he provided.*

Nearly a decade had passed since Caroline had last seen her mother. They had said farewell when she was a starry-eyed, naive bride-to-be. Years of fending off vicious royal scheming and emotional abuse had forged a damaged, stronger and even more willful woman. Caroline was still often optimistic, and may have hoped that her relationship with her often-absent, constantly neglectful mother might change now. At least, she knew this would be one more person on Caroline's side. Augusta had a decades-long rivalry with Queen Charlotte, meaning chances were slim she would ever side with Prinny.

Without a royal residence on offer, Augusta came to stay

* Although, due to past bad blood between Augusta and Queen Charlotte, she was not offered a royal residence.

with Caroline. Prinny offered to come by and visit, but only if Caroline was absent; Augusta explained that Caroline might visit at any time, so she could not guarantee a time when he would find her alone.

Within a month, friction between Caroline and Augusta led to plans to live in separate households. Augusta had often avoided her daughter as a girl and teenager; therefore, when presented with this high-spirited, opinionated adult version of Caroline, she preferred again to flee. In September, Augusta moved to nearby Chesterfield House, renamed Brunswick House in her honor. Today known as Ranger's House, it is a public museum.*

Princess Charlotte, now eleven, was permitted to visit her grandmother much more frequently than her mother. Caroline took advantage of this proximity to stop by and spend as much time with her as she could. George III had forbidden Charlotte from being in the same room as Willikin, and so Caroline's adopted son was tastefully omitted from family conversation.

In this era, Caroline became good friends with the Scottish poet Sir Walter Scott. He wrote an ode to Caroline's father in his poem *Marmion*, which so moved her that she sent him a vase in thanks. He praised her in poems, and she invited him to visit whenever he came to London or Blackheath. Scott wrote about her as follows: "She is an enchanting princess, who dwells in an enchanted palace, and I cannot help thinking that her prince must labour under some malignant spell when he denies himself her society."

Caroline was never without a romantic interest, and found her latest beau in Lord Rivers of Stratfield Saye and Sudeley Castle, a fifty-seven-year-old bachelor and former Tory mem-

* Fun fact: exterior shots of the *Bridgerton* family home are filmed there for the Netflix series.

ber of Parliament. Rumored to be her new lover, as were all men she spent time with, Prinny sent a private detective to subtly investigate. Surely aware of the gossip, Caroline delighted in having Rivers on her arm as an escort to her new London life of parties and events.*

That May, Caroline attended a party celebrating her role as godmother to the son of Henry "Anastasius" Hope. Caroline loved any opportunity to dance, leading another attendee, Miss Mary Berry,† to write:

> *Such an exhibition! but that she did not feel at all for herself one should have felt for her! Such an over-dressed, bare-bosomed,‡ painted eye-browed§ figure one never saw.*

But Caroline took a liking to Berry, who, along with her sister Agnes Berry, was a celebrated travel writer. Caroline was always intrigued by writers, especially those who were women. Berry lived with her partner,¶ sculptor Anne Damer, at Strawberry Hill house. A few months after this initial interaction, Caroline paid them a visit, and, as ever, Berry was soon won over. After having hosted Caroline at Strawberry Hill, Berry wrote:

---

* Caroline also continued to troll Prinny, who was responsible for paying all her bills, by purchasing things like a donkey-driven chariot for her to ride around Greenwich. To be clear, she also had him pay for the donkey.

† Not the former host of *The Great British Baking Show.*

‡ Caroline was often criticized for her filmy, low-cut dresses. These had been the fashion when she was younger, but fabrics had gotten sturdier since around 1810.

§ Caroline, whose eyebrows were naturally pale blond, had developed a fondness for overdrawing them in a dark color, likely using burnt cork or fine soot as those were the options for brows in this era.

¶ The two women lived together for many years and were certainly life partners; the romantic nature of their relationship is assumed by many historians, including me.

*She was on her very best manner, and her conversation is uncommonly lively, odd, and clever. What a pity she has not a grain of common sense! not an ounce of ballast to prevent high spirits, and a coarse mind without any degree of moral taste, from running away with her, and allowing her to act indecorously and ridiculously whenever an occasion offers! Were she always to conduct herself as she did here today, she would merit the character of having not only a remarkably easy and gracious manner, but natural cleverness above any of her peers [members of the royal family] that I have seen.*

Caroline became a regular visitor at Strawberry Hill, and Berry and her sister became frequent guests at Caroline's Kensington Palace parties. About one of these events, Berry wrote:

*Went with my sister to Kensington. A numerous ball; the Princess mighty gracious. I had a long and almost an affecting conversation with her, because for the first time she seems to feel her own situation, while she continues very good-natured to others.*

This may have been Berry's first glimpse of Caroline's true feelings, which speaks to how much the Princess had come to trust her. Caroline had hardened herself from her younger habit of trusting people too easily, perhaps after the fallout with Lady Douglas. She had also become practiced in hiding her emotions behind a cheerful mask, exerting great effort to prevent others from noticing how much she had been suffering all these years in England. Often, she used humor to distract from her sadness and anxiety, and only those closest to her could tell when she was faking joy.

Caroline's lady-in-waiting, Lady Charlotte Campbell, recalled Caroline confiding in her: "If I had not been miraculously supported, I could not have outlived all I have done: there are moments when one is supernaturally helped."

When initially approached to take a role in Caroline's household, Campbell turned to friends for references as she worried the stories of Caroline's debauchery were true. Their responses illuminate how others saw Caroline at this time.

Mr. G. Lewis wrote:

> *[Caroline] is extremely good-humoured and obliging, and seems very much attached to the persons in whose favour she conceives a prepossession . . . She seems grateful for the slightest indication of good-will (probably, poor soul! the ill-treatment which she has at times received since her arrival in this country have made such doubly acceptable to her), and she is generous, indeed I may say profuse, in her manner of returning them.*

A second reference, known only as Mrs. ____ wrote:

> *I believe the Princess to be exceedingly amiable—a true and zealous friend to all those whom she once takes [in friendship]; and is moreover an excessively agreeable companion, full of natural talent, and combines in a surprising manner the dignity of her position with an unaffected and natural ease very rarely seen in a Princess. It is, indeed, only fair to add that she makes it a point to draw about her all the clever and agreeable persons she can; and that, particularly in a royalty, is no small merit.*

As regards to the people in Caroline's household, Mrs. ____ wrote:

> *I am able to say I am sure you will find them all particularly honourable and superior persons . . . the Princess's selection of such persons does her infinite credit, as they are of a very different quality from those who generally occupy places at a Court.*

Caroline's parties were frequented by Berry, Byron, and other notable writers as well as an increasing number of Whig politicians as she and Prinny had again switched sides. Prinny now sided with the Tories, led by recently named Prime Minister (and Caroline's former best friend) Spencer Perceval. Caroline was now so pro-Whig that she publicly criticized her ex-bestie Perceval as unfit to serve as prime minister.

Sir Walter Scott would later characterize this switcheroo:

"[The] Opposition picking up the Princess of Wales so soon as they had lost the Prince was like a game of commerce, a popular card game, in which exchange or barter was the chief feature."

Despite her frequent hostessing, Caroline preferred smaller groups of her closer confidantes. Inspired by a party she'd heard Napoleon enjoyed, she led games of blindman's bluff. When she felt the party atmosphere was lagging, she jumped to begin an impromptu dance party, usually preferring the most strenuous ones. Dancing was one of the few forms of physical exercise women were permitted to indulge in, and Caroline was always enthusiastic on the dance floor.

Monk Lewis recalled that the "pleasant evenings I have spent at Kensington, her Royal Highness's hospitality, and the delightful assemblage of persons she had the good taste to congregate around her, will ever form the most agreeable reminisces in my life."

Her guests might also enjoy a reading from one of the authors present, or play a game of cards. All of these standard activities were exaggerated when shared with Prinny, who was still on the lookout for grounds to divorce her.

Campbell,* who chose to work with Caroline despite concerns about her etiquette, soon came to regret her decision. A stickler for protocol, Campbell was frequently horrified by

* Who later betrayed Caroline by publishing their private correspondence.

Caroline's casual style and fondness for pranks. Caroline enjoyed adventuring outside Kensington Palace grounds, either in disguise or in her own ensembles. On one occasion, she rang the bells of nearby houses and asked if they were available for rent. Most scandalous to Campbell was the way that Caroline would easily converse with the everyday people she encountered in Kensington Gardens.

Much as Princess Diana would go in disguise to nightclubs to dance with Freddie Mercury in the 1980s, Caroline arranged incognito escapades into town. On one occasion, Caroline and two of her ladies snuck out a back exit to Kensington Palace, where they connected with other conspirators. Caroline changed into a plainer dress, including a mask, and the party all went to attend a masquerade at an acquaintance's house.

Caroline's interest in music led her to befriend the Sapios, a family of Italian musicians. Like many other wealthy people, she welcomed high-status foreigners with open arms. The patriarch Antonio Sapio had been Marie Antoinette's music tutor, and he'd fled to England to escape the wrath of the French Revolution. He first worked in England with Caroline's sister-in-law Frederica, Duchess of York, before joining Caroline's household. The Sapios were sought after for their skill, but the xenophobic and classist Campbell* was horrified at the way Caroline treated them as friends.

Following a Kensington Palace soiree, Campbell wrote:

> *The horrible din of their music hardly ever stopped the whole evening, except when it was interrupted by the disgusting nonsense of praise that passed between the parties . . . to hear her let herself down so as to sing paeans to the Fiddler's son . . . it is more than human patience can bear, to witness such folly.*

---

* Whose obsessive observations of Caroline are reminiscent of Cady reporting on Regina George in *Mean Girls*.

Caroline's informality with the family led to the inevitable rumors that she had taken one of the Sapio men as her lover, especially when word spread that she had hired handsome Pietro Sapio as her private vocal instructor and paid for the family to live in their own cottage, which she visited often.

As this was all going on, continental Europe was still busy with the Napoleonic Wars. We haven't discussed this much in the book so far because Caroline was not very interested in the minutiae of military strategy, and this is a book about Caroline. But it is now necessary to get into the Napoleon of it all.

Napoleon first came to power in France in 1799, two years after Caroline had given birth to Princess Charlotte and the same year she and Prinny separated households. In 1803, Napoleon declared war on Britain. One year later, he declared himself Emperor of France and held an extraordinarily lavish celebration at Notre Dame Cathedral.* He then set about using his Grand Army to storm around continental Europe, taking over various duchies and kingdoms and putting one of his Bonaparte relations in power there.

In 1806, Caroline's father, Karl Wilhelm Ferdinand, was called up to lead the Prussian army against Napoleon's troops and then died.† This left Caroline's younger brother, Friedrich Wilhelm, as the new Duke of Brunswick. However, Napoleon had his sights set on most of these German duchies and took it over, declaring Braunschweig part of his new kingdom of Westphalia in 1807, ruled over by his brother, Jérôme.

Friedrich Wilhelm understandably developed a raging hatred of Napoleon and the French in general. He bided his time until an opportunity presented itself for him to avenge his father's death and reclaim his homeland. In 1809, the Austrian

---

* Prinny, impatiently waiting for his father to die so he could become the next King, was taking notes for his later coronation ceremony.

† As we discussed in Chapter Seven.

Empire and the United Kingdom joined together in the Fifth Coalition against Napoleon. Friedrich Wilhelm immediately approached Austria for support, financing the formation of a new military force by mortgaging his principality in Oels. He called upon volunteer troops and more than two thousand recruits arrived. As they had come from a variety of units with different colored jackets, it was decided that everyone was to dye their uniform black (it was one of the simplest dyes to use on a variety of colors, and was also representative of mourning, both of the death of Karl Wilhelm Ferdinand as well as their country). The regiment, therefore, became known as the Black Brunswickers. And Friedrich, their leader, became known as The Black Duke,* which we will now call him in this book, because that is an incredible nickname.

The Black Brunswickers, filled with righteous fury, descended upon Germany and briefly reclaimed control of Braunschweig. Napoleon's forces soon reclaimed it, and the Black Brunswickers journeyed Westward, holding off the attacking armies on the continent so they could make their way safely across the sea to England.

And so it was that Caroline's brother arrived in town, a swashbuckling war hero in a cool uniform with a skull and crossbones on it. She and her mother were thrilled to have him in town, as was much of the population, who offered him a hero's welcome much as they'd welcomed his father decades earlier. He summoned his sons, who had been sheltering with their maternal grandmother in the German riverside town of Glückstadt, to join him in England. This was Caroline's first meeting with her nephews, who she loved as she loved all children. Their grandmother Augusta perhaps

---

* Their uniform also included black beret-like hats with skull and crossbones pins on it, representing how they did not fear death. Their motto was VICTORY OR DEATH.

loved them even more, changing her will to make them her heirs rather than Caroline.

When Prinny invited Augusta to visit him at Carlton House, both Caroline and The Black Duke were appalled at her agreement. The Black Duke advised Caroline to write to their mother: "This must not be. You must not suffer her to think of going." Caroline wrote a lengthy letter to Augusta, explaining that her visiting Prinny would indicate that she approved of the way he had been treating Caroline.

By now seventy years old, Augusta was mostly deaf and tended to be forgetful. She also wanted to appeal to her brother, whom she entirely depended on for money. She had been forced to leave her dowry behind after fleeing Germany and was trying to play both sides in this situation. She told Caroline's messenger: "I love my daughter above all things, and would do anything in the world for her; but I must go to Carlton House."

But ultimately, she sided with Caroline. Relieved, Caroline noted that this "was so evidently a trap to inveigle [Augusta] into a tacit condemnation of me."

The Black Duke met with the King,* who agreed to take the Black Brunswickers into the British armed forces. Caroline and many of The Black Duke's other admirers were sad to see him have to shave off his distinctive blond mustache and switch from the deadly black to British red.

Caroline's life otherwise continued on in this new normal. She spent most of her time in her Kensington apartments, was able to visit regularly with her now teenage daughter, kept company with her broad circle of interesting friends, read novels, and enjoyed herself.

In November 1810, tragedy struck the family as twenty-

---

* Who was, remember, his uncle because Friedrich's mother was Augusta, sister of George III.

seven-year-old Princess Amelia, Prinny's youngest sister, died from a bacterial infection. She had been a favorite to many of her family members, including him. He was said to never again sleep without several candles lit in her memory, and burst into tears at the mention of her name years later. She had also been Caroline's favorite of the sisters-in-law. Most crucially, Amelia had been close to her father, George III.

As many expected, the King's health declined after this tragedy. The old King had been ill for decades and had already been worsening. Seventy-two years old, in cognitive decline, nearly blind from cataracts and incapacitated from rheumatism, rumors he would step down were everywhere.

Caroline was staying in London at this time, and took advantage of the six daily mail deliveries to stay in constant communication with her local friends. She shared her thoughts with nearly the frequency of today's text messaging. Regarding the King's health, she wrote:

> *Some people think the King will die, others that he will remain as he is; but at his age a complete recovery is not to be hoped, though the royal family have most wonderful constitutions. As for me, no changes, I feel sure, will make any different in my lot; so I remain very indifferent to them all. The world is decidedly cutting me, right and left, since my poor uncle's relapse. [But what can you do?]*—'tis the way of the world.*

During the King's previous illness in 1788, Prinny had mocked him in London clubs, sharing intimate details of his "madness," mimicking him, and openly planning a coup d'etat in which he would take over. Presumably, this time

* Caroline's English letters often contain words or phrases in French, which was her first language. For ease of reading, these French phrases will be translated and put in brackets.

was no different, as he waited eagerly for his turn to take charge.

In a later letter, Caroline wrote:

> *Here I am again, in the solitude of this sequestered place. I found it useless to remain in London, for everyone has flown away, the poor King's increased illness have put a stop to all gaieties. Every body thinks he is going to die. Though he is not able to befriend me, yet I shall feel more desolate still when he is gone, and there will then be no restrictions on the tyranny of the Regent. I am not a coward . . . and [think] I could bear most suffering; yet I felt my heart smite the other day when I had a curious letter, sent [to] me by an anonymous, written well, and full of fearful predictions as to my future fate. I cannot suppose why it was sent to me since the writer asked for no money or bribe nor appeared to wish me evil but rather to lament my fate.*
>
> *Amongst other things it contained, the writer said . . . they thought I might very likely be sent to Holyrood House, and play the part of a second Mary, Queen of Scots.* Everybody except me is longing for the change, and hoping they know not what from the poor old King's death . . . I have been much tormented lately by the advice of different friends—some commending my plans—some abusing me and telling me I was ill-advised and my time ill-chosen for bringing forward my wrongs. Think of Miss___ telling me the other day that the royal family never abused me; I laughed in her face and said, 'Does it not rain?' pointing out of the window where it was pouring . . . The King may die, or there may be a Peace, or a destruction of the 'Beast,' as Lewis calls [Napoleon], which might be all in my*

---

* Mary, Queen of Scots was Caroline's ancestor, who had been forcibly removed from power first by her husband and his coconspirators, and then by her cousin Queen Elizabeth I. Holyrood House was the Edinburgh palace where she was at one point held hostage.

*favour, as making more money going; and I should gain praise from [the public] by enduring my present state patiently a few months longer perhaps.*

In January 1811, she wrote to Campbell:

*the most violent pain, which you must remember I had once in my loins at the time you were with me at Kensington, paid me again a visit on the eve of New-Year's Day, and wished me joy (I suppose) on the season. This visitor gave me the most insinuating pain imaginable; and the spirit of turpentine, which I used most unmercifully upon my old carcass, has vanished the phantom who destroyed my peace . . . I am now about writing a novel, of which the scene lies in Greece.*

On February 5, 1811, the King's condition was found to be so far gone that he had to be removed from power. Prinny took on the role of Regent and thus began the infamous Regency Era.

CHAPTER NINE

# THE REGENCY ERA

Prinny had waited his entire adult life to become King. He had watched enviously as other rulers, like Napoleon, got to hold extravagant coronation events. Like a young girl imagining her future wedding, Prinny had long been dreaming of his own coronation. Yet the circumstances of his being named Regent (his father becoming incapacitated) meant that to hold a luxurious party would be in poor taste. Not that Prinny had ever paused his plans due to matters of tackiness, but not even he could bully the government into celebrating the removal of his mentally ill father from responsibility.

Instead, the Regency Era began with a small paperwork-signing meeting in Prinny's drawing room at Carlton House, where a small group of Privy Council members arrived to complete this bureaucratic task. His own heir, Princess Charlotte, was excluded—much to her annoyance. The now fifteen-year-old Charlotte made her presence felt by riding a horse* back and forth past the room where the ceremony was being held, trying to catch a glimpse of the action.

Had George III died, Prinny would have become King and Caroline his Queen. But the role of Regent had no equivalent promotion for Caroline. In fact, the prestige of his new

* Unlike Caroline, who preferred humans to animals, Charlotte was a BIG horse girl.

position led many of Caroline's friends to desert her to curry favor with him.* Ever resilient, Caroline found new allies amongst the Whigs who, out of power, sought to ally with her as they all hated Prinny.

Prominent among these allies was the handsome lawyer Henry Brougham. Brougham was an ambitious member of Parliament with a long-term scheme to eventually become prime minister. Like Perceval, he didn't personally back Caroline, but knew that her popularity could improve his political ambitions. As is the way of the best contestants on *Survivor*, Caroline knew that siding with him would help her for the time being and was prepared to later turn on him.

Caroline, Brougham, and the rest of the anti-Prinny faction worked to clear a path for Princess Charlotte's eventual takeover. Prinny was not expected to live long, as he'd been in poor health for decades and, like his father, had a history of becoming incapacitated by health symptoms. When he fell ill at around this time, Caroline wrote:

> *The Regent is dangerously ill; still I am not sanguine enough to flatter myself that the period to all my troubles and misfortunes is yet come. Yet one must hope for the best.*

Prinny recovered, much to Caroline's disappointment, and was able to convince the government to let him throw a ball three months after being named Regent. Rather than celebrating his father's illness, Prinny claimed this Carlton House Fête was actually to celebrate his (absent) father's birthday as well as to celebrate members of the French royal family who had been living in England.

---

* This did not just organically happen, of course. Prinny intentionally let it be known that he expected Caroline to be excluded from polite society and also dissuaded people from accepting positions in her household.

It had been eighteen years since the execution via guillotine of King Louis XVI and Marie Antoinette. Napoleon seized power six years after that, leaving the remaining members of the French royal family to seek asylum outside the country. Louis XVIII, French King in exile, had been staying in Britain for three years along with his brother, the Count of Artois, the Duke of Berry, and Marie Antoinette's daughter Marie Thérèse of France.

Two thousand people were on Prinny's guest list, but Princess Charlotte was not among them. He did not permit her to attend as he feared her popularity and youth might distract from a celebration he wanted to be all about him. She was sent away to spend the evening with her grandmother and spinster aunts at Windsor. This was one of Charlotte's most hated places, with these women her least favorite company.*

Maria Fitzherbert was invited but did not attend, as she was offended that Prinny would not seat her at the head table. Queen Charlotte also refused to attend and forbade Prinny's sisters from going, as she felt it was in poor taste to be celebrating when George III was so ill.

Caroline, also excluded, spent that evening with her friends Mary and Agnes Berry. She extended personal invitations to the French royals to join her another night for a dinner party. When Louis XVIII and Marie Thérèse sent regrets, Caroline suspected (correctly) that Prinny had dissuaded them from attending. Her party was still well attended with The Black Duke, Caroline's mother, eight of the other French royals, and a guest list including several British lords and ladies.

Prinny's fête officially set the tone for the Regency Era, energizing society after decades of more staid entertainments overseen by George III and Queen Charlotte. After the event,

* She referred to their home, drafty old Windsor Castle filled with unmarried women, as *La Grande Convent*.

Prinny permitted the public to enter Carlton House and its gardens to view the decorations for three days; over thirty thousand people arrived on the final day. He may have been unpopular, but his subjects were nosy and wanted to view the spectacle of his famous home.

As Prinny settled into his role, his efforts to ostracize Caroline increased. By October 1811, Caroline's friend Lord Glenbervie wrote that she "seems tired of Kensington, and disgusted with it, and complains that nobody comes to her there." Campbell recorded Caroline venting that those who had abandoned her were dead to her forever: "No, I repeat it, so long as that man [Prinny] lives, [things are going from bad to worse] for me—whoever comes in to serve him, even those calling themselves my friends, are just the same; they will set me aside and worship the Regent."

Caroline was unrelenting in her determination to fight back. One suggestion she repeatedly brought up to her advisers was to finally publish *The Book.* These plans did not come to pass, but a related title soon became the talk of the town: *The Spirit of the Book* by Irish author Thomas Ashe. Ashe, who wrote this book over six weeks while in prison, imagined a fictional version of Caroline's life, starting with her having a teenage affair in Braunschweig with an Irishman named Algernon. He slightly changed everyone's titles (Caroline was Princess of Hasburgh, rather than Brunswick; Prinny was a Prince of Edinburgh, not of the United Kingdom) but otherwise used Gothic romance tropes to share the saga. As he had written it in the form of letters sent from Caroline to her daughter, it had the veneer of authenticity, and it was widely read not only in the United Kingdom but on the continent as well.

Knowing it was the best way to hurt her, Prinny continued to keep Caroline separated from their daughter. In late

1811, Caroline wrote to Campbell without the assistance of a secretary, thus explaining her awkward grammar as English was her third language:

> *I have seen my daughter once; she do not look well, and I think they not love her very much, poor soul, but I no say anything to make her grumble; it is best she should be satisfied with what is. She sees little of the Sultan [Prinny], and he do not take the way to win her heart.*

Caroline's mood was changeable; happy one moment and full of despair the next. Her lady-in-waiting Lady Charlotte Bury wrote:

> *One day, I think her all perfection—another, I know not what to think. The tissue of her character is certainly more uneven than that of any other person I was ever acquainted with. One day, there is tinsel and tawdry—another, worsted—another, silk and satin—another, gold and jewels—another [the mud, the dirt] . . .*

In November, Prinny processed through the streets in a carriage for the opening of Parliament. While crowds stood to watch him pass, no one cheered or applauded him. Charlotte, following in a carriage behind him, was warmly greeted with loud cheers. Prinny's resentment of his daughter's popularity led him to keep her isolated both from the public and from her own confidantes. Forbidden to communicate with her mother, Charlotte arranged couriers to secretly pass letters between them.

Charlotte wrote pages-long daily letters to her mother. Even separate, their shared victimization via Prinny had bonded them more than ever. Caroline wrote they were "now so united that no event could make a disunion between us."

Unlike the fraught relationship Caroline had with her own mother, she was determined (in a time and place where this concept did not yet exist) to break the generational trauma and forge a loving relationship with Charlotte. Given Caroline's lack of understanding of boundaries, she could take this too far. When Caroline found out that Charlotte had been forbidden from seeing her crush, Lieutenant Charles Hesse,* Caroline arranged for the lovers to meet at her Kensington apartments. At one point, she pushed them into a bedroom together, called out to "have fun!" and closed the door behind them. She wasn't a regular mom. She was a cool mom. But when your daughter is the heir to the throne, this was not the most appropriate choice.

That being said, Charlotte was empathetic to her mother's struggles and failings, writing: "My mother was wicked, but she would not have turned so wicked had not my father been much more wicked still."

Charlotte had long lived in fear of her father's mercurial moods, and he had become more cruel to her the more she rebelled. While Caroline never spoke well of him, Charlotte had developed negative opinions of Prinny from her own lived experience. Caroline wrote:

> *[Charlotte] has a complete contempt of her father's character, which she obtained, not from influence, but from her own sagacity, and experience which she has made of a similar ill-treatment. She abhors the Queen . . . She has no confidence in any of the princesses, not in either of the dukes.*

This fraught family system took a back seat on May 11, 1812, when Caroline's former ally Perceval became the first

---

* Likely the illegitimate son of Charlotte's uncle Prince Frederick, Hesse had previously been one of Caroline's rumored lovers.

British prime minister to be assassinated.* His killer was John Bellingham, an unemployed clerk from Liverpool who had been attempting to get compensation from the British government for the time he'd spent in a Russian prison. Like Prinny trying to woo a new paramour, Bellingham inundated Perceval, other government officials, and Prinny with letters pleading his case. He viewed the lack of response as part of a vast conspiracy against him.

Bellingham was waiting in the lobby when Perceval left from the day's parliamentary sitting. Using a pistol, Bellingham shot Perceval at close range. The prime minister's final words were reported to be, "I am murdered! Murdered!"

Within an hour, a mob was gathering in nearby Parliament Square. Among the politicians, who'd locked themselves in their offices in fear, was a concern that this was the first parry in a vast antigovernment revolution.† The increased violence of recent mob activity led the wealthy to fear that a widespread *Purge*-like riot could overtake the city. A Welsh army officer later recalled, "In the riots and meetings of those troublesome times, the mob really meant mischief, and had they been accustomed to the use of arms and well drilled, they might have committed as great excesses as the ruffians of 1793 in France."

Clearly thinking along the same lines, Prinny sent word from Brighton that all arms depots should be secured so the mob couldn't access firearms.

When a coach arrived to take Bellingham to Newgate Prison, members of the mob rushed the carriage. A military guard was then brought in to escort him to Newgate.

The mob was very into graffiti, which at this point meant using coal, ash, or paint to write lengthy sentences on the walls of public buildings. The sentiments for this movement

---

* And as of this writing, the only British prime minister to be assassinated.

† Prinny, off in his pleasure palace in Brighton, was not in any danger from the mob.

included *Rescue Bellingham or die!* His grievances were not part of a larger movement, but the starving, unemployed and angry people of London were keen to see more of the wealthy elites killed, as had happened recently in the French Revolution.

As word spread of Perceval's murder, riots broke out in other cities, including Nottingham and Leicester. There was great enthusiasm throughout the kingdom for revolution.

Perceval's widow insisted on a private funeral, as the famously humble man would have wanted. The funerals of prime ministers and royals traditionally included having the body lay in state at Westminster Abbey for two days, allowing for mourners to come in and pay their respects. This was omitted in Perceval's funeral for fear of crowds coming to violence. The traditional procession through the city was retooled to depart early in the morning, and would travel down lesser populated roads to avoid large gatherings that could lead to riots. The procession included far fewer participants than usual, both to honor Perceval's private wishes and also so it could pass through as quickly as possible while raising the least amount of attention.

Bellingham was put on trial; the jury took only ten minutes to find him guilty. He was condemned to death, and denied until the end that he'd had any accomplices or that he had acted as part of any political movement. The mob did not riot at his execution, and his brief time as a would-be martyr to instigate a revolution passed quietly.

Though their friendship had been on the outs at the time of his death, Caroline mourned him for the friendship they had previously shared. She wrote: "I have lost my best friend. I know not where to look for another. Though even he changed towards me since he had become one of the ministers." Out of respect for him, she canceled all her public engagements in the weeks following his death apart from attendance at court, "as that cannot be attributed to any love of pleasure."

Perceval's replacement as prime minister was one of Prinny's friends: Robert Jenkinson, second Earl of Liverpool. With the new government leader's backing, Prinny revealed stricter guidelines surrounding Caroline's ability to visit their daughter. On June 17, he wrote a letter declaring that the pair could only meet once every two weeks, and never on any of Prinny's property.

Later that year in September, Prinny sent a messenger to inform Caroline that Prinny had refused her request to have Charlotte visit her that Saturday. Caroline was at the time being attended by her loyal friend, the six-foot-tall Lady Anne Hamilton, when she received his refusal. Hamilton "behaved like Joan of Arc in the whole of this business; she was immovable; not a muscle of her face altered at the eloquent speech of this knight errant." Caroline was unsurprised by this latest turn, accustomed as she was to disappointment that "one more or less makes not much effect upon my temper."

But she was never without a plan. On October 4, she went to Windsor to demand to see her daughter. Upon this request being refused, Caroline demanded to speak with the Queen. Queen Charlotte received her, but only to refer her to take up her issues with Prinny directly.

And so began a months-long battle, fought via letters in which Caroline and her entourage squared off against Prinny and the government with no détente on the horizon. In November, Caroline wrote a letter (edited by Brougham) to the Queen, complaining both of being kept separate from her daughter and also criticizing the way Charlotte was being kept away not only from her mother but from all of society.*

* In a manner similar to how Caroline had been treated at the same age.

When Charlotte fell ill with a cold, Caroline was not permitted to pay her a visit. Caroline wrote:

> *I have not had the power to [think] of anything else. She was very unwell for some days, and though I begged hard, the Regent and the old stony-hearted Queen would not let me see her . . . I know not how long I shall be able to go on bearing all my sorrows.*

Princess Charlotte took up her mother's cause. Brougham reported that she "is extremely solicitous that her mother should be openly vindicated, and [Caroline's] wish for this proceeds almost as much from the desire of gratifying her as of punishing her husband. [Charlotte] is quite furious at their treatment of [Caroline]. I mean Queen, Princesses, Dukes, and her father as much as any."

Charlotte became further irate when her governess resigned and, despite being now seventeen, Prinny arranged for her to get a new governess. She wanted to be treated as an adult, with her own establishment and ladies-in-waiting rather than governesses. Charlotte fought this decision until Prinny finally compromised to provide her with two lady companions, one of whom, Cornelia Knight, became Charlotte's absolute ride or die.

A new issue among the warring family was that of Charlotte's debut into society. She would be turning eighteen in January 1813, and Caroline had privately arranged with Charlotte that she would present her. Meanwhile, Prinny and his mother had decided that Charlotte's aunt Princess Frederica, the Duchess of York, should make the presentation. On the date in question, all were present in the drawing room at St. James's Palace. Charlotte, waiting outside, was told of her father's wishes. Standing firmly on Caroline's side, she said, "Either my mother, or no one." Her debut was, therefore, postponed.

The same week as this failed debut, a letter Caroline had written to Prinny was leaked to the press. She had first sent it to him in November. When it was returned, unopened, she had Campbell resend the letter. It was returned again. Campbell attempted to send it again, and finally, it was leaked to the press.

Caroline begins the letter by protesting her innocence from the Delicate Investigation:

> *Let me implore you to reflect on the situation in which I am placed; without the shadow of a charge against me—without even an accuser—after an inquiry that led to my ample vindication—yet treated as if I were still more culpable than the perjuries of my suborned traducers represented me, and held up to the world as a mother who may not enjoy the society of her only child.*

The rest of the lengthy letter focuses on the unfairness of keeping Caroline separated from her daughter:

> *The plan of excluding my daughter from all intercourse with the world, appears to my humble judgement peculiarly unfortunate. She who is destined to be the Sovereign of this great country, enjoys none of those advantages of society which are deemed necessary for imparting a knowledge of mankind to persons who have infinitely less occasion to learn that important lesson.*

Prinny had years earlier sworn to never open or read any of Caroline's letters as a show of his contempt for her, and he never wavered. Her letter made its way to Liverpool, the new prime minister, who told Caroline that Prinny had been made aware of its contents and had no response. Shortly thereafter, someone* shared the full text with the Whig newspaper, the *Morning Chronicle*.

---

* Someone named Caroline of Brunswick and/or Henry Brougham.

The letter was a sensation nicknamed *The Regent's Valentine* as it was published so close to Valentine's Day. Caroline and Charlotte both gained even more public sympathy, and a frenzy ensued, with excerpts from the letter being merchandized for sale on prints, plates, and jugs. Jane Austen wrote about the matter to a friend:

> *I suppose all the world is sitting in judgement upon the Princess of Wales's letter. Poor woman, I shall support her as long as I can, because she is a woman & because I hate her husband . . . I am resolved at least always to think that she would have been respectable, if the Prince had behaved tolerably by her at first.**

The letter's publication made Prinny even more firm in his conviction that Caroline would never see their daughter. Upon receipt of a letter from the prime minister on Prinny's behalf, canceling Charlotte's planned visit to her mother, Caroline dictated a letter to Liverpool to her friend Lady Anne Hamilton. In this, Caroline defended herself against the insinuation that she had been involved with *The Regent's Valentine* being made public. Furthermore, Caroline protested that she would not have written about this at all except that the effect of this rumor operated "to deprive her Royal Highness of the sole real happiness she can possess in this world—that of seeing her only child." She continued that preventing a mother and daughter from meeting was "positively against the law of nature."

Using the publication of *The Regent's Valentine* as grounds to reopen the Delicate Investigation, Prinny instructed a com-

---

* Despite Austen's dislike of Prinny, he was a superfan of hers, retaining a full set of her books in each of his residences. He also bullied her into dedicating her 1815 book *Emma* to him, much to Austen's distaste.

mittee to reevaluate all evidence from this investigation and to come to a new conclusion as to whether her moral character was suitable to visit Princess Charlotte. Again, this was held in secret and again, Caroline was not officially informed it was happening. Again, she was unable to defend herself.

When Caroline inevitably found out about the Delicate Investigation 2.0, she submitted a formal protest against the proceedings to the Lord President of the Privy Council. She wrote, in the third person, that she "has not had any power to choose the judges before whom any inquiry may be carried out; but she is perfectly willing to have her whole conduct inquired into by the persons who may be selected by her accusers. The Princess only demands that she may be heard in defense or in explanation of her conduct, if it is attacked; and that she should be either treated as innocent, or proved to be guilty."

One week later, she wrote a similar letter to the Speaker of the House of Commons.

If Prinny had hoped to ruin Caroline's reputation among her fans with this reminder of the Delicate Investigation, things backfired spectacularly. The Princess of Wales's appeal to the House of Commons created a great sensation throughout the country, as the notion of fair treatment was held by many as one of the virtues of British identity. The concept of a secret investigation instigated by the already unpopular Regent and Queen only made them more widely loathed.

The public made their feelings known when any of the royals stepped out in public. The Queen was booed. The crowds who viewed Prinny's carriage remained aggressively silent. Caroline and Princess Charlotte were widely and enthusiastically cheered.

With a public eager for any updates, news soon spread that Caroline and Charlotte had been spotted meeting up. This had been purely coincidental; both had been taking carriage rides at the same time around Hyde Park. The park was like the main street in a small town, where people drive back and forth to see and be seen. Spectators would assemble to watch the rich and famous slowly drive in open-top carriages along the park's paths, one row going one way, one going the other, with gentlemen on horseback riding throughout as well.

Caroline and Charlotte happened to be there at the same time, heading in opposite directions in their carriages. The audience who had come to watch the elite on parade were nearly as excited as these two were to see one another after so long. The number of witnesses to this reunion led to word quickly spreading about how unfair it was that these two were only able to interact in this brief manner, and within weeks news of the run-in was common knowledge.

Public sentiment was so clearly on Caroline and Charlotte's side that the Delicate Investigation 2.0 members were forced to take this into account. After a number of delays, the committee again unanimously declared Caroline's innocence. They wrote that Caroline's "innocence is acknowledged entire—complete. To such restrictions as the Prince Regent, in his capacity as father of the Princess Charlotte, or by the advice of his Ministry, might think proper to impose upon her intercourse with her daughter, she must submit. It is her lot. But she has the satisfaction of knowing that her reputation is, by the confession of all, without imputation or reproach."

Across London, cheers went up as pub-goers toasted their heroine's latest victory. The public, forever loyal to Caroline, celebrated her second victory by inundating her Kensington Palace apartments with letters and notices of congratulations. Caroline took to the streets herself, where well-wishers mobbed her, causing her lady-in-waiting Bury to wonder if this was "the proudest moment of the Princess's troubled life."

And yet, her situation was largely unchanged. "After all this farce it leaves you just where you were before," the annoyed Charlotte commented, correctly. Caroline's ability to visit with Charlotte remained unchanged: only with Prinny's permission and only on his terms.

Caroline was furious to have been again put in this humiliating position by Prinny, writing to Campbell: "Though it is in some measure satisfactory, I AM NOT YET SATISFIED."

CHAPTER TEN

# The Royal Pariah

One result of the Delicate Investigation 2.0 was that Prinny permitted Princess Charlotte to read about her mother's behavior. She had long been aware of Caroline's flirtatious personality, but these documents outlined alleged liaisons and sexual relationships resulting in children. Charlotte was shocked to read these details, writing:

> *The publication of things I was wholly ignorant of before, really came upon me with such a blow and it stagger'd me so terribly that I . . . shall not ever recover from it . . . The horror of the knowledge of the whole can never make those feelings ever return again that might have allowed influence.*

However, she felt sympathy for her mother's social ostracism, further writing:

> *She has a great deal of pride and high spirits and feels mortified, and fears she may be lower'd in people's eyes. She likes society, hates being shut out of it, and yet if she were to give parties people would then see who she is reduced to.*

Caroline faced another blow when her mother died following a brief illness. As the mother of the controversial Princess of Wales, but also the elder sister of the current King and grandmother to the second in line to the throne, Augusta's funeral needed to be, to some extent, public.

Caroline and her advisers also saw this as an opportunity to further influence public opinion in her favor. They began making serious plans to finally publish *The Book*. Prinny attempted to get some public goodwill by allowing Charlotte to visit her mourning mother at Blackheath.

Caroline had long had a good relationship with London's Lord Mayor, through their mutual friend, Alderman Matthew Wood. Wood wrote a formal address to deliver publicly on behalf of the city in appreciation for Caroline's fortitude in the face of ongoing persecution. This read, in part, that the city council viewed "the foul conspiracy against the honour and life of her Royal Highness and their admiration at her moderation, frankness, and magnanimity under her long persecution."

The formal address was set to be delivered on April 12, a month after Augusta's death. A massive crowd congregated to celebrate Caroline, necessitating her to take an alternate route to avoid the road blockage. Prinny, notably, made sure he was out of town. In her Kensington apartments, Caroline received the Lord Mayor and aldermen and delivered a response to Wood's address. Her voice shook initially, but she gained confidence as the speech progressed. It read, in part:

"It is to me the greatest consolation to learn, that during so many years of unmerited persecution . . . the king and favourable sentiments with which they did me the honour to approach me, on my arrival in this country, have undergone neither diminution nor change in the hearts of the citizens of London. The sense of indignation and abhorrence you express against the foul and detestable conspiracy, which, by perjured and suborned traducers, has been carried on against my life and honour, it is worthy of you, and most gratifying to me . . .

"I shall not lose any opportunity I may be permitted to enjoy, of encouraging the talents and virtues of my dear daughter the Princess Charlotte; and I shall impress upon her mind my full sense of the obligation conferred upon me by this spontaneous act of your justice and generosity . . . she will ever be found to the City of London in ties proportioned to the strength of that filial attachment I have had the happiness uniformly to experience from her."

Suspecting that Prinny would soon evict her from Kensington Palace, Caroline set about to lease a town house in London. Despite Prinny's active interference, through which several potential rentals fell through, Caroline eventually rented Connaught House in Westminster.

Charlotte requested permission for another visit for her mother's birthday on May 17 and was permitted to only stay there for the morning, lest she witness the alleged debauchery of Caroline's evening parties. Charlotte, still loyal to her mother despite Prinny's ongoing slander, wrote that Caroline "was ill-used, and is still more now than before, after this double clamor."

As 1812 turned to 1813, Caroline's life remained status quo. She was still adored by the public, being given a standing ovation just for showing up to attend the opera. Yet, like so many public figures then and now, Caroline was insurmountably sad in private. Mary Berry wrote in April 1813 that Caroline "was tired, body and mind." In July, Berry wrote that Caroline "is melancholy, and almost in ill-humour, now seeing more nearly the truth to her position." In October, Berry wrote that Caroline was "in good humour, but not very cheerful, and appearing to find her situation more hopeless, without the death of one of the two*—which is very true."

* Namely, either the death of Caroline or of Prinny.

Caroline herself wrote that year from Kensington Palace to Campbell:

*I am becoming more and more insignificant every day, and cannot say I feel sure of having a single friend in England! It is a melancholy position . . . to be so [isolated], but I must bear my fate, and keep up a good courage so long as I can. How long that may be, God He knows. I am ashamed of wearying you with my lucubrations, but you are always indulgent to my miserable self, and truly one must confide one's sorrows to somebody.*

Though Caroline had been declared innocent in Parliament, many of her former friends continued to choose Prinny over her due to his superior position in society. That being said, many continued their friendships with Caroline this year with recorded visits, including Princess Sophia of Gloucester,* Lord Byron, Earl and Lady Grey,† Lady Anne Hamilton and Mary Berry.

Caroline continued to enjoy the company of writers and was delighted to hear that French author Germaine de Staël was coming to London. De Staël was well-regarded at the time as a philosopher and author. She had been a leading figure in the French Revolution and later so annoyed Napoleon that he banned her from Paris for ten years. She spent the decade traveling around continental Europe, arriving in London in 1813.

Caroline's love of interesting guests, women writers, travel, and scandalous figures made her determined to have de Staël attend one of her house parties. Upon her arrival, as per Lord Byron, de Staël "preached English politics to the first of our English Whig politicians . . . preached politics no less to our Tory politicians the day after."

---

* The daughter of Prinny and Caroline's uncle, Prince William Henry.

† The inventors of Earl Grey tea!

Caroline wrote, "I am in expectation of seeing Madame de Staël, and I shall fairly give my opinion upon this new meteor, which is now in full blaze upon our atmosphere."

Soon, Prinny's influence became apparent, as de Staël refused all of Caroline's invitations. Caroline wrote, "I begin to suspect that Madame de Staël will be guided by the torrent . . . I am determined to be very proud, and not to take one single step, if it is not entirely from Madame de Staël's own impulse that she becomes acquainted with me." Ultimately, the two women did not meet.

Charlotte was still being mostly kept apart from Caroline, who continued to be anxious to spend more time with her. In March 1814, Caroline wrote, "Princess Charlotte I have now not seen for six weeks past."*

Prinny, meanwhile, was working behind the scenes to remove Charlotte from England entirely. He had begun to pick a man for her to marry, ideally a royal Prince from continental Europe. His plan was for her, like her mother and grandmothers, to depart the country to go and live with a foreign husband. Charlotte was not informed that she would be asked to leave the country. All she knew was that a marriage was being planned for her.

Prinny chose twenty-three-year-old Crown Prince William of Orange. William was heir to the throne of the United Kingdom of the Netherlands, "Prince of Orange" being the title given to this heir to the throne like "Prince of Wales" is the title of the British heir. An alliance between the two kingdoms could be cemented with a marriage alliance between Charlotte and William.

William came to England, briefly met Charlotte, and an engagement was publicly announced. Caroline learned about

* Charlotte had been permitted to visit Caroline on her eighteenth birthday, January 4, 1814.

this simultaneously as the rest of the public despite being in regular correspondence with her daughter.

Charlotte soon discovered her father's plan to have her shipped off and begged him to include a clause promising her an establishment in England and that she should not be taken or kept out of England against her wishes. He refused to allow her to see the marriage contract, noting that it was a matter for him to sort out with the King of the Netherlands. Charlotte flatly refused to accept the terms of this contract.

Caroline wrote in May 1814:

> *I have not seen Princess Charlotte for nearly five months. She is outrageous at the thoughts of leaving this country; and her unnatural father assured her that she should never have an establishment in this country; but I have advised her to be firm, and not frightened; and I think she will conquer. She is no child of mine if she submit [sic] to such tyranny.*

Prinny continued to ostracize Caroline in the pettiest of ways. When Caroline requested a seat at St. Paul's Cathedral for a Thanksgiving service, she was informed that all the seats had already been reserved for Prinny and his guests. As biographer Lewis Melville wrote, it was doubtful if Prinny succeeded "in doing anything beyond causing her distress and exposing his own pettiness. He did, indeed, prevent his guests from going to Kensington."

In the midst of all this, in June 1815, Napoleon was soundly defeated by Prinny's friend Lord Wellington and his troops. The monarchy was restored in France, leading to celebrations across London (a place that never needed an excuse for a party or a riot). Windows were aglow with candlelight and people took to the streets in joy. His defeat meant the reinstatement of the French royals, leading other foreign royals to arrive in England to join the party. These visitors included the King of Prussia and the Russian Czar. Among this delegation was the quietly handsome Prince Leopold of Saxe-Coburg, who caught Charlotte's eye.

Prinny took this opportunity to humiliate Caroline. When the Czar of Russia was about to enter his carriage to visit her at Kensington, one of Prinny's representatives intervened, requesting he skip the visit upon Prinny's request. The Czar, feeling badly, wrote a letter of apology to Caroline for missing their visit. When Charlotte noted that Caroline had been left off the guest list of one soiree, she refused to attend herself out of loyalty.

Caroline wrote to the Queen to question being left out of the festivities, and the Queen responded:

> *[The Prince Regent] desires it may be directly understood, for reasons of which he alone can be the judge, to be his fixed and unalterable determination not to meet the Princess of Wales upon any occasion, either in public or private. The Queen is thus placed under the painful necessity of intimating to the Princess of Wales the impossibility of her Majesty's receiving her Royal Highness at the drawing-room.*

Not willing to accept this, Caroline wrote back with barely disguised threats to go public with more gossip about the royal family:

> *Your Majesty will, I am sure, not be displeased that I should relieve myself from a suspicion of disrespect towards your Majesty, by making public the cause of my absence from Court at a time when the duties of my station would otherwise peculiarly demand my attendance.*

With the Queen holding firm, Caroline wrote again, more desperately:

*Since his Majesty's lamented illness I have demanded, in the face of Parliament and the country, to be proved guilty, or to be treated as innocent. I have been declared innocent; I will not submit to be greeted as guilty . . . Can your Royal Highness have contemplated the full extent of your declarations—never to meet me upon any occasion, either public or private? Has your Royal Highness forgotten the approaching marriage of our daughter, and the possibility of our coronation?*

White's, the preeminent private members club of this era, often hosted soirees for the wealthy. When they announced plans to host a ball for the visiting monarchs, Prinny (a club member) ensured that Caroline had no method to acquire a ticket. Caroline's loyal friend Lord Sefton declared that he intended to provide her with one of his tickets; fourteen others expressed the same intention, which led to Prinny canceling the ball entirely.

He could not stop Caroline from attending a gala performance at the opera, which Prinny and the foreign royals also attended. Caroline entered as "God Save the King" was being sung. When the song concluded, the orchestra turned toward her box and applauded her. Caroline did not acknowledge this tribute, despite her friend Sir William Gell encouraging her to.

"No, no; Punch's wife is nobody when Punch is present," she joked. "I know my business better than to take the morsel out of my husband's mouth. I am not to seem to know that the applause is meant for me, till they call my name."

When the opera concluded, the crowd yelled, "Where's your wife?" to Prinny. In contrast, Caroline was warmly applauded as she left, then cheered on the street by a large mob that blocked her carriage for a few minutes.

"Shall we burn Carlton House?" they offered.

"No, my good people," Caroline replied. "Be quiet—let me pass, and go home to your beds."

As she left, they called after her, "God save the Princess!" and "Long live the innocent!"

Campbell recalled that Caroline "was pleased at this demonstration of feeling in her favour, and I never saw her look so well, or behave with so much dignity."

Through all of this, her daughter, Charlotte, was working to break off her engagement to the Prince of Orange. Relocating to the Netherlands would mean leaving her mother, and she worried about what might happen to Caroline if Charlotte wasn't around to help fight for her and support her. Several of Charlotte's most explosive arguments with Prinny had involved her desire to spend more time with her mother. She had stood up for Caroline when she could, like when she'd refused to attend balls her mother wasn't invited to. Charlotte also knew that, powerless as she may often feel, her role as heir to the throne gave her some amount of power she could wield in her mother's defense.

Caroline was impressed with her daughter's strength as she stood up for herself against Prinny. Caroline wrote:

> *My daughter has acted with the greatest firmness, promptitude, and energy of character possible, in the very intricate business concerning her marriage. She has maneuvered and conquered the Regent so completely, that there can be no more doubt that the marriage is broken off . . . Charlotte declared to [the Prince of Orange] that she would never leave this country, except by an act of Parliament, and by her own special desire . . . I am quite transfixed with astonishment that my daughter at last has resumed her former character of intrepidity and fortitude . . .*

Prinny became obsessed with forcing Charlotte's hand in marriage in order to get her out of the country. Caroline's friend Brougham wrote that Prinny "is jealous of [Charlotte] to a degree of insanity, and has been for some time."

Seeing this stalemate between Prinny and Charlotte and knowing that her own presence in England was an impediment to Charlotte getting her way, Caroline began to plan to leave the country herself for the sake of her daughter. Caroline also knew that aside from moral support, there was little she could do to help her daughter from England. Prinny had socially isolated her, and the Whig support Caroline relied upon could just as easily help Charlotte with Caroline out of town.

Caroline had in some ways grown to resemble her mother: arranged marriage landing her in a country she hated, desperate to return to her birthplace. More than anything, Caroline needed distance from all of the misery she'd experienced from Prinny and his family. She wrote to a friend, "I rejoice in the thought of so soon being far off from all of them."

Her childhood dreams of travel and adventure seemed possible now that the Napoleonic Wars had ended. She undertook negotiations with Parliament, who offered her a generous allowance in exchange for her return to Braunschweig. What they didn't know was that while she *did* plan to stop by her hometown, she ultimately aimed to settle in Italy and stay there until Prinny died and Charlotte became the new monarch.

Of course, she hadn't shared any of this scheming with Charlotte yet. And her teenage daughter was busy with bold plans of her own.

CHAPTER ELEVEN

# A Royal Escape

Caroline was visiting friends in Blackheath late one night in July 1814 when a messenger arrived, bringing forth the startling news that Princess Charlotte had run away and was waiting for her mother in London at Connaught Place. Caroline set out right away with Lady Charlotte Lindsay.* By the time they arrived at Connaught Place, Princess Charlotte had already assembled a team of advisers, including the ever-present Henry Brougham. Dinner was served for the company, and Charlotte regaled her mother with the story of her escape.

She had been staying at her London residence, Warwick House, using the excuse of an injured knee to avoid spending time with Prinny. When he commanded she return to her aunts and grandmother at Windsor Castle, she fled Warwick House through a back entrance.

But where to go? She knew of the existence of hackney cabs, the yellow-painted carriages similar to a modern-day taxi, but she didn't know how to hail one. Luckily, Charlotte looked so flustered that a nearby man offered to hail one for her. She gratefully climbed inside and instructed the driver to

* Lady Charlotte Lindsay had been one of the couriers involved in getting correspondence between Caroline and Charlotte.

take her to her mother's residence.* The driver assumed she was a lady's maid until, upon arrival, she entered Connaught House through the front door, and servants bowed to her.

From there, Charlotte sent a messenger to bring Brougham to her. He later described her as behaving with the high spirits of a "bird set loose from its cage" as she excitedly enjoyed her first-ever evening of freedom.

Several of their political supporters were out of town or unable to be found, but Brougham suggested they call upon Charlotte's uncle Prince Augustus, who had recently spoken in her favor in Parliament. Shortly after Caroline and Lindsay's arrival, Charlotte's best friend, Margaret Mercer Elphinstone, arrived. Prinny sent emissaries from Carlton House, all of whom Caroline and Charlotte commanded to wait outside.

Caroline was eager to hear the litany of Charlotte's longheld resentments against her father and the other royals. Charlotte was appalled by her forced arrangement with William. She was furious that she was being separated from her mother. Every time Charlotte grew close to one of her female aides, spies let Prinny know and her friend was removed. Charlotte declared it her "fixed resolution" to live entirely with her mother.† After airing out her grievances, Charlotte asked for advice. All present, including Caroline, advised she return to Prinny. Charlotte refused.

The time passed, and soon it was midnight. Brougham advised Charlotte her only options were to leave of her free will, or wait to be forcibly removed. Her reaction was notable, as he later wrote: "I have told many a client he was going to be

---

* This was the first time a member of the British royal family rode in a taxi on their own.

† Caroline hadn't yet shared her Italian plan with her daughter.

Augusta of Great Britain, Duchess of Brunswick-Lüneburg and Princess of Brunswick-Wolfenbüttel, was Caroline's mother and Prinny's aunt. This portrait shows Augusta dressed in the highly feminine, structured style fashionable during her young adulthood. This contrasts with Caroline's preference toward undone hairstyles and looser-fitting, more sensual gowns, similar to the way Augusta's and Caroline's personalities clashed throughout their relationship. Augusta is painted here by Anna Rosina de Gasc.

Photo Credit:
Richard Borek Stiftung

This portrait of Caroline is from 1804, two years before the Delicate Investigation. Her rumored lover Sir Thomas Lawrence has included three visual messages in the portrait. First, her wedding ring is in shadow, decentralizing her role as Prinny's wife. Second, a bust of her father's head is just behind her (usually a married royal woman would pose with her husband's bust). And third, she is staring straight ahead, as though challenging the viewer to judge her. She holds a sculpting tool, indicating that she is the artist of the bust in the background. She wears red, her favorite color, showcasing her irrepressible personality.

Photo Credit:

This portrait of Caroline's brother Friedrich Wilhelm, the Black Duke, was painted by Friedrich Barthel. In the painting, we see the Black Duke's impressive uniform, including skull and crossbones imagery on his hat and on the horse's saddle. Prinny liked to be painted in this manner, but unlike him, the Black Duke actually wore a uniform and was a real war hero, so this portrait accurately represents him.

Photo Credit:
Richard Borek Stiftung

Karl Wilhelm Ferdinand, Prince of Brunswick-Wolfenbüttel and Duke of Brunswick-Lüneburg, was Caroline's father. A scholar by personality, he was forced by circumstances to lead a military career, which he was highly successful in. Caroline adored him and was devastated by his death in battle in 1806. This portrait is by Johann Georg Ziesenis.

Photo Credit:
Richard Borek Stiftung

George, Prince of Wales (aka Prinny), was ruthlessly mocked by the press throughout his adult years. This image was printed in 1792, the year he married Caroline. Easter eggs include a view of Carlton House's unending renovations through the window, unpaid bills stacked under a chamber pot by his elbow, and various medications to cure digestion, bad breath, hemorrhoids, and sexually transmitted infections behind him.

This portrait of Caroline by Gainsborough Dupont was commissioned by her uncle/father-in-law, George III. Her breathtaking wedding gown is on full display here. As described in issue 65 of *The Gentleman's Magazine*, 1795, she wore "A royal robe; silver tissue petticoat, covered with silver Venetian net and silver tassels; body and train of silver tissue, festooned on each side with large cord and tassels." A miniature of Prinny is pinned at her breast.

Photo Credit: © Royal Collection Enterprises Limited 2025 | Royal Collection Trust

This painting of Caroline and Prinny's nuptials by John Graham was painted in 1795, the year of their wedding. A droopy Caroline resembles a melting wax figure, while Prinny seems about to topple over from his drunken misery. Between them, the officiant gazes heavenward as though for the strength to get through the ceremony. On the right, Queen Charlotte (seated) looks at the viewer as though to say "I never approved of this match," as other women gossip among themselves about, probably, how drunk Prinny is.

Photo Credit: Royal Collection Enterprises Limited 2025 | All Rights Reserved

Caroline with her daughter, Charlotte, who is around five years old. Caroline is painted here as Minerva, the Roman goddess of music, wisdom, justice, law, and victory. The artist, Sir Thomas Lawrence, spent so much time at Caroline's home while working on this portrait that they were rumored to be lovers. This painting was exhibited at the 1802 Royal Academy Summer Exhibition to great acclaim. Caroline kept this painting with her until her death, when it was acquired by Queen Victoria (first cousin of Princess Charlotte).

Bartolomeo Pergami, Caroline's chamberlain and probable lover, was a muscular, six-foot-tall ex-soldier. His handsome picture was popular in England at the time of her trial.

Photo Credit: © National Portrait Gallery, London

Princess Charlotte of Wales, Caroline's daughter, was adored by the public from the day she was born. Painted here, pregnant at age twenty-one, she is depicted with hints of her artistic interests as indicated by the portfolio under one arm. This maternity dress is currently in the collection of the Museum of London.

Photo Credit: © National Portrait Gallery, London

This bust of Caroline of Brunswick was made in 1821. The neckline of her gown is lowered to slightly expose one shoulder, perhaps the same "impertinent shoulder" that was noted by Lord Malmesbury years earlier. The artist, Peter Turnerelli, also created a bust of Princess Charlotte late in her pregnancy. Presumably Caroline spoke with him about her daughter as she modeled for this bust.

Photo Credit:
Richard Borek Stiftung

Caroline of Brunswick, sketched as she attended her "trial" at the House of Lords in 1820. Her dark hair (a wig) is topped with a headdress featuring large ostrich feathers, the symbol of the Prince of Wales. This sketch was used as a reference for a large painting of the trial, later completed by Sir George Hayter.

convicted, but I never saw anything like her *stupefaction*; for a quarter of an hour she was lost."

At around 3:00 a.m., Prinny's brother Prince Frederick arrived, authorized to remove her physically if necessary. Caroline went down to chat with him while Charlotte remained upstairs with Brougham and Augustus.

Dawn was beginning to creep through the night, and Brougham pulled out one last strategy to convince Charlotte to return home. He pointed out the window at Hyde Park, noting that come daylight, it would be filled with people coming to vote in that day's by-election. If they saw her in distress and heard of her grievances, they would all be willing to riot in defense of her. This riot may reach Carlton House, which they might burn down, leading to bloodshed. Did she want this to be her legacy as Queen?

Perhaps it was his way with words, perhaps it was exhaustion, or perhaps Charlotte had run out of fight, but after speaking with Brougham, she agreed to leave her mother's house. She had one condition, though: Brougham was to prepare an official document stating that she refused to marry William, and that any announcement of their marriage would be against her will and without her consent. Six copies were made and signed by Charlotte, Caroline, Prince Augustus, Lindsay, Elphinstone, and Brougham.

When Charlotte was to be escorted from Connaught House without her lady's maid, Caroline stood up for her and insisted she be permitted along. After the long night, Charlotte was put back in her cage at 5:00 a.m.; her freedom had lasted twelve hours. But she had managed to achieve one of her goals: the Orange match was off.

Word of the Princess's extraordinary night spread quickly through town, fueled by the Whig newspapers decrying it all as Prinny's fault. Most people were already sympathetic to Charlotte's desire to spend time with her mother, and Prinny was blamed for bringing her to such a desperate act. Tory newspapers did their best to paint Prinny as the victim in the situation, claiming this escape attempt was the sort of rash behavior he was trying to prevent through his strict rules for her conduct. Ultimately, few minds would have changed. Those who supported Caroline and Charlotte used this as evidence they were right, as did those who sided with Prinny.

Charlotte met her father at Carlton House days later for an emotional meeting. Both were moved to tears and to her surprise, he claimed to forgive her. The Orange match may be off, but she was still living a strictly controlled life entirely on his terms. Her ladies-in-waiting, working for Prinny, were under order never to let her out of their sight, even at night when she was asleep. She was forbidden to write letters to anyone, but managed to steal paper and pencil to send a letter each to her uncle Augustus and to her friend Elphinstone. In both, she blamed herself for bringing trouble to others.

Depressed, Charlotte saw little hope in her future. And at the end of the month, her father came to share the news that Caroline was planning to move to the continent. He assumed she knew, but nobody had told her. She felt humiliated to have to learn this from him, rather than from her mother.

This plan had been in the works for a few weeks. Caroline had approached Prinny, requesting permission to visit The Black Duke in Braunschweig and wrote to prime minister Liverpool, noting that she, "after very mature reflection, has resolved to take such measures as may enable her to go abroad . . . The Princess of Wales would perhaps have postponed her intended departure till the marriage of the Princess Charlotte had taken place, had she not been informed that the unprotected state of the Princess of Wales, in these peculiar circumstances in which the Princess Charlotte must have left her mother, formed the chief impediment to the union with the Prince Hereditary of Orange. It is the sincere wish of the Princess of Wales to remove every obstacle to the welfare of her daughter, and to the tranquillity and peace of mind of the Prince Regent, which induces the Princess of Wales to request that Lord Liverpool will lose no time in communicating to his Royal Highness the Prince Regent her wishes, and her intention to go to her native country, to pay a visit to her brother, the Duke of Brunswick."

Caroline was delighted to be granted permission to leave the country. She wrote in third-person to her friend, Whig politician Samuel Whitbread:

> *She is about to take the most important step in her life. She has embraced the resolution of quitting this country for a time . . . she has been intending to travel ever since 1806, although reasons, too long for explanation, have prevented her . . . The Princess having obtained this public satisfaction cannot in conscience remain a [burden] to her friends any longer.*

She clarified that she would not have left so soon "had not the marriage of the Princess Charlotte with the Prince of Orange been broken off at her own instance. Dear as her daughter is to her, she could not resolve to leave her without protection in a situation so critical. The Princess, aware that the match was ardently desired by the people, wished neither to impede the happiness of the nation nor that of her daughter. On this account, she is solicitous to depart at once, for it is pitiable to see a child rendered on all occasions a source of dispute between her parents. The Princess of Wales is assured, that in future the Princess Charlotte will be more happy and tranquil; and she is led to make this sacrifice that if she remains some time longer unmarried, there may be fewer obstacles to her appearance in public."

She continued, "The Princess Charlotte will the less feel

the deprivation of her mother's society as she has been deprived of it for the last two years. During that time, five or six months in succession have passed away without the mother being allowed to see her daughter . . . although living in the same capital, they were not allowed to speak, even when they met in their airings . . . Thus to quit her will be but the grief of a day, whilst to remain is to plant daggers in the bosom both of mother and child."

She suspected that her absence might cause Prinny to begin divorce proceedings so he could take a new wife and father a son to supplant Charlotte as heir to the throne.* Caroline wrote that if she heard even hints of such a scheme, Prinny "could be surprised at the Princess's sudden return to this country."

She was permitted to see Charlotte for an in-person farewell. Given Charlotte's ongoing restrictions, the meeting was also attended by chaperones ensuring that she would not attempt to escape. In her usual manner, Caroline kept her emotions hidden so as not to reveal any personal weakness. The more emotive Charlotte misinterpreted this as her mother's indifference to being separated and wrote to Elphinstone:

> *After all, if a mother has not feeling for her child, or children, are they to teach it her or can they expect to be listened to with any hopes of success?*

But Charlotte's and Caroline's friends all knew once she had set her mind on a course of action, there was no room for change. "Nothing can stop her," wrote Lindsay, in a version of Brougham's words about Charlotte's own stubbornness. "I never saw so fixed a determination."

---

* Because until 2013, younger sons could always outrank older sisters in becoming heir to the throne in the United Kingdom.

Though she had acquired permission to return to Braunschweig, as mentioned previously, Caroline already had plans to settle in Naples for the winter. And so in early August 1814, Caroline of Brunswick set out with a small entourage, including her wards Willikin and Edwardina, as well as her lady-in-waiting Lindsay and her trusted messenger John Hieronymous. She stopped en route in the town of Worthing where she went for an evening walk to the beach. She sat there for two hours, contemplating the moonbeams dancing on the waves. In London, Charlotte was so distressed at being abandoned by her mother that she was overcome with nervous spasms. Prinny raised a toast to "the Princess of Wales's damnation and may she never return to England."

On August 8, a small crowd gathered to see her off. They were quiet and apparently somewhat confused at why she was leaving. It is from them we have the description of the unique hat she chose to wear: a military-style tall hat of violet and green with a towering plume of green feathers. Caroline decided to travel under the pseudonym the Countess von Wolfenbüttel, though her true identity was evident to anyone who saw one of her trunks painted with the words *Her Royal Highness the Princess of Wales, to be always with her.* Allegedly, its contents included her as-yet unpublished tell-all memoirs. Caroline had made no secret that she had written memoirs, the prospect of their publication one of her frequent threats to her in-laws. According to a friend, Caroline spared no details in the writing:

> *[The memoirs] begin from her early youth, and continued in detail to the epoch of her marriage, and in still greeted detail since. Every circumstance of the Prince's behaviour to her at and after her marriage . . . his character, which she knows perfectly; the Queen's, which she abhors, and whom she believes to be her greatest enemy . . .*

Of this alleged document, the *Examiner* wrote:

> Who would give their ears . . . to know what is inside of this mysterious receptacle.

It had been nearly twenty years since she had first arrived in England. Then, she had been filled with joy by the prospect of her impending marriage, to a man she wrote of as the "finest and handsomest prince in the world." As the ship set sail this time, the forty-six year old Princess wept.

# PART TWO

# CAROLINE ABROAD

CHAPTER TWELVE

# No Fucks Given Era

As Caroline traveled across German territories, she was greeted by a public that was overjoyed by their release from Napoleon's grip, and was equally thrilled to see their hometown Princess return. Her attendants were also excited to be traveling on the continent, setting foot in places that had been out of bounds to British subjects for more than twenty years due to the wars. And Caroline? She was ecstatic to finally be in charge of her own life, able to travel as she pleased without having to worry about overbearing parents or Prinny's interference.

In Braunschweig, she was greeted by her brother, The Black Duke, back in charge following the eviction of Napoleon's brother. Her time in her hometown was filled with "excursions, plays, and balls"* in a nonstop celebration of her visit. While there, she made the impromptu decision to marry her twenty-one-year-old ward Edwardina to one of The Black Duke's aides-de-camp. This decision perplexed no one so much as Edwardina herself, left behind in Braunschweig with a new husband she'd only known for two hours.† Leaving one protégé behind, Caroline's beloved Willikin remained by her

* As described by her companion, Sir William Gell.

† Edwardina quickly divorced him and took a second husband, of her own choosing, one year later in Rome.

side as she left Braunschweig for adventures in Italy.* She was to spend the winter in Naples, then return to Braunschweig in the spring to set up a permanent home.

Also joining her entourage at this point was Charlotte's former fling, Captain Hesse, on leave from the military and assumed by most to be Caroline's lover. Caroline and Hesse may have been lovers during the Blackheath era as well; it is unclear what the timeline was between his affairs with mother and daughter.†

The Black Duke accompanied her to her next stop in Pyrmont, handing over responsibility for her protection to local royals who hosted her in their homes. By September, she had begun dressing the gentlemen of her entourage in a costume of her own invention. Like her brother designing uniforms for the Black Brunswickers, or Prinny designing military uniforms for his own brigade/himself, she enjoyed fashioning military costumes, and designed an outfit of black coats with gold embroidery lined with crimson silk, and hats with high feathers.

In Strasbourg, France, Caroline's party encountered François-Étienne-Christophe Kellermann. Kellermann had been a hero of the French side of the wars, fighting on behalf of Napoleon. He had also led the French troops at Valmy, the battle that claimed her father's life.

Upon Caroline's arrival, he was called upon to ceremonially review the eight thousand troops lined up to greet her. Her attendants were not sure how Caroline would react to his presence, but she was only gracious to him. This was the

---

* She'd only gotten permission from Parliament to travel to Braunschweig but she assumed (correctly) that they'd be so glad to be rid of her they wouldn't chase after her across Europe.

† Remember too, he was likely the illegitimate son of Prinny's brother Frederick, making him Charlotte's first cousin and Caroline's nephew.

first hint of her current point of view. Though the French had killed her father, forced her brother into exile, and captured her homeland, they were also the enemy of Prinny. And at this point in her life, hatred of Prinny (and, by extension, England) trumped her family loyalty. Caroline was officially a fan of the French.

She made her way slowly toward Naples, stopping to visit royals along the way. In Geneva, she attended a dinner alongside Napoleon's second wife, Empress Marie Louise.* The two women, both separated from their husbands in wildly different circumstances, hit it off extremely well; they even sang duets at the postdinner celebrations. Caroline wrote to Charlotte that she was "much pleased with her reception" there. Prinny had forbidden Charlotte to write to her mother, but she wrote to a friend of her hopes that Caroline "will derive much benefit from her tour . . . at all events, change of air must do her health good. It would require more than novelty of place and society, I fear, to do her spirits service. However, I hope time and Providence may yet have much happiness in store for her."

While in Geneva, Caroline purchased a new black wig, which she wore most of the time afterward. Her thought process seemed to be a desire to fit in better with the dark-haired Mediterranean people. And it also matched the dark eyebrows she had preferred to draw on for several years now. She also continued to apply blush with a strong hand, perhaps now also as a way for her pale complexion to blend in better with the suntanned locals.

With most of her household staff remaining back in England, she needed a trusted lady's maid. In addition to the usual tasks of hair, clothing and makeup, Caroline required

---

* Napoleon was in exile in Elba at this point. Marie Louise chose not to accompany him there, and in fact took a lover in his absence.

someone to help with her correspondence. While she was mostly fluent in English, her grammar and spelling had not improved during her time in England, and she needed someone trustworthy to serve as her assistant. In Geneva, she hired a young Swiss woman named Louise Demont to take on this important role.

When word reached London that Caroline's ultimate destination was actually Naples, Liverpool pleaded with her to reconsider, stating: "[Britain] and Naples are not at peace (an armistice only existing at present between them). I should think therefore her Royal Highness would upon reflection take up her residence under present circumstances in the territories of any other sovereign in Italy."

Caroline, of course, did not heed his warning. In fact, her contrarian nature made it more likely she would go there if England didn't want her to. After all, this would be one more way to annoy Prinny.

Her party continued on toward Naples, stopping in Milan long enough to be received by the Austrian governor and his chamberlain, Conte Filippo Ghislieri.* As she had come to expect, crowds cheered for her in the streets as well as in the opera house.

She paid a visit to Lake Como, a region she found immediately enchanting, at the invitation of Napoleonic General Domenico Pino and his wife, the former ballerina Vittoria Peluso, who had inherited Villa del Garrovo, a luxurious Lake Como property, from her first husband. Caroline greatly admired the estate and promised to return again for a visit.

Caroline asked her new friends Pino and Ghislieri for recommendations of an Italian man she could hire to join her entourage, as she was in need of someone who knew the language and the region and could help arrange lodgings and

* Austria was currently in charge of several Italian territories.

accommodations for her. Pino recommended a thirty-year-old Italian man named Bartolomeo Pergami, who had served under him in the army, and who had performed a similar job for Vittoria.

Pergami was instructed to present himself the next day at Caroline's lodgings. He arrived to find no one around. He wandered through the rooms until he came across a woman struggling to disentangle her skirt from a piece of furniture. The woman, of course, was Caroline. And after Pergami gallantly assisted her, she hired him on the spot.

Pergami was well over six feet tall and muscular, with flowing black curls and a spectacular mustache. Caroline knew how impressive he would look, riding a horse at the head of the royal entourage, and she'd always had a weakness for handsome men. At this point, she was widely understood to have taken Hesse as a lover, so Pergami was initially hired as eye candy.

On October 31, Caroline arrived in Rome, where the nobility expected her. Her entourage was annoyed at this point that their luggage had not yet arrived from England. The delay was partly due to Caroline having planned to move eleven cases of dishes that had been given to Caroline by George III years earlier. The Crown* insisted that the dishes were Crown property, on loan to Caroline only as long as she stayed at Kensington Palace. Caroline argued the case through intermediaries, but Prinny's decision was final: He would keep the dishes. And so it was that their luggage did not arrive in Italy for four months.

Prussian diplomat Friedrich Wilhelm Basilius von Ramdohr wrote about seeing Caroline in Rome. She had aged since he'd last seen her, and he wrote:

---

* Prinny, being the worst, as always.

*[Her] assured expression make her face appear hard, which it was not formerly . . . her toilette is rich but bizarre, and recalls the dress of Guercini's sibyls.**

In other words, Caroline was delighting in her new freedom to dress, act, and style herself exactly like she wanted. Black wig, lots of red blush, drawn-on eyebrows, see-through dresses, the biggest feathers in her caps: She was a woman untethered and having the time of her life. However, she was distressed not to have heard from her daughter as much as she wanted. She wrote:

*The only misery I feel is, that I have never yet heard from Princess Charlotte. Mr. St. Leger saw her at Weymouth after his return to England. She was much better, but she never wrote once, though I write every week.*

Having already met Napoleon's wife Marie Louise, she continued seeking out other Napoleon-connected people during her travels. She met with Prince Lucien Bonaparte, the former Emperor's brother who had fled to Rome after the fall of the empire. She was also seen dancing at a ball with Louis Bonaparte, Napoleon's other brother, the former King of Holland. Lord Sligo, who traveled with Caroline to Rome, noted that "to be Bonaparte's friend or relation appears to be a claim upon her friendship."

Another new Napoleonic friend, former marshal of the French Empire Prince Józef Antoni Poniatowski, asked her when she planned to return to England.

"Not before my daughter is Queen," Caroline replied.

She went out dancing as often as she could, leading Ramdohr to note:

---

* He was referring to paintings by seventeenth-century artist Guercino, who often painted women whose tunics are falling off their shoulders.

"She did not quit her place all evening. Waltzes, contredanses, English, French . . . all executed with pretensions and graces, and with a frivolity hardly fitting her age and figure."

Yet, Ramdohr explained her charismatic personality as her having "a need for vague activity, a desire for distractions, quite a strong dose of vanity. . . . One understands as easily how the most serious accusations could be lodged against her as how she was able to get so many to leap to her defence." He did also note that the proportions of her stomach seemed to hint at pregnancy.*

Word inevitably got back to England about her no fucks given behavior. Prinny hoped she would continue to behave outlandishly so he'd finally have grounds for divorce. Wannabe ambassadors and diplomats quickly realized they could further their careers by gaining Prinny's gratitude for stories of Caroline's scandalous behavior. And so reports on Caroline (true, embellished, or made up) made their way continuously to his notice from ambitious men like Sligo, who sent regular letters to Prinny, hoping to prove himself capable enough to become a paid spy.† Yet there was nothing in her public behavior for them to report, as she was living "the most peaceful life in the world, and [was] not connected with anyone" who she could get in trouble for fraternizing alongside.

Caroline was aware that people in her orbit were passing along messages to Prinny and fed them lies to test their loyalty to her. In December, she summoned Sligo, tearfully asking if he had heard anything about Prinny potentially divorcing her. She pondered making a statement in England, perhaps even finding a way of reconciling with Prinny. Sligo,

* Drink! Also, Caroline's lady-in-waiting Lady Charlotte Bury did write about Caroline's habit of going without a corset, which Lady Charlotte warned could lead people to suspect things "exceedingly injurious to her character."

† Prinny gratefully accepted the letters, but never paid him for his services.

excitedly, wrote home that he had succeeded where all others had failed.

But Caroline, who likely knew about his espionage and hoped to confuse the people he was reporting to, never spoke again of this alleged reconciliation.

So it was then that Prinny hired a man to infiltrate her household in order to find definitive proof of her adultery.

CHAPTER THIRTEEN

# A SPY IN THE VILLA D'ESTE

Prinny's chosen spy was Baron Friedrich Ompteda, former Hanoverian ambassador to the Pope. Why him? Because of the connection between Britain and Hanover at that time.

In 1714, around one century before the events of this story, Britain and Hanover were joined in a personal union. This meant that the same person, Georg Ludwig aka George I, would serve as Elector of Hanover and King of Great Britain and Ireland.* Following the defeat of Napoleon, the Electorate of Hanover became the Kingdom of Hanover. So, since 1814, Prinny's role as Regent meant that he was overseeing both places. Hanover had a simpler governance structure without the checks and balances required by the British Parliament, so Prinny was able to enact his wishes there without requiring a Parliament to approve them. And so it was that Ompteda became the not-really-official Caroline spy.

Ompteda's instructions, conveyed via his bosses in Hanover, read in part:

> *The Baron is to approach as near as he can to the Princess, and write an exact account of her conduct. If that conduct is not as it*

---

* Despite there being over five hundred miles and several countries between London, England, and Hanover.

> *ought to be, it is extremely important to obtain sufficient proofs to legitimate the fact. . . . In pursuit of this end naturally Baron Ompteda is authorized to employ all honest means thereto—given that this is with moderation and discretion.*

Just as Ompteda headed off for his spy mission, Caroline arrived in the kingdom of Naples. She was met by the King, Joachim Murat, and a corps of soldiers, to escort her into the city. Murat, handsome in his military uniform, had long curly black hair that made Caroline joke that, in her wig, they resembled one another. She had Willikin accompany them for propriety's sake so they weren't alone in a carriage. But behind closed doors, she had taken a new lover: Pergami.

They may have spent the night together for the first time in Naples, as Caroline had sent Willikin off to sleep in his own room that night. The morning after their arrival, she requested that Pergami be moved to a room adjoining hers.

Murat, a marshall in Napoleon's army, was married to Napoleon's younger sister, now Queen Carolina Maria of Naples. The royal couple doted upon Caroline, inviting her to many events, tiring her entourage. When an invitation came for a masked ball, Caroline attended with only her maid, Demont, and Pergami attending her. These four months were described by Caroline's attending physician, Dr. Holland, as "a time of continuous fete and revelry."

Caroline became quick friends with Queen Carolina Maria, ordering fifty bottles of Colley's Chemical Cream (her preferred black hair dye) from England on her behalf. Queen Carolina Maria was already a fan of Caroline's and apparently kept a copy of *The Spirit of the Book* on her bedside table. Caroline was also fond of the Naples princesses, particularly Princess Louise, who was close in age to Charlotte. Her daughter was often on her mind, as Caroline had barely heard from her since she left. Prinny had long ago forbidden Charlotte from writing to her mother, but the distance meant the women's usual couriers couldn't pass along messages.

On New Year's Eve, 1814, Caroline hosted a grand fete on behalf of the Murats, with three hundred guests in the royal casino at Chiatamonte Gulfi. She arranged for illumination in the gardens and a fireworks display. Ompteda, among the guests, recorded every action she took.

In February, Naples held its annual carnival. Caroline was front and center among the partygoers, throwing confetti from her carriage. Ompteda's obsessive records also share that she went dressed to another party as an "immodest Sultana," and wrote that Caroline was "the talk of the Court and town. . . . Her unguarded conduct, especially towards men, exposes her to scandalous suspicions . . . in a town where chastity has never had much of a ministry."

Ompteda initially believed that Pergami was a eunuch* and, therefore, incapable of being Caroline's lover. However, he soon suspected that the pair were involved. Rumors weren't enough for Prinny, so Ompteda knew he'd have to find a way to catch them having sex.

There were some household changes as she prepared to travel to Lake Como, including the addition of two men Pergami had met in Naples and taken a liking to: Moritz Crede, hired to work in the stables, and Teodoro Majocci, a former employee of the Murats, hired for household duties. Caroline arranged various outfits for Pergami, all of which Ompteda dutifully rendered in watercolors to send back to his handlers.

Caroline's fixation on Napoleon reached a new level when

* Probably told to him as a joke.

his mistress, Countess Walewska, met her at a party. Walewska's appearance was unexpected, but even more surprising was the news that quickly spread through attendees: Napoleon had escaped from Elba with over one thousand troops seven days earlier and was headed to Paris to regain power. The Murats had known beforehand that he was planning to do this, and Caroline inserted herself into the narrative by claiming she had also known. Not many believed her, but the ever-credulous Ompteda did, dedicating pages of his reporting to outline his investigations into Caroline's potential involvement in Napoleon's escape.

With the continent plunged again into war, Caroline's role as Princess of Wales set her apart from others in Naples. Despite her bad reputation in England, Parliament knew she had to be protected, and a frigate was sent to fetch her and remove her from Naples. The captain of her ship was Captain Samuel Pechell, who immediately irritated Caroline with his many careless habits. She annoyed him right back when, during a shipboard dance, she suggested Pergami and her maid, Demont, join in so they had enough numbers for the routine.

Caroline wrote Mary Berry: "Thank God, here I am and out of Naples in four-and-twenty hours. I left it after Napoleon made his escape!" She further described how she had grown to "hate Naples from all [her] heart, and [would] under no consideration, ever think to return there."

She settled next in Genoa, delighted to receive three letters smuggled from Charlotte. There, she went for daily rides in a phaeton she had acquired from the Murats in exchange for her English carriage. Phaetons were lightweight, two-person carriages that women could use to drive themselves around. They were fast, dangerous, and eye-catching, ideal for Caroline's high-spirited lifestyle and love of attention.

Speaking of her grand theatrics, she had also assembled a dramatic entourage when she drove around. In the front of the pack was the handsome Pergami, dressed to resemble King Joachim Murat, riding a large horse. Next came a child dressed as a Cupid, leading a miniature phaeton made of a conch shell and driven by two miniature horses. Caroline took up the rear in her phaeton next to Willikin, her trendy shorter-than-usual skirts exposing her feet and ankles.*

Caroline took on a new lady-in-waiting in Milan: Pergami's sister, Angelica Pergami, Countess Oldi. Her maid Demont's sister Mariette Bron also joined the household. Ompteda noted darkly that Caroline's diversely staffed household was a sign she wanted to be rid of the vigilance a British staff would provide her.

This new international entourage accompanied Caroline as she excitedly toured many Italian cities to visit their historical sites, including her ancestor Ariosto's tomb in Ferrara. Her ultimate aim was to purchase her friend's villa on Lake Como. Pergami, proving his worth as a household manager, as well as arm candy, worked to finalize the paperwork for the villa.

In England, Henry Brougham entreated her to live frugally and pay off her debts. Paying him no mind, Caroline signed the documents to purchase the villa in July.

While waiting to move in, Caroline rented rooms at the nearby Villa Villani. While there, notable people in the area flocked to her just as they had in her early years at Montague House in Blackheath. Her party-throwing reputation continued unabated, and her charismatic personality drew people

* She and her daughter had always liked to show off their pretty feet and ankles, which was a trend of the time among nonroyal women. It was their rank that made this choice shocking to some.

into her orbit. As always, Ompteda was one of her most frequent visitors to the extent that Caroline provided him with his own rooms. From there, he obsessively recorded her actions in lengthy letters. He hoped that from these close quarters, he would witness incontrovertible proof of Caroline's affair with Pergami. Much to his frustration, none could be found.

Allied forces continued to wage war against Napoleon, including The Black Duke, who died in combat on June 16 at the Battle of Quatre-Bras. When Caroline was informed of her brother's death, she reacted in public with the same stoicism she'd displayed after bidding farewell to Charlotte. Arrangements were made for his body to be moved to Braunschweig, where he would be laid to rest in the same tomb as his heroic father and their ancestor, Henry the Lion.

Caroline was appalled that the British royals did not write condolences to her upon his death, swearing that she was resolved "never to write to them again, nor even to answer them, if they ever take it into their heads to write again."

The Black Duke's young sons left London to take over the Duchy.* Caroline offered to move back to Braunschweig to serve as Regent to her young nephew, but her services were not required as he'd already been assigned someone with previous Regent experience: Prinny.

Which was well enough, as her new villa was ready for her to move in. She renamed it the Villa d'Este, in honor of her Guelph and Este ancestors who had lived there. She signed her name as Caroline d'Este on the invitations for the first party at her new home, held on August 24 (the feast day of St. Bartolomeo, presumably in honor of Pergami).

Ompteda felt he had finally found something worth pur-

* Two days after The Black Duke's death, Napoleon's forces were decidedly defeated at the Battle of Waterloo.

suing. Other Guelph descendants had recently organized secret societies to throw off Austrian rule. Caroline's sudden embrace of her ancestry, Ompteda was sure, meant she was involved with these groups and, therefore, committing treason. He was also intrigued when Caroline destroyed some papers in a fireplace before the move to Ville d'Este, coincidentally around the same time that King Joachim Murat had been captured and shot by a firing squad. These papers, he was sure, were secret correspondence between Caroline and the Murats.

In fact, Caroline was during this time mainly concerned with improving the local infrastructure. She hired laborers to extend a nearby carriage road, providing work for recently unemployed soldiers and other townspeople. She self-funded numerous improvements to the villa. When her British allowance did not cover the costs, she turned to a local lender in Milan.

More of Pergami's family members joined the household, including his brother Luigi and cousin Bernardo. His three- or four-year-old daughter Vittorine also came to live at the villa, much to Caroline's delight.* Willikin, by now a teenager, remained at the home, but much of Caroline's attention had transferred to the newer, youngest child in the house.

By November, Caroline's wanderlust had come upon her again. She left the home amid renovations and additions as she planned more trips: to Sicily, Sardinia, Cairo, Greece, Turkey, and Tunis, with the ultimate goal of visiting Jerusalem. Her choice of locations was inspired by the tales of friends and other acquaintances, and a longing to follow in the path of her ancestor Henry the Lion's twelfth-century pilgrimage.

---

* Pergami was, it should be noted, married. His wife remained back in Milan with another, younger daughter.

These plans had no place for Ompteda, who could only follow her as far as Genoa. He attempted to bribe a crew member to spy on his behalf, but found no takers. Ultimately, he was forced to hope someone's stories could be bought when the party returned to the continent.

CHAPTER FOURTEEN

# Eat, Pray, Fuck

Before the Napoleonic Wars consumed continental Europe, it had been expected of young upper-class British men to take what was called the Grand Tour, a sort of gap year spent touring around Europa à la *Eat, Pray, Love*—eighteenth-century style. Heavy emphasis on *Love*, which to these men meant *fucking as many European people as they could find.*

The purpose of this trip was to expose these men to the wider world, showing them archaeological sites and museums and giving them the opportunity to improve their language skills. For centuries, wealthy young men had taken this trip. Wealthy young women were expected to wait back in Britain until they could be married. Older British women were not expected to tour around like Caroline was doing, and if they did, convention would expect them to travel with British household staff. Everything Caroline was doing was unprecedented for a woman in this era, let alone the Princess of Wales. And she was loving it!

Caroline set sail on November 14, 1816, aboard a ship called the *Leviathan*. She insisted they make a stop on the island of Elba so she could visit Napoleon's former home. While there, she took his billiards cue as a souvenir.

She wanted to designate Pergami chamberlain, the chief officer of her household, but he was too low-ranking. So, she led her party to the small town of Augusta,* where an estate was for sale that would make the buyer a baron. With Pergami's efficient help, the land purchase was completed in two days, and he left the town as Barone Pergami della Franchina, her chamberlain.

Throughout these travels, she maintained an unusual sleeping arrangement. As she herself described:

"I remained night and day upon deck . . . a sort of tent was contrived for me; I lay there without ever taking off my clothes, and the rest of the persons who remained on deck with me did the same."

Despite Caroline's description, Pergami was the only other person to share this tent. Her other friends and aides came into the tent to speak with her, but no others slept on the deck. Caroline only left the tent to bathe.

Her plans for Tunis were to be a white savior, like Daenerys in Season 3 of *Game of Thrones.* Basically, Caroline wanted to free the white Christians forced into slavery there by the Barbary corsairs. She may have gotten this idea from Henry Brougham, who had been lobbying for years to abolish slavery and free Black enslaved people from Europe and the Americas.

However, Caroline's lofty goals to free enslaved people left her mind when she met and was won over by the ruling Bey,† who offered her use of his new palace. He also presented her with gifts of horses, which she happily maneuvered onto the small ship, creating a challenge for the captain and his crew. Meanwhile, the Bey provided Caroline with an honor guard and permission for her to visit the ruins of Utica.‡

---

* Coincidentally, a city with the same name as her mother's.

† The local ruler, who employed corsairs and supported their slave trading.

‡ These ruins, which can still be visited as of this writing, are those of an ancient city considered to be the first founded by the Phoenicians in North Africa. It was later taken over by the Romans.

While in Tunis, Caroline received word that her daughter, Charlotte, was now engaged to Prince Leopold of Saxe-Coburg.* Caroline must have been pleased that her plan worked. By removing herself from England, Charlotte had been able to pursue a new marriage for herself. Charlotte first met Leopold (whom she nicknamed The Leo) two years earlier. It took two years of her best behavior to convince Prinny to agree to the match.

The Leo was ideal in many ways for Charlotte. Most importantly, he seemed kind and treated her with consideration. He was also close to her age and looked hot in a soldier's uniform. His position as the younger son of a King meant she would not be expected to leave Britain to live with him. And in a welcome change for the family's convoluted gene pool, the pair were barely related.

News of her daughter securing what neither she nor her own mother had managed—a marriage of her choice to a man of her choosing—must have cheered her up as her trip continued.

But then, similar to when the Napoleonic Wars burst into her Naples holiday, some shit went down, getting in the way of an otherwise carefree tour.†

One year earlier, American forces had secured the release of all white Americans enslaved by the Barbery corsairs. While Caroline was enjoying being a tourist, British forces were coming to ensure the same for their enslaved white people. Twenty-five ships arrived, causing the Bey to call off other planned entertainments for Caroline as he dealt with twenty-four hours of cannon-based attacks.

The British forced her to leave, much to her annoyance, and so she sailed off to see the sights in the hopefully less

---

* Upon news of the engagement, Prinny's personal librarian suggested to Jane Austen that she write a novel about the royal love story; Austen politely refused.

† Other than slavery, which she'd moved on from worrying about.

war-torn Athens, which had been recommended by her Greece-obsessed friend Lord Byron. After two weeks there, she headed via Corinto to Constantinople, where she got her shopping spree on, purchasing four embroidered gold brocade dresses and "other gold clothes."

An outbreak of bubonic plague forced her to end this visit earlier than intended, and she took a leisurely route along the Mediterranean to Acre, then known as St. Jean d'Acre, part of the Ottoman Empire. It had been a popular destination during the Crusades centuries earlier, and Caroline retraced the steps of her heroic ancestor, Henry the Lion, as she visited the land of the Bible. As she wrote:

> *I travelled on horseback through Palestine to Jerusalem, Nazareth, Bethlehem, Canaan—by the Dead Sea, and the rivers of Jordan and Jericho—and I returned by Jaffa.*

Her entrance into Jerusalem was commemorated in artwork, both complimentary paintings as well as gawkish political cartoons. These images show her arriving in grand style, dope as hell (and culturally insensitively), riding on a donkey amid a convoy of camels, Pergami by her side. Like other royals who had visited Jerusalem in the past, she founded an Order of Knighthood to reward the men who had accompanied her. These included Pergami as Grand Master of the order, and his children would succeed him and continue to wear the same Order "from generation to generation, to the end of the world." Willikin was named Knight of the Holy Sepulchre, a title that would carry on through his future descendants as well.

Caroline enjoyed the unpredictability of her journey, leaning into the discomforts associated with this pilgrimage. Her party traveled only at night to avoid the sun; she and the others slept under trees, in a cowshed, and under canvas as needed. Prinny would never.

In her writings, Caroline emphasized the boundaries she was breaking as the first lady of her rank to take this pilgrimage and visit these sights.

Her party left in July, and their plans to next visit Cairo were forced to change due to another bubonic plague outbreak. As the ship made its leisurely way back to Italy, she relaxed in her shipboard tent, feeling independent, happy, and satisfied for perhaps the first time in her life. That being said, the journey back was challenged by storms and periods of quarantine required for people returning from the Levant.

On September 16, she returned to the Villa d'Este, having been away for ten months. She had acquired new servants from her travels, adding an international element with Turkish, Arab, African, and Italian people, including some from Pergami's hometown of Crema. With the villa's renovations now complete, Caroline was happy to settle into a quiet life. Willikin was sent to a nearby school, leaving Pergami's daughter Vittorine as her only young companion. Pergami's mother, Signora Pergami, called Madame Mère, also joined the household as a laundress.

Life had settled into a new normal until a new scandal—not one caused by her, for a change—upended everything.

CHAPTER FIFTEEN

# Villa Cabrile

Caroline had employed a maid named Annette Presinger since her time in Braunschweig. When Annette became pregnant, she parted from Caroline's household back in Naples. Caroline rehired her later on, only for Annette to become pregnant again. The father was Caroline's stable manager, Moritz Crede. Crede was fired for this "intrigue" with Annette, and, hoping to get back on Caroline's good side, confessed to an even greater wrongdoing: he had been helping Ompteda spy on Caroline.

As Crede explained in a written statement, while Caroline was on her Mediterranean trip, Ompteda had paid Crede for access to her rooms in the Villa d'Este. Crede had allowed him inside to look around and had also provided him with a set of keys so that Ompteda could, at a later date, catch Caroline in a compromising position with Pergami.

Caroline, horrified and furious at this breach of her privacy, reported this to the governor of Naples, who banished Ompteda from the region. Ompteda admitted to all of his espionage and resigned from his position as Caroline's spy. This salacious gossip reached England, where various politicians and aristocrats were keen to win Prinny's favor by reporting on Caroline to him (even as the public continued to support Caroline). Any news of scandal emerging from Caroline's home delighted Prinny, who continued in his efforts to prove her so debauched he could be granted a divorce.

Caroline, concerned that there were further double agents in her midst, demanded soldiers be provided to stand guard at her gates. They left when fights broke out between them and her servants. The whole ordeal had damaged her reputation throughout the region. Local nobles and aristocrats began to avoid her. Her New Year's party in 1817 was attended only by local farmers and their families.*

Much as Caroline preferred not to think about her financial situation, the long trips and constant house-purchasing had begun to catch up with her. She headed to Germany with a scheme to acquire more funds. She first stopped in Munich, making some money selling some of her antiques to the Prince Royal of Bavaria. She then continued on to Karlsruhe, home of her cousin Karl Ludwig Friedrich, Grand Duke of Baden.

Her scheme was to get him to cash in an IOU for £5000 ($560,000 today) she claimed to have acquired from her late brother, The Black Duke, prior to his death. She felt that Karl Ludwig Friedrich would be more persuasive to claim the amount from Braunschweig than she would be. The negotiation for these funds was lengthy, but Caroline found ways to amuse herself while in town. One day, while out for a hunt, Caroline came upon the idea of wearing a half-pumpkin on her head to stay cool, to the astonishment of all.

She then went to Vienna, hoping to visit with Emperor Francis. Claiming to be in mourning, he did not receive her; a cartoon of her being turned away was published in Britain, where tales of her travels were always a sure bet to sell papers.

Caroline continued on to Rome, arriving in June 1817, where

* This party was held at a new property, La Barona, named for Pergami and being worked on by him as a fixer-upper.

she was provided housing at the Villa Rufinella by Prince Lucien Bonaparte, younger brother of the late Napoleon. Her plans here were also financial, as she hoped to sell the Villa d'Este to her Roman banker. She needed money from the sale, but also, still shaken from Ompteda's actions, she wanted to move to a more isolated property where it would be harder for Prinny's agents to spy on her. Within a month, the sale was made.

She leased her next property, the elegant Villa Caprile, in Pesaro on the Adriatic coast. There, she bathed in the ocean water similar to the cold plunges she'd taken in her tub back in Blackheath. To her delight, there was a small open-air theater nearby that she put to immediate use putting on shows featuring her own musical performances. She made friends with the artists and poets who lived in the area, though at least one worried for his daughter's safety as there were rumors someone (Prinny) might be attempting to poison Caroline, and her friends may also be at risk.

Caroline kept distracted and cheered up by updates about her daughter's impending marriage. As Charlotte was not permitted to contact her, Caroline acquired portraits and news from friends in England. She learned that the couple had been granted their own household, where Charlotte could finally live as the adult she was. Caroline was not invited to the wedding, which disappointed but did not surprise mother or daughter.

She passed the summer and early autumn in relaxation. She wrote:

> *I find myself very happy here, in a delightful climate. The situation is truly enchanting, and the best society in all of Italy . . . I am now busy writing the travels I have made in Sicily, Africa, Greece, Athens, Constantinople, Syria, and Palestine, as far as the Jordan, with the drawings I have made myself, and those of the people who have accompanied me on this long journey.*

Following her daughter's two miscarriages, Caroline learned that Charlotte was pregnant with a due date in October. Campbell forwarded Caroline a print of Leopold "The Leo," which Caroline added to her existing collection of portraits of her daughter and son-in-law.

In late October, the grandmother-to-be wrote of her blissful situation, where she considered staying into her retirement years:

> *I shall now soon be a grandmother . . . and I trust to heaven that then all libels about me will be at an end. I am then a well-established old lady and no more scandals can be created about little old me.*

Now married and largely freed from Prinny's control, Charlotte disobeyed him to write to her mother, keeping her updated about her impending childbirth. Charlotte had been paying attention to Caroline's lifestyle as well, writing in late October 1817 that "I have it not in my power at present to repay any services shown to the Princess of Wales; but if I ever have, those who remain steadfast to her shall not be forgotten by me."

Keen for any news of her grandchild's birth, all members of Caroline's household were on notice. When word spread an English messenger was passing through en route to Rome, Caroline's staff sought him out and brought him to her. Little did they expect that he had been sent with the devastating news of Charlotte's death.

He reported that on November 6, after an agonizing labor, Charlotte delivered a stillborn baby boy. Early the following morning, she died from birth complications. Upon hearing this news, Caroline, who had always remained stoic in the face of hard news, fainted dead away.

CHAPTER SIXTEEN

# The Triple Tragedy

History books are filled with women dying due to complications during pregnancy or childbirth. It occurs so often that it can read as a historical shorthand, like dying of "old age." But what happened to Charlotte can be reasonably deduced by symptoms others saw in her pregnancy and childbirth experience, and while Caroline wouldn't know these details, it seems correct to walk through how this tragedy occurred.*

As soon as their married life began, Charlotte was "happy and contented" with The Leo, as diarist Princess Dorothea von Lieven wrote. "[T]hey are both of them prodigiously in love—he with his wife, and she with her husband and freedom."

Charlotte wrote to her bestie Elphinstone that The Leo was "the perfection of a lover." They spent most of their time together in their new home, Claremont House. For Charlotte, this was the first time she had ever been able to express herself fully, choosing the decor of her house, their dinner plans, how she dressed. She miscarried a few months after the wedding and, despite Prinny's instructions

* I consulted with two twenty-first-century obstetricians about this and both agree this is likely the sequence of events. Both also want me to mention that Charlotte's death occurred decades before doctors realized they should wash their hands, which just exacerbated everything.

forbidding her from communicating with Caroline, wrote to her mother:

> *Why is not my mother allowed to pour cheerfulness into the sinking heart of her inexperienced and trembling child? . . . I have but one mother.*

One year after their marriage, Charlotte was pregnant again, and the press reacted as excitedly as *People* magazine does now when one of the modern-day royals has a new baby. Charlotte put on a concerning amount of weight as her pregnancy progressed, to the extent that her grandmother, Queen Charlotte (who had survived fifteen pregnancies), was alarmed. Charlotte's medical team was led by Sir Richard Croft, Prinny's private physician. He put her on a diet, encouraged her to increase her daily activity level, and began bleeding her because that's what every physician did.

Charlotte, overdue and very large with a very large baby to deliver, began labor on November 4. She promised her nurse, "I will neither bawl nor shriek."

She labored for fifty hours, likely because the baby was too large to easily emerge vaginally. This was in an era before doctors knew about germ theory, so nobody washed their hands, and they especially did not wash their tools. The use of forceps was avoided as those tended to result in the death of the mother. A Cesarean section would surely lead to her death. Her role as heir to the throne made the doctors all value saving her life above all else, which wound up being a disastrous decision. At some point during the labor, the baby died.

Charlotte was presented with a ten-pound, stillborn son. Much like her mother, she appeared stoic in the face of tragedy, and she reassured The Leo that they were still young and would try again. Charlotte also tried to comfort the despairing nurses and maids around her. The Leo took an opiate and went to bed, having been by her side through the fifty hours.

Three hours after the delivery, Charlotte complained of abdominal pain and began vomiting. The medical team found her cold to the touch, having difficulty breathing, and bleeding. They placed hot compresses on her, but the bleeding did not abate. While some texts suggest she suffered a pulmonary embolism, interviews with modern-day obstetricians theorize that she likely had an infection. A long labor with a dead baby can cause infection in the uterus, not to mention the doctors' unwashed hands. Her large size during pregnancy suggests she had gestational diabetes, another potential source of infection. The more infected she became, the lower her blood pressure fell, and she started vomiting and experiencing pain in her infected uterus. Infections cause the coagulation system to go out of whack, causing uncontrollable bleeding. Ultimately, this infection became septic, and her death was hastened by the bleeding that ensued.

In the twenty-first century, gestational diabetes can be diagnosed early and managed. If an infection like this occurs during childbirth, the parent can be given powerful antibiotics, blood pressure support, and drugs to slow down bleeding. If all of this fails, a hysterectomy can be performed. In a modern context, her death could have been avoided. With modern medications and a knowledgeable doctor or midwife, most women would survive this situation in contemporary times.

But this happened to Charlotte in 1817, and she died at age twenty-one. Upon seeing his dead wife and child, Leopold turned to his friend and whispered, "I am now quite desolate. Promise to stay with me always."

The public, who had been placing bets on the baby's sex and planning great celebrations, was equally devastated. Princess Charlotte had been beloved by the nation since she was born, and she was mourned by many like their own family member. Lady Charlotte Bury captured the overall sentiment when she wrote, "A greater public calamity could not have occurred to us."

Charlotte's funeral was held in St. George's Chapel in Windsor Castle, the place she'd always hated to stay with her grandmother and aunts. So many members of the public attended that some members of the ceremonial procession were unable to get in. Prinny did not attend, as he was too overcome with grief. Public mourners were able to pay their respects in London at Madame Marie Tussaud's touring exhibition, where a waxwork of Charlotte laying at rest with her child drew many visitors.

There was no plan to inform Caroline of her daughter's death. Prinny maintained his long-ago vow never to contact her, and so it fell to The Leo to send word. In shock with grief, he did not write a letter. And so it fell to a courier, stopped by Caroline's staff while en route to inform the Pope of Charlotte's death, to share the tragic news.

Upon hearing of the death of her daughter and the stillbirth of her grandchild, Caroline fainted. The stress triggered her chronic illness, which, along with her profound grief, contributed to extreme headaches and a deep depression. She had often been treated with bloodletting for other physical symptoms, and her physicians used the latest trend: leeches. Medicinal leech use had become popular in this era, preferred by doctors for its precision and the gradual way that blood was drawn as opposed to traditional lancing. She took to her bed for weeks.

While her physical symptoms could be treated, her grief was unfathomable and untreatable. Caroline wrote shortly after receiving the news: "I have not only to lament an ever-beloved child, but one most warmly attached friend, and the only one

I have had in England! But she is only gone before—I have her not [lost]—and I now trust we shall soon meet in a much better world than the present one."

One month later, Caroline's page Hownam wrote: "Her Royal Highness's state I leave to your imagination. My pen is unequal to the task." Caroline refused all visitors, who Hownam noted "can only tend to make her more unhappy."

All of Britain mourned the tragic loss of their beloved Charlotte, and there was much sympathy for Caroline. One supporter wrote that they heard "her sighs wafted on the gales, and we feel the crash of the thunderbolt which tore asunder the last tie that bound her affection to the British Isles."

In January, Caroline wrote of herself in the third person:

> *She has been all her life a child of misfortune and wretched and miserable for so many years, that this last blow for her future prospects of life has been almost the death [warrant] to her feelings. The rest of the few years which may perhaps have been allotted to her by the Almighty. . . [she trusted] to passe tranquille without any [further] persecution and insultes. Her political interest for England and also for Europe is now for ever at ende . . . She must for ever look as a very severe punishment upon the English nation the dreadful melancolique death of the hope and glory of the British nation.*

She mourned her beloved daughter, the girl for whom Caroline had given up everything. She mourned the life she herself should have had, returning to Britain as the mother of the next Queen. She mourned the role of grandmother that she would have cherished. Caroline, ever the optimist, always ready to distract herself from her pain, was unable to escape this grief.

Caroline's usual habit was to feign indifference and good

cheer in the face of misfortune, which often led people to presume she was unfeeling. She was devastated and struggled to cope with this tragedy. She turned to those around her, namely Pergami and his family, for support. They were able to empathize with her, especially since his younger daughter, living with her mother back in Milan, had died earlier that year. Together, Caroline and Pergami planned a monument in their garden to commemorate Charlotte's memory. Both found comfort spending time with his surviving daughter, Vittorine, who lived with them.

Caroline was not alone in her hopelessness. In February, three months after Charlotte's death, Charlotte's primary physician, Sir Richard Croft, took his own life out of guilt at not being able to save her or her son. His death, in combination with that of Charlotte and her child, was referred to as The Triple Tragedy.

Household staff drama played out at around this time as well, as Caroline's longtime maid and secretary, Louise Demont, was let go for helping a courier steal coins from Caroline's private box. Caroline had long relied on Demont to take dictation and write her letters. At this time the volume of Caroline's correspondence waned, both for the lack of a scribe and her indifference in communicating with those back in England. Her interest in the entire nation had evaporated with the loss of her daughter. Pergami took over both her legal and business correspondence, as well as most of the household tasks, as Caroline uncharacteristically remained at home for the time being.

Back in England, Prinny was obsessed with the possibility she may one day return to annoy him. Charlotte's death renewed his determination to divorce Caroline. He did not specifically want to marry again, though a new heir was needed. He had thirty-five rumored illegitimate children, but none of these could inherit the throne (nor could any of the rumored fifty-two illegitimate children of his brothers). Three of his brothers took up this cause, separating from their non-royally-approved longtime partners to marry and impregnate foreign princesses, in a race to father the next heir.

On New Year's Day 1818, nearly two months after Charlotte's death, Prinny submitted paperwork to his ministers, calling for a new investigation into Caroline's possible adultery. They refused, largely because public sympathy was so completely on Caroline's side that he would never win such a battle.

That September, Prinny sent his own investigators to Milan to secretly interview people about Caroline's conduct. He was given approval for this on the understanding that this was his own private matter, and that proceedings against Caroline were not guaranteed to follow receipt of this report.

This was good enough for Prinny, and so began The Milan Commission.

CHAPTER SEVENTEEN

# THE MILAN COMMISSION

The three men appointed to Prinny's Milan Commission were solicitor John Allan Powell; the King's Counsel William Cooke; and military attaché seconded from the British Embassy in Vienna, Major James Browne.

Powell, the youngest of the trio, saw immediately that the entire operation was a fool's errand, and as a nonfool, he was reluctant to join the task force. He was won over when it was made clear that if his work led to charges filed against Caroline, it would "lead to results highly advantageous."

Cooke, the elder of the group, was mostly retired from a career that included writing on bankruptcy law. He readily accepted the job, but on the condition that they would be given official authorization for their mission from either Prinny or the government. This was hard to procure since it was entirely unofficial. He found it curious that the government ministers were reluctant for their names to appear on documents pertaining to this matter, but Prinny happily approved the hiring of the trio as effectively private detectives on his behalf.

Browne, an officious military man, was pleased that Prinny could cut through the bureaucratic obstacles that usually hindered investigations of this kind. He already had apartments in Milan, where it was agreed they would hold their interviews.

Prinny had gotten the Austrian authorities to cooperate with his agents, and the Hanoverian government was also entailed to provide support. The papal government was also happy to help. The three commissioners planned to travel separately in Milan and meet up, pretending to be "chance travellers who had become acquainted with each other on the road." One of their first actions was to conscript Baron Ompteda.* Now Hanoverian minister to the Vatican, Ompteda planned to join them in Milan.

Meanwhile, Caroline was minding her own business in Pesaro. She ended her lease on the Villa Caprile, moving instead to a new home she named Villa Vittoria, after Pergami's surviving daughter. Her new home was more secluded than her previous Italian villas, away from the prying eyes of British spies or visitors who might intentionally snub her. Surrounded mainly by Pergami's family members, she had downsized her life to suit her current needs.

She was so settled in Italy that when asked, she permitted her brother-in-law, Prince Edward, to take over her Kensington Palace apartments. Edward, like his brothers, had married a young princess in order to try and conceive a new heir to replace the late Princess Charlotte. His chosen wife, Princess Victoria of Saxe-Coburg-Saalfeld, was the younger sister of Charlotte's widower, The Leo.†

As planned, the commissioners pretended to have met by

* As though the project wasn't already doomed, why not bring in the world's worst spy?

† Prince Edward and Princess Victoria did have a daughter, Alexandrina Victoria, later to become Queen Victoria, who therefore grew up in Caroline's former apartments at Kensington Palace.

chance in Milan, where they joined up with Ompteda. Despite his brief hiatus from Caroline-stalking, he was super hyped to be back on the beat. Ompteda suggested some disgruntled former servants who were fired for criminal acts would be good character witnesses against her: Teodoro Majocchi (fired for fighting), Giuseppe Sacchini (fired for allowing Ompteda to access Caroline's room), and Louise Demont (fired for helping her friend steal Caroline's money). What could go wrong?

Ultimately, twenty-four people of interest were brought in for questioning. The interviews were held at Browne's lodgings in Milan. Each witness was asked to swear to tell the whole truth and nothing but the truth with their hand on a crucifix. Bribery and payment for information were strictly forbidden in this "official" context, but the commissioners were allowed to cover the costs of the witnesses' travel, food, and lodgings. They planned to complete all interviews in two weeks.

But they hadn't counted on how quickly gossip would spread about what they were up to, and how many locals were in need of money, food, and lodgings. Each witness was encouraged to get their friends to testify as well, and soon, there was an understanding throughout the regions that these British men would pay anyone willing to speak against Caroline. Witnesses arrived from throughout Lake Como and other Italian territories, many of whom had never met Caroline but claimed they had insider information on her debauched actions. Ultimately, the commissioners collected statements from eighty-two people, with even more turned away for their obvious lying.

Caroline quickly deduced that she was yet again under investigation, after hearing through the grapevine that, "Lord Stewart at last succeeded to have a few vagabond of servants who speak ill of me and he took them to Vienna . . ."

All of those who testified were from the lower or working classes; nobody in high society turned against Caroline. Though Ompteda was optimistic they could find nobles as well, the commissioners came to realize that this was impossible. As a beloved figure in Pesaro, renowned for her charitability, she was simply too popular. Local authorities filed reports about her behavior, as the commissioners insisted, but also provided guards every day to help protect her.

As her household was predominantly filled with loyal Pergami family members, they turned to past employees to testify against her. Their star witness was disgraced Swiss maid Louise Demont.* Caroline was aware of Demont's involvement but dismissed her as "a great w— and undoubtedly bribed." We don't know about the w— allegations, but records show that Demont was being paid by the commissioners to live in Vienna along with other sequestered witnesses.

By January 1819, Caroline was fed up and went on the offensive against this attempted smear campaign. She sought out her own witnesses—noble friends from Como—who would speak well of her.

In March, Henry Brougham's brother James arrived in Pesaro on his behalf. The elder Brougham had continued to represent Caroline's interests in London, and wanted his brother to assess Caroline's financial situation. James went over the books Pergami had been keeping and found everything perfectly in order. Caroline had some debts, but not much, and far less than Prinny's. He wrote, "She is solvent if she were to die tomorrow . . . the debt compared to her income is a flea bite." Living low-key in Pesaro helped her stay within her means.

---

* When Demont finally deigned to be interviewed, she kept the investigators enthralled for twenty-two days with exaggerated tales of Caroline's scandalous ways.

James provided a fresh and objective point of view on her private living situation, specifically that Caroline and Pergami had adjoining rooms and seemed to be living as man and wife. More concerning to him was the outsize influence Pergami held over the household. Despite Caroline far outranking him, Pergami's name, image, and coat of arms were on display all over, including on the dishes from which they ate. Every room seemed to contain a portrait of the man. He oversaw every household matter to an extent that James found troubling, especially since his family was living off Caroline's income.

This does beg the question of whether or not Pergami was a grifter. If he was, he also responsibly maintained Caroline's household, cheered her up, and had been steadfast by her side for years. Through their relationship, he had elevated his status, and found a way to keep his family employed and housed in quasi-luxury. Did Caroline know? And if Caroline knew, did she mind? Seemingly not. But the nature of their relationship was the single question that the members of the Milan Commission were intent on defining.

James was surprised when Caroline revealed she was ready to negotiate a formal divorce from Prinny. All she wanted was enough money to live as she was accustomed and for Prinny to leave her alone. However, current law prohibited divorce unless one party admitted to adultery. As Prinny never would, this meant Caroline would need to make the claim. She told James, "That is impossible." While James genuinely wanted to help Caroline end her marriage, back in London, Henry Brougham was intent on using this situation for his own political benefit.

Caroline had long relied on Henry Brougham but had never fully trusted him, and for good reason: He was a shady character. He changed allegiances to fit his own ambition to one day become prime minister. To do so meant he had to stay on good terms with both the Whigs and Tories, as well as the royal family. With Prinny as Regent, this meant helping him get his greatest desire: to be rid of Caroline. So, while working ostensibly on Caroline's behalf, Brougham became a double agent for Prinny.

Brougham used his brother's suggested separation terms as a template to bring to Prinny. These included Caroline remaining in Italy, renouncing her right to be crowned Queen when Prinny ascended to the throne, and ceasing use of the title Princess of Wales.* In exchange, she would be provided with an increase in her annual allowance. Despite these terms coming from Caroline and James's conversations, Henry Brougham suggested that these terms were his own idea and that only he would be able to negotiate with Caroline in a way that would please Prinny.

While the prime minister and Cabinet approved plans for a separation, Prinny rejected the proposal as he would only be satisfied by a divorce. He pinned his hopes on the Milan Commission's report, which he felt would convince both Parliament and the public of Caroline's utter depravity and, therefore, allow him to emerge as the hero in divorce proceedings. When the Milan Commission's report finally arrived in London, the Cabinet found it unconvincing. Prinny thus instructed Cooke and Powell to hold further interviews.

Brougham never told Caroline that the prime minister and Cabinet had approved the plan. Rather, he manipulated her by claiming that public hearings would soon be held against her. Secretly meeting with Prinny at Carlton House, Brougham

* The title suggested for her would be the Duchess of Cornwall, which was used by Camilla Parker-Bowles prior to the coronation of Charles III, when she became Queen.

reassured him that he'd worked Caroline into such an agitated state she would surely agree to Prinny's terms.

But unbeknownst to him, Caroline was not falling for his manipulations. She had secretly been corresponding with other allies in England, such as Alderman Matthew Wood.* Caroline was always most herself when she was working on a scheme, and with their help, she was now involved in a big one: to bring about the downfall of the current government (their hope) and to destroy Prinny (her hope).

What brought Caroline to this point? Having left the country to ensure her daughter's happiness and successful eventual coronation, Charlotte's death not only devastated Caroline emotionally but also removed her main reason for not burning it all down. She'd have happily spent the rest of her life retired in Pesaro, cold plunging in the ocean and playing billiards with Napoleon's pool cue, but Prinny wouldn't leave her alone. And so the full force of her hatred of him, combined with her love of drama, led her to team up with Wood and other Radical politicians. She planned to return to England and destroy Prinny. And on August 17, she and her household left Pesaro with vengeance on her mind.

---

* Former Lord Mayor, and longtime Caroline supporter.

CHAPTER EIGHTEEN

# Caroline's Scheme

At first, no one knew where she had gone: not the members of the Milan Commission, not the agents they had paid to keep an eye on Caroline, not the Vatican authorities, not the local authorities. Caroline and her entourage remained under the radar from mid-August until early September, during which time Brougham, Prinny, and others feared she might already be en route to England.

However, this is the same woman who attempted to travel incognito years before while transporting a trunk with the name *Property of the Princess of Wales* on it, so it was only a matter of time before she was spotted. The size and exuberance of her traveling party, along with her distinctive painted eyebrows and feathered hats, made her arrival obvious in Parma, where she rented out the Villa San Bono in the Piacentine Hills.

This trip was different from her past tours as Caroline remained relatively low-key while at San Bono. Like Taylor Swift removing herself from the public eye between albums, rumors swirled about what she was up to. Some thought she was waiting for British visitors. But who? Had they already arrived secretly? And how could her enemies stop her if they didn't know what she was doing? She had been issued a passport to go as far as France under a fake name;* was that her ultimate destination? Or somewhere else, like London?

Members of her household, primarily Pergami and Willikin, were often seen coming and going. At the nearby post office, workers reported that she had been corresponding with Wood, the Radical MP Sir Francis Burdett, and cloth merchant-turned-London-sheriff Robert Waithman. Police records showed that two English travelers passed through town, named "Guglielmo Wood" (who was likely Wood's son, William) and Joseph Broadley.

On September 12, a courier delivered a letter for Caroline from England. That night, she left San Bono under cover of darkness, destination unknown to all but her and her staff. Her next stop was the castle of Montuè de' Gabbi in the provinces of Alessandria, under the purview of the King of Sardinia. Since her motives were still undefined, and suspicions against her were rising, the King ordered his officials to make her feel as unwelcome as possible; they stopped clearing the road leading up to the castle and did not provide guards at her gates.

She remained there as mysterious as before, receiving no visitors or letters from England. Pergami, Willikin, and others rode about to Como and Milan, seeking out positive character references for her. Clearly, part of her plan was to mount a defense against the Milan Commission's report. She requested a passport for her Como lawyer, who she wanted to defend her in England. After one month, she departed.

This was her first time leaving Italy since Charlotte's death. The British government and all the spies in Italy were flummoxed by her actions. The Sardinian and French governments were instructed to prevent her from traveling. Yet still, Caroline managed to evade every roadblock, arriving in Lyons,

---

* She procured this document in the name of Pergami's sister, Countess Oldi.

France, where she took out a paragraph in the local newspaper to announce her arrival. This ostentatious move, seemingly incongruous with her stealthy travel plans, was meant to warn Prinny that she was en route to England and to stir up anticipation of her imminent return.

On November 5, she received a letter from Brougham full of vague promises and mistruths. He was still playing all sides in the current drama, hoping to stay on the good side of whoever wound up leading the next government. Currently allied with the Whigs, he was helping to fan anti-Prinny sentiment in the hopes that it would lead to the downfall of the Tories. Bringing Caroline to town to cause a scene had been his plan now for several months, and she had been following his instructions to do so. Therefore she was confused by his latest letter, encouraging her to stay put. This was a classic Brougham move, hoping to keep her as a backup plan; but Caroline was never content to be anyone's plan B.

What Brougham didn't mention was that he no longer needed her to return to England for his plans to work because a separate crisis had caused the increase in anti-Prinny sentiment her return was intended to create.

On August 16, Radical leaders had organized a massive rally in St. Peter's Fields in Manchester, with attendance estimated at around sixty thousand people, including women and children, demanding universal suffrage and parliamentary reform. The attendees did not bring any weapons, only banners bearing wordy phrases like "Taxation Without Representation Is Unjust and Tyrannical."

The event began with a merry, carnival-like atmosphere. However, the recent French Revolution was fresh in the minds of the authorities, who feared similar riots would break out in Britain. A crucial difference was that Paris had its own police force that had sided with the revolutionaries. Britain didn't yet have a centralized police force, so enforcing the law fell to local communities to monitor themselves. Each parish would appoint a constable or constables, whose job was to arrest wrongdoers and present them to the local magistrate.

On the day of the Manchester rally, the local magistrates assembled one thousand five hundred military troops to monitor the protest. Most of these were regular soldiers of the same working class as the protestors. The magistrates instructed them to treat the demonstrators as an unlawful assembly before the assemblage had even begun.

The magistrates ordered the arrest of keynote speaker Henry "Orator" Hunt before he'd even begun his speech. Forty inexperienced young men from the Manchester and Salford Yeomanry charged into the crowd, aiming to reach him on the stage. They assaulted all those in their way with sabers, injuring and terrifying all they passed. They were soon assisted by the 15th Hussars, many wearing their medals from their recent success at the Battle of Waterloo, who forced the crowds to flee.

During these fifteen minutes of conflict, fourteen people were killed, and 654 were injured as a direct result of the soldiers' and Yeomens' actions. Robert Poole described this as "the bloodiest political event of the nineteenth century on English soil."

Newspaper reporters who had been in attendance helped to quickly spread word of the tragedy. That women had been present and among those attacked was used to villainize the troops and, by extension, the government. *Sherwin's Political Register* claimed that "Women appear to have been the particular objects of the fury of the Cavalry Assassins. One woman . . . was sabred over the head . . . some were sabred in the breast; so inhuman, indiscriminate, and fiend-like, was the conduct of the Manchester Yeomanry Cavalry."

Because the Hussars had been wearing their Waterloo medals, *The Manchester Observer* called the event "Peterloo Massacre." The tragedy was commemorated by Percy Bysshe Shelley in his poem *The Masque of Anarchy* and by Lord Byron in his poem *Don Juan*.* The soldiers were blamed along with the government who had sent them there. In response, the government passed the Six Acts of 1819, which banned public meetings of more than fifty people and cracked down on what the press was able to publish. Prinny, forever unable to read the room, publicly congratulated the soldiers. Public opinion was even more riled up than before against the Tory government, which the Whigs and Radicals saw as a way for them to seize power.

Caroline's correspondents Wood, Waithman, and Burdett busied themselves, turning this tragedy to their political advantage. Their plan had initially been to use Caroline's dramatic return as a way to turn the public against Prinny and the Tories. The massacre meant her involvement was no longer needed.

It seems she had gone to Parma to meet with these men; by the time she got there, they were already busy with the Peterloo fallout. The Tory government cracked down even further on dissent, arresting Hunt and other speakers and further muzzling the ability of the press to report on the matter. Armed rebellion seemed increasingly likely, with Caroline's Radical ally Matthew Wood now focused on calling the government to task for its handling of the debacle. Wood had sent his son to explain his father's absence. By then, she had received word from Brougham that he could meet her in Lyons in a month (which was a lie, as he no longer intended to meet with her).

---

* Despite neither man having been present at the actual massacre.

Caroline, frustrated by the sudden changes in plans, cast aside by her collaborators, and not fully understanding how Peterloo had changed the landscape of British politics, decided to head to England on her own. She left Lyons for Marseilles, sending word to Brougham that he should meet her there. If her divorce trial didn't happen in a timely manner, she would return to Pesaro for the winter. She would no longer wait around on Brougham's schedule.

Another complication arose in everyone's scheming when word spread that King George III's condition was worsening.* The King's death would thrust Prinny onto the throne and would also mean Caroline would ascend to the role of Queen. Practically speaking, this would mean a new negotiation with Parliament about her allowance.

The closer Prinny came to the crown, the more frantic he became about the idea of Caroline's potential return and her being crowned Queen. He turned again to the Milan Commission's report, urging state law officials to reconsider pressing charges against her, hoping that the new political situation might make them more amenable to the idea of a public trial.

In January, the law officers of the Crown and of the Duchy of Cornwall agreed that a parliamentary bill of divorce would be appropriate. Caroline could not be tried for treason, as that charge only applied if she had committed adultery with a subject of the British Crown. Pergami, as an Italian, could not commit treason against a King who was not his own. Caroline, being with him, was also not committing treason. Though this bill was legally sound, the law officers worried that pursuing this as a public trial would bring (more) scandal to Prinny's name, particularly as discussion of his marriage to Fitzherbert could make him known publicly as a bigamist.

---

* Remember him? He's still been alive this whole time, mentally and physically incapable of ruling, hence Prinny's Regency.

Prinny could not be seen breaking one of the foundational laws of the Anglican Church he was soon to preside over: that marriage was sacred between one man and one woman, not even considering that Fitzherbert was a Catholic as well.

Caroline, having by now given up on Brougham, caught up with her friends Agnes and Mary Berry in Marseilles. The sisters found her quiet and contemplative. Caroline had decided to return to Pesaro and was waiting for better weather to sail back. In January 1820, she boarded a ship to Toulon.

Her usual bad travel luck caught up with her, and a near-shipwreck left her stranded in Monaco. After a few days recuperating at the palace of Prince Honoré V,* she headed off to Livorno. Upon arrival there, she was presented with a letter from Brougham. In Caroline's own words:

> *On my arrival at [Livorno] I found Mr Sicard with a long letter from Brougham communicating the demise of our good old King and the new title I had obtained.*

George III had died. Prinny was now King George IV. And Caroline was now Queen.

* A man who had spent time with Napoleon, which surely Caroline chatted to him about.

PART THREE

# QUEEN CAROLINE

CHAPTER NINETEEN

# CAROLINE ON THE MOVE

The instant George III died, Prinny became King and his wife, Caroline, became Queen. These are the rules of succession, no coronation ceremony required, no need for Caroline to return to Britain. Her first letter written after this news was signed, for the first time, *Caroline R.** In this, she requested to reside at Queen Charlotte's former residence in Green Park.

No official communication of his death or her new position was sent to Caroline by the British royals or government, and other European courts were not informed of her new role. Rather, the British ambassadors in various kingdoms communicated that their new King did not want Caroline recognized as Queen.

Brougham's letter, in which he shared the news of George III's death, instructed Caroline to head to northern France to meet him. The wound of her recent snubbing in France was still fresh, and, clearly over Brougham's two-faced ways, she instead made plans to travel south to Rome, where she assumed she would be treated appropriately to her new role.

---

* Caroline Regina, which means Queen Caroline.

But there were shitty men everywhere, and in Rome, this role was filled by Baron Reden, a replacement for Baron Ompteda as Hanoverian minister to Rome. Reden took Prinny's message to heart and also seemed to have been told that proceedings were imminent against Caroline, which would strip her title of Queen. Papal Secretary of State Cardinal Ercule Consalvi believed Reden's point of view and, therefore, treated Caroline with a lack of respect.

Pergami, in his new role as chamberlain to the British Queen, had sent ahead for a guard of honor and an audience with the Pope. Consalvi wrote back that the Vatican had not received official word from England about the death of George III and, therefore, did not accept that she was Queen.

Caroline wrote back:

*I desire from the Secretary of State a categorical answer, why the honours due to my birth are not rendered to me. I will not now enter upon the subject of the political views which may influence your Eminence, relative to the new title I have acquired by the will of the Almighty, and the acclamation of the noble and generous people of England; I shall always endeavour to merit their good opinion, and to sustain my own dignity, not allowing myself to be vilified under false pretences.*

Consalvi replied:

*His Holiness's Government cannot grant the guard to my lady the Countess of Oldi.* * *No guard is given to private persons; and when even royal princesses travel incognito, under a private name, they do not receive this distinction . . . But as no communication has been made to his Holiness's Government by the*

* The pseudonym under which Caroline was traveling.

*Government of his Majesty the King of England and Hanover upon the change that has taken place, nor upon the rank of the said royal person, the Papal Government does not know that the Queen of England is in Rome, and in consequence cannot grant a guard to the same.*

Caroline then wrote to her friend:

*If I were not obliged to stay here to settle finally all my accounts with my banker Torlonia, I should set out immediately for Pesaro and, after that, directly to dear old England. When few English persons have called on me, I see, too well, the spirit of independence and of true chivalrous feeling towards ladies in distress no longer exists in the world.*

By early March, word reached Caroline of Prinny's latest cruelty, which she initially assumed she had heard incorrectly. As the monarch was head of the Church of England, every Anglican service in England included a liturgy in which prayers were offered for the royal family individually and collectively. Prinny ordered that all members of the royal family should be named, apart from her. This informal new protocol was performed at Westminster Abbey. Hearing about this, Caroline wrote to a friend, "you may tell the world that the Queen is well, and alive to all their insults . . . and the Queen will certainly come to England, even if the people are not allowed to say the usual prayers for her."

Prinny requested a bill that would formally exclude Caroline's name and title from being mentioned in prayers. He furthermore was seeking to have her excluded from the coronation.

These insults sped up her plans. Rather than wait until the

end of the year to return to England, she returned straightaway. Back in Britain, bookies were making bets on whether or not she would return. Even some of Prinny's ministers doubted she would actually show up. Lord Eldon wrote, "Our Queen threatens approach to England; but, if she can venture, she is the most courageous lady I ever heard of."

Eldon wrote in another letter, "The town here is employed in nothing but speculation whether her Majesty will or will not come. Great bets are laid about it. . . . [Some] assert that they know she will come, and that she will find her way into Westminster Abbey and Westminster Hall on the Coronation, in spite of all opposition. I maintain my old opinion that she will not come, unless she is insane."

On April 12, Cardinal Consalvi told his friend Elizabeth Cavendish that Caroline had gone "in such anger that she has vowed vengeance in every paper, French and English, and that it would not stop there."

Caroline was in a burn-it-all-down era, and nobody was going to get in her way.

"The 30th of April I shall be at Calais for certain," Caroline wrote. "I have seen no persons of any kind who could give me any advice different to my feelings and my sentiments of duty relatif of my present situation and rank of life."

The day after she left town, a letter arrived in Rome from the British Secretary of State for Foreign Affairs, clarifying that George III had died, Prinny was King, and Caroline was indeed Queen. In Britain, Consalvi's rude letter was published in newspapers,* rallying the riot-happy public to Caroline's side once more. More exciting news soon reached English shores: Caroline was en route.

News of her imminent arrival caused widespread panic

---

* Caroline had submitted it to them for publication.

among the royal family and the government. Bear in mind that only Brougham knew at this point that Caroline had never learned that the June 1819 separation proposal had been approved; the others all thought she had been informed, rejected the terms, and was coming back for vengeance. Her ally Wood claimed to be visiting his son, but instead left town to meet up with her.

Caroline's return was delayed in Pesaro when she fell ill with rheumatic fever, her symptoms emerging as usual when she was under strain. She did not know that at around the same time, Prinny had also become very ill with his own chronic symptoms, such that many around him assumed he might die. If he did, the question of Caroline's role would then become moot; she would be Dowager Queen and likely permitted to return to her retirement in Italy. But both of their physicians used the latest leech technology to revive the pair, and both lived on to fight another day. Not even health concerns would stop either one from the face-off both had been working toward since the day of their first meeting.

Caroline had most of her household items packed to bring over to England to fill her new home (wherever it may be) with all her finest belongings as befitting of a Queen. Ever aware of the importance of fashion as soft diplomacy, she commissioned new gowns in the English style to replace her Italian-inspired wardrobe. Her plan was to show up looking as British as possible, ensuring everyone who saw her knew she was *their* Queen.

Caroline wrote, "England I now sigh to visit. Over the tomb of my dear Charlotte I long to weep and again to partake of the pleasure of the society of my sincere friends. I have been perpetually exposed to annoyance for these last two years by d'Ompteda and his emissaries, and now other spies have lately arrived at Milan. The object of my enemies appears to be to destroy all my happiness, and thus accelerate my death. I am determined to come to England and face all my accusers."

She fell ill twice more en route, in Milan and Turin, with rheumatism and sciatica. Her physician suggested she avoid traveling until August, but she refused to delay. In a letter that April, she wrote that "my health is good and my spirit is perfect," though she did admit that her "health has suffered much since the melancholy death of my ever-beloved daughter." Charlotte's death continued to sit heavily with her. When considering where she would settle in England, she refused to consider Windsor as "I could never live at a place where my poor daughter was buried."

Her symptoms increased when crossing the Alps, where she had a "most dreadful spasm" in her stomach and was forced to rest in the French town of Mont-Cenif. She reached Geneva in May, already exhausted from the strain of the journey. Still, on she went, finally reaching Montbard where she reunited with Wood and her former lady-in-waiting, six-foot-tall Lady Anne Hamilton.

Back in England, her Radical allies were ecstatic at her approach and the way it would surely unsettle the status quo. Prinny was also eager for her arrival, as he'd gotten Parliament to agree to start proceedings against her the minute she stepped on British soil. Brougham was poised and ready to use her to advance his career, with his latest gambit being to present himself as her loyal champion.

Brougham went to meet Caroline at St. Omer near Calais, where she had already been conferring with Wood. He found her mind made up as firmly as Charlotte's had been the night she ran away, writing, "I never saw a resolution more fixed than that which she has taken to go to England without loss of time."

Despite Brougham's best efforts, Caroline would not change her mind or accept any of the proposals of separation he suggested. In fact, she left her hotel and fled in a carriage without telling him, leaving Brougham to watch her retreating carriage through his window.

Brougham's colleague, who witnessed the meeting and Caroline's escape, wrote:

> *[On] this occasion we have been entirely out-generaled—the violence and the determination of this woman have had the effect for the moment of wisdom and arrangement and she has completely succeeded in all her plans.*

Caroline parted from Pergami, as she could not arrive in London with her alleged lover, with whom she was rumored to have committed adultery. As soon as Pergami set foot on British soil, he would be deemed to be under the protection of the King, and therefore, their affair became legal treason. He and the other Italian members of her household headed back to Pesaro, other than his sister, who remained in Caroline's service.

Brougham followed Caroline to London. Headlines about Caroline's movements were already in the papers there, as the *Times* editor had been in St. Omer and was given copies of her correspondence by Wood. This editor traveled ahead of her and reported on the high spirits of the crowds awaiting her arrival. On her return to Britain, *The Times* reported:

> **There have been disembarkations on the British coast, bringing war and producing revolutions in the state, ere now . . . Henry VII and William III brought with them . . . a train of armed followers. But this woman comes arrayed only in native courage, and . . .**

**conscious innocence; and presents her bosom, aye, offers her neck, to those who threatened to sever her head from it, if ever she dared to come within their reach.**

A hotel room had been prepared for her in Calais, but Caroline chose instead to immediately board a public ferry (she had not been provided with a royal yacht, as she'd requested).

*The Times* reported breathlessly:

**Neither at the landing of William the Conqueror nor at that of William III had any arrival in England caused such a sensation.**

The Caroline fandom was not new. She had been popular ever since she first arrived in England, and her popularity always outshone that of Prinny or his parents. The Delicate Investigation and her exile had maintained her popularity, especially as a symbol of anti-Prinny sentiment. Her return reignited her previous supporters.

She landed in Dover to find a crowd that had been waiting for hours. Caroline's plan was to travel to London, following the same route that Charles II had taken in 1660 when he victoriously returned to England to restore the monarchy. Caroline was greeted as enthusiastically as Charles had been, with crowds prepared to cheer her all along the route.

In Dover, the commandant of the garrison gave orders for a royal salute, and so was Queen Caroline greeted upon her return to England by a roar of cannon along with the cheering crowds. Not willing to wait for a ship to bring her to shore, Caroline boarded an open boat and landed ashore to cheers of "God bless Queen Caroline!"

The Queen had arrived.

CHAPTER TWENTY

# Chaos in the Streets, a Queen in the Sheets

To understand how rapidly the kingdom of Britain descended into nonstop pro-Caroline riots from the moment she set foot in the country, we need to pull back a little to talk about what had been going on there while she was out of town.

Prinny was odious and constantly hated, as we have previously discussed. The government he oversaw was seen as corrupt and out of touch, which it was. Britain had been poised and ready for its own French Revolution moment for at least a century, evidenced by the riots and rebellions that kept breaking out. The general population was unhappy with the status quo, the royal family, and the government in particular. Caroline had arrived in town to a population primed and ready to side with her because she had been used and abused by Prinny and the government, like they had been. They were all on the same side: burn it all down.

There had been numerous riots across Britain for centuries, many of which wound up in tragedy when government forces intervened and protestors were killed. Even just looking at the time since Caroline's birth, the country had seen crises including the Massacre of St. George's Fields (1768), the Spitalfields Riots (1765–1769), the Gordon Riots (1780), the Old Price Riots (1809), the Luddite Riots (1811–1817), the Spa Fields Riots (1816), and the Peterloo Massacre (1819).

What were people so upset about? Similar things as people are protesting in the twenty-first century: the rising cost of living, lack of governmental support for the poor, machines replacing jobs, the elites living in luxury while ordinary citizens starve. The concept of rebellion was in the air following the American, Haitian, and French Revolutions, and anarchist and socialist writings were becoming more widely available.

In reaction to widespread plots to overthrow the government, Prime Minister Pitt the Younger suspended habeas corpus from 1794–1795, during which time anyone could be arrested on a whim and held in captivity without a trial. In 1795, it was made illegal to hold political gatherings of over fifty people or for anyone to think of imagining the King's death.

American politician John Quincy Adams, in London in 1816 as US minister, wrote that "the extremes of opulence and of want are more remarkable, and more constantly obvious, in this country than in any other I ever saw." One reason for this was the sudden increase in population. The population of London increased by two-thirds in forty years at this time, the most rapid period of growth in its history. The bigger population brought greater wealth to those who owned land, as they were able to sell and rent more. But it left less food and land for the people in need, with greater competition for low-paying work. The growing population was also younger than in previous generations, with one-third of the population under age fifteen. Around one in five families in Great Britain were not earning enough to feed, house, and clothe themselves.

The same year that Adams made his observation, food was even scarcer than usual. The volcanic eruption of Mount Tambora in Indonesia threw weather patterns into disarray around the world, leading to Western Europe's "year without summer," destroying crops throughout the United Kingdom.* There was frost and flooding in June, and snow in August. Other than these weather events, it rained constantly, with overnight temperatures as low as -4 degrees Fahrenheit.

This weather led to the worst harvests in living memory, which, in the wake of the Napoleonic Wars, caused many to starve. Strikes, riots, marches, and armed uprisings occurred throughout Britain, exacerbated when the government chose to loot the Elgin Marbles from Greece rather than put bread on the table for their population. Public anger coalesced around Prinny and the royal family, with several attempts on their lives. Prinny's beloved Carlton House was tagged by graffiti scrawled on with coal or chalk, and crowds spat and jeered him in his carriage. On one occasion, a projectile broke through his carriage window, narrowly missing his head. While he claimed it had been an air gun pellet, it may have also been a rock. In either case, the mob's anger at the monarchy was becoming increasingly violent.

In February 1820 (four months before Caroline set foot in Dover), a conspiracy to murder all of the British Cabinet ministers, including the prime minister, was discovered. Known

* And was also the setting, in Switzerland, for Mary Shelley to write her first draft of *Frankenstein*.

as the Cato Street Conspiracy after the conspirators' meeting place, it led to the arrest of thirteen men and the death of one policeman. Five conspirators were publicly hanged and beheaded, and five others were deported to Australia.

It was into this powder keg of anti-monarchist and anti-government fury that Caroline arrived, like Katniss Everdeen in *Catching Fire*, an emblem of wronged innocence for the riot-happy public to rally behind. Caroline's particularly feminine victimhood resonated with women who sympathized with the plight of a wife treated cruelly by her husband. A large number of women were among the cheering crowd at Dover. *The Times* correspondent noted that "Well-dressed ladies, young and old" were on the scene; another witness noted that the windows above closed storefronts were "filled with females waving their handkerchiefs."

The size of this gathering far outnumbered the limit of fifty as per the Six Acts. The streets were so crowded that Caroline and her party were not able to walk to the nearby hotel. She climbed into an open-top carriage with Wood and Hamilton, and before horses could be untied to pull them along, men from the crowd had begun pulling the carriage along themselves. The crowd booed soldiers stationed outside the hotel, attacking them such that the guards had to take shelter indoors. Once settled into her hotel room, Caroline stood at a window and bowed to the crowd, which burst into riotous cheers.

Caroline and her entourage had intended to remain in Dover for only a short pit stop before continuing on to London, but the crowd's enthusiasm led her to stay long enough for a formal greeting from local officials. When she finally went to leave, the crowd again replaced her horses to drive her and her carriage back out of town.

She stopped for the night in Canterbury at the Fountain

Hotel. She arrived in the rain and found the gates illuminated by candles, with over ten thousand people waiting to cheer her entry. After being formally received by local dignitaries, Caroline again waved from the window of her hotel.

The Queen's grand progress left the next morning for her next stop in Sittingbourne. She sat in her carriage facing forward, Wood by her side and Hamilton sitting opposite. She likely chose this seating arrangement to make it clear to all who saw her that she was side-by-side with the Radical faction represented by Wood. Caroline leaned out the window, waving a handkerchief and calling out greetings to her throngs of fans as the carriage passed. The young woman from Braunschweig who was sequestered away from society, hidden behind castle gates, and denied affection for so many decades was finally getting the attention she'd longed for since childhood. She would never have imagined the circumstances that brought her to this moment.

She attended mass at Sittingbourne where, though forbidden to mention her name during the liturgy, the clergymen greeted her warmly and rang the church bells to honor her. The local crowd prepared again to personally pull her carriage, and had to be dissuaded by Caroline herself, explaining she hoped to reach London that day and horses would be faster than a mob. She was cheered by large crowds in every town she passed through, which surely increased her confidence that her popularity might help her defeat Prinny's latest scheme.

Larger crowds had been waiting for hours on the outskirts of London, waving Union Jack flags, bursting into cheers when her procession came into view. Pamphleteer William Cobbett was among them and claimed that the crowd which greeted her numbered two hundred thousand. When she was near her old home in Blackheath, the crowd could no longer be dissuaded, and the horses were again removed so the mob could pull her carriage. People waited alongside their own carriages to join her procession and accompany her.

All of London seemed to have turned out to cheer on her arrival throughout the streets, coinciding with the bright rays of sunshine that peeked through the rainy skies. Caroline opened her carriage door to provide the crowd with an outfit reveal: She was wearing a black gown with fur ruff, and a black satin hat that was adorned with her huge trademark feathers.

This color palette was perhaps chosen due to the new reality of life in London, where brightly colored clothing would more clearly show the effects of now ubiquitous smog. The city had changed from the one she'd left; even the air was different now, as the increased number of factories had led to a new permanent haze hovering overhead. Small particles of soot permeated the air like grim, omnipresent snow that stuck to clothes and skin. This was one of the reasons that Prinny, and others who could afford to, left the city in the winter, when the smog was thickest.

As Prinny had refused to provide her with a royal residence, Caroline went to stay in Wood's town house at 77 South Audley Street in Mayfair. Even before she'd left England, many great lords chose to demolish their old mansions and turn the land into elegant town houses, providing luxurious residences for the wealthy. Wood's was similar to others, mostly three- or four-story terraced buildings. She emerged on a balcony to wave at the street full of fans.

As night fell, the crowd turned more riotous. They castigated Wood's neighbors to put candles in their windows in honor of the Queen. Those who did not comply had rocks thrown at their houses. Princess Dorothea von Lieven wrote that "The mob streamed through the streets all night making passers-by shout, 'Long live the queen!'"*

This celebratory rampage continued for days. Mayfair resident Lady Jerningham wrote, "This country is I fear nearer disaster than it has been since the days of Charles 1st . . . a constant mob cheering her and for two nights past breaking every window† which did not illuminate . . ."

Prinny and Parliament may have thought that refusing to permit her a royal residence would humiliate her. Rather, it brought her closer to her strongest supporters: the regular people of London, particularly women. Prinny's parents had worked to establish the monarchy as a sort of parental force, one in which the royal couples' affection for one another and their children represented their love for their subjects. Prinny's cruelty to Caroline merged in the minds of the subjects with the way the government and armed forces didn't seem to care for them. Regardless of Caroline's guilt or innocence, many agreed that Prinny was unquestionably worse. Jane Austen had passed away, but Caroline's cause was supported now by fellow novelist Mary Shelley, who wrote, "I wish with all my heart downfall to her enemies."

Caroline agreed to allow Brougham to defend her, and he got to work speechifying in Parliament even as Prinny and his allies were again poring over the Milan Commission's report for evidence to use against her.

Meanwhile, the mob continued to enthusiastically support Caroline in the way they best knew how: mayhem. They began attacking the residences of Prinny's ministers

---

* By contrast, Prinny was booed when he went to the House of Lords and the crowd shouted, "The Queen! Where's the injured Queen?"

† Remember, the wealthier the owner, the larger the panes and therefore, the greater the damage when broken by the mob throwing a rock!

and closest friends. His former mistress, Lady Hertford, had all her windows smashed (the mob couldn't keep up with his womanizing to know that his latest conquest was actually Lady Conyngham).

William Benbow, the Radical printer, plastered signs all over the streets, encouraging everyone to keep candles lit in their windows to show support for their Queen. The mob, staying put on South Audley Street, stood guard on all corners and encouraged* passersby to raise their hats and huzzah for the Queen. At regular intervals, chants of "Queen!" or "Balcony!" would break out, and Caroline would dutifully emerge to smile and wave at them from above.

At night, when Caroline went to bed, the mob fanned out around London to encourage everyone to light candles for her in their inimitable way, yelling "Lights!" and throwing rocks at houses that did not comply. Soon many houses had broken first-floor windows on nearby streets. The mob headed down to St. James's Square to throw rocks at the home of the leader of the House of Commons. The chant then changed to "Carlton House!" and they headed off for Prinny's place. But Prinny had guards at the gates, and, unable to attack, the crowd dissipated.

It should be stated that this mob was currently aligned with Caroline, but this was also a freelance mob that had been protesting the monarchy and government for half a century. She had not driven them to mob violence; the mob happened to hate the same people she hated, so they worked in her favor. And for the time being, their support terrified her enemies, fearing a sort of French Revolution might happen but instead of killing the monarchy, they'd appoint Caroline as their leader.

---

* "Encouraged" by throwing mud at anyone who did not comply.

Threatening letters were sent to the Cabinet ministers' offices, including numerous death threats aimed at politicians, the King, and Prinny. Despite crowds all over chanting, "no Queen, no King," a man named Reverend Crowther was put on trial for saying this publicly.

Caroline allowed Wood to return to his home when she went to stay with Hamilton at 22 Portman Street, nearby. The mob followed her, celebrating in the street below. Upon Brougham's advice, Caroline wrote to Prime Minister Lord Liverpool. In his reply, he revealed what Brougham had still not told her: that Parliament had accepted the terms of her offer to divorce Prinny.

Getting over her surprise at learning of Brougham's betrayal, Caroline responded that she was amenable to negotiation; Prinny, however, would not relent. Brougham encouraged her to take a deal. Wood and the Radicals encouraged her natural impulse to fight.

The lack of a police force meant that the army, like at Peterloo, was called upon to control the crowd. Additional troops moved into London in anticipation of the riots. This led to a new twist in the whole crisis: The 3rd Regiment of Guards mutinied, angry at their cramped living arrangements and low pay. The Duke of Wellington, famous for defeating Napoleon, was still in charge of the army and was pretty panicked at this turn of events—particularly that neither he nor the government heard about the mutiny until several hours afterward. The defeat of Napoleon had been a victory for Britain, but it also led to a surplus of soldiers that were no longer needed in battle. These men found it hard to find work and had reasons to potentially act against the government.

As local magistrates and constables weren't numerous enough to combat the mob, Wellington advocated the government to set up a special military corps, separate from the regular military, to keep peace in the streets. This idea was not pursued.

Local businesses banked on pro-Caroline sentiment, offering free ale and meat to any soldier who drank to the Queen's health. In Brighton, two regiments shared a celebratory dinner where one of the sergeants proposed the health of the Queen. He was kicked out of the party by monarchist loyalists only to return with a mob, who ran the hosts and other guests out of the residence.

Diarist Harriet Arbuthnot reported that Liverpool said, "the aversion to the King was rising to the greatest possible height, that the Guards in London were all drinking to the Queen's health and had the greatest possible contempt for the King, from thinking him a coward."

Among the widely hated royal family, Prinny's younger brother Prince Frederick was marginally more popular than the others due to his lengthy military career. As such, Liverpool floated the idea of sending Prinny to Hanover until the crowd died down, leaving Frederick as Regent.

Prinny's advisers were throwing out whatever strategies they could to get Caroline to agree to leave the country without a public trial; they knew that would only instigate more mob violence, ruin Prinny's reputation, and potentially topple the government, leaving room for the Radical faction to take control. Brougham also wanted Caroline to agree to a negotiated truce so he could present himself as a savior, the one man capable of handling this mediation, the rightful candidate for prime minister. He brought up the deal that his brother had helped negotiate in Pesaro, in which Caroline agreed to stay out of Britain in exchange for an increase in her allowance. Wood advised her to stay firm and refuse their offers, forcing the public trial that the members of Parliament so gravely feared.

But Caroline understood Prinny in a way the others didn't. She knew he would never rest until he got what he wanted: to humiliate her. She was determined to have a public trial to vindicate herself. She hadn't come all this way, triggering her chronic illness symptoms, leaving her peaceful Italian life and lover to sign a piece of paperwork. To that end, she wanted the same thing he did: a public showdown of Caroline versus Prinny, winner takes all.

CHAPTER TWENTY-ONE

# Court of Public Opinion

On June 6, the same day Caroline arrived in London, Prinny contacted the House of Lords and the House of Commons, declaring that the Queen's arrival had forced him to hand over "disclosures and discussions" about her conduct. Namely, the contents of the Milan Commission's report, tidily packed into two of the large green bags (which will have a breakout moment soon, stay tuned) used to transfer legal documents at that time. Each house gathered more secret committees to go over these documents and advise on Prinny's legal options.

Brougham was present at the discussion in the House of Commons, where he gave one of his charismatic speeches, so quotable that the newspapers reported it the following morning. His remarks, alluding to various matters he had been quiet about until now, led to further speculation. If he chose to reveal Prinny's marriage to Maria Fitzherbert, it could threaten Prinny's role as King as marriage to a Catholic disqualified him from the role as King.

Prinny wanted three things: to be granted a divorce from Caroline, to humiliate her publicly, and to become more popular than she was. Despite needling every politician he knew, the only way to divorce her was to prove her adultery.

A big reason his advisers didn't want to pursue this as a public matter was because chances were high that his own string of mistresses, illegitimate children, and bigamy would also be brought to light, further tarnishing the poisonous reputation of him and his family.

As Brougham's speech was publicized in the newspapers, he arrived at the House of Commons with a message from Caroline. In it, she objected to secret proceedings and insisted that the investigation be public and, crucially, that she "may see both the charges and the witnesses against her—a privilege not denied to the meanest subjects of the realm." Cheers broke out in the House as Brougham read the letter aloud.

In response to further debate, Brougham continued with his pro-Caroline talking points, stating:

"Could you wonder that any person, but more especially a woman, and still more especially this woman, born a princess, niece to Frederick of Prussia, niece to George III, daughter to the heroic Duke of Brunswick, and consort to his present Majesty, the first sovereign in Europe; could you wonder that this exalted female should feel acutely when the ministers of her own country wanted to treat her with indignity?"

Parliamentarian William Wilberforce, known today for his role in the abolition of the slave trade, pleaded for permission to mediate between Caroline and Prinny. He suggested she accept the payout that Brougham claimed to have offered her in Italy. This was the first time that Caroline learned that her offer had been accepted by Parliament, as Brougham had until now led her to believe they had turned this down. Despite her shock at yet another Brougham betrayal, Caroline, buoyed by the support she experienced whenever she looked out the window,* acted on the advice

* The mob's latest chant was "No Queen, no King!"

of her Radical allies and refused any offer that did not restore her name to the liturgy.

Lady Charlotte Lindsay disagreed with Caroline's stubbornness, writing to Mary Berry:

> *The weakness of her adversaries makes her rash. She thinks that everything that embarrasses them [Prinny and the government] must be for her advantage, not recollecting that they may all fall to the ground together.*

And now it was the green bags' time to shine. On June 27, they were opened, and a fifteen-member secret committee read their contents. The public, enthralled by this new plot twist in the ongoing reality show, was excited about what would be revealed.

Caroline's friend Sir Walter Scott wrote that, in his estimation, many people were "privately glad we are to have the reading of all the scandal, especially now that we have made [some show of] decent reluctance to it . . . I cannot see why these two great personages should remain [ . . . ] without the public knowing which is right, which wrong."

Newspapers, pamphlets, and flyers featured drawings of the infamous green bags. Though they were the same type of container that legal documents were always transferred in, they became symbols of corruption. An editorial in the *Morning Chronicle* declared that the committee's decisions were a foregone conclusion, as they had been put together by Prinny specifically to torment Caroline. "Everyone has heard that persons of all ranks and situations of life, from Hanoverian barons down to the lowest scum of Italy, had been employed to beset the Queen." The alleged witnesses had all been paid to lie, and the green bags contained evidence of this bribery.

On July 4, the secret committee announced that after

having read the green bag papers, they felt these charges should become the subject of an official legal inquiry to be held at the House of Lords.

The House of Lords sits in parallel to the elected House of Commons. All titled male members of the British nobility had automatic membership in the House of Lords, known as the peers. New members were added at the monarch's leisure when he appointed someone new to a lordship. Caroline's case was likely brought before the House of Lords because noble people could only be tried by other members of the nobility.

Historically, there had been only fifty peers in the House of Lords at a time. But during his tenure, George III had created so many new peerages that by the time Caroline's case was before them, the membership had risen to 367 members. These included several of her friends, such as her past protector Malmesbury and her frequent dinner guest Lord Byron.

On July 5, a day after raising Caroline's case to the House of Lords, an act was introduced that would force Caroline out of the country and strip her of her royal titles. The full name of the bill was "An Act to deprive her Majesty Queen Caroline Amelia Elizabeth of the Title, Prerogatives, Rights, Privileges and Exemptions, of Queen Consort of this Realm, and to dissolve the Marriage between his majesty and the said Caroline Amelia Elizabeth."

This act was being introduced as a terrifyingly named Bill of Pains and Penalties. Society hostess Emily, Lady Cowper wrote: "A Bill of Pains and Penalties is an awkward name; it sounds to the ignorant as if she was going to be fried or tortured in some way." *The Times* declared the bill was a "violation of the law of God."

The Bill of Pains and Penalties was normally a parliamentary procedure to impose ramifications where recourse to the criminal courts was deemed unsuitable. There had only been one Bill of Pains and Penalties enacted in the previous two hundred years. This would be, effectively, a trial by Parliament as there wasn't enough legal basis to attempt a divorce case in the normal legal manner.

The not-really-a-trial would lead to a vote on Caroline's innocence by the peers of the realm. As it was not an actual trial, she would not be afforded the rights of someone legally accused. She and her team would not be told in advance who the witnesses would be to testify against her; it was as though the peers would be both prosecutors and judges.

As Pergami was specifically named in the act as Caroline's alleged lover, he became a celebrity without being in the country. Madame Tussaud added a waxwork model of Pergami to her preexisting Caroline and Prinny figures.

Prinny's coronation was postponed indefinitely because he hoped the trial would strip Caroline of her rights to a crown so she wouldn't have to be invited.

Princess Dorothea von Lieven wrote to her lover Prince Metternich that "The radical families are already urging the populace to take up arms in defence of the Queen; and she herself . . . makes an appeal to the people."

Remember, the American, Haitian, and French Revolutions, all of which had overthrown monarchs, were still within recent memory, and troops who had fought against rebels in America and Haiti were living in England. Spain's Ferdinand VII had only recently retaken his throne after being overthrown following an army mutiny; the unrest spread to nearby Portugal. The same month that proceedings were announced against Caroline, Ferdinand I of Naples was forced by the mob to grant a constitutional monarchy; the revolutionary spirit spread next to Milan from where one Colonel Browne wrote:

*Constitution and insurrection are in every one's mouth. I cannot, perhaps give your lordship a better idea of the extent to which the question of the Queen is mixed up with politics here than by mentioning that a leader of the democrat party said in society a few evening since "The Queen of England shall triumph"; and two or three questions of a similar nature are all that are now wanting to restore the rights of man, and to rid us of all our tyrants at once.*

While the country was poised on the brink of war and societal collapse, Caroline was second-guessing keeping Brougham as her advocate. She knew he was entirely out for himself, but his passionate speeches in her defense would be persuasive in the not-a-trial. However, she did not like how much control he had over her legal case. At one point, she was seen pacing around her room, saying, "If my head is upon Temple Bar,* it will be Brougham's doing!"

Also frustrated with Wood's advice, she sought out an additional political adviser. She turned to Sir George Canning, her rumored lover from the Blackheath era. Canning had recused himself from this trial due to his past relationship with Caroline, so she hoped he could come and work for her side. He refused.

Next, Caroline approached pamphleteer William Cobbett, to his great delight. Cobbett, recently back in London after a period of exile in America, had been writing and offering his services to her for some time. He had been among the crowd greeting her in Blackheath, and had already published a successful pro-Caroline pamphlet called *A Peep at the Peers*.† This not only helped keep the public on Caroline's side,

---

* In previous centuries, executed criminals would have their heads mounted on pikes and displayed at Temple Bar, the ceremonial entrance to the City of London.

† The pamphlet outlined the nepotism and paychecks of the House of Lords, exposing how they weren't objective in judging Caroline's case. Dedicated to Queen Caroline, the publication sold over one hundred thousand copies.

but also helped Cobbett pay off his debts. Cobbett's daughter Anne wrote that, "Papa would never have got through that hard time so well, if it had not been for the Queen's Affair."

Cobbett wasn't the only one to profit from public interest in the trial. More volumes of public verse were published in 1820 than in the decade before or since. The pro-Caroline *Times* saw its circulation increase to twenty thousand copies sold per day during the trial. Literary elites also discussed Caroline and the trial, including Lord Byron in *Don Juan* and Bysshe Shelley's play *Swellfoot the Tyrant.*

Cobbett dedicated space in his weekly newspaper the *Political Register* in defending her. He was the one to blend nascent nationalism (still at a high level following the British defeat of Napoleon at Waterloo) with support for Caroline. He wasn't advocating for an end to the monarchy; he respected it so much that he was defending it, through her. He also had the ability through his writing to connect with women, and leaned into this by emphasizing Caroline's status as a symbol of female fortitude in the face of great peril led by scheming men.

Working-class women became a backbone of pro-Caroline sentiment. Among the eight million working-class people in England at this time, half were working women. They and their children might work in factories or mills, as domestic servants, or selling goods on the street. Thirty years earlier, French market women had been instrumental in the early stage of the French Revolution when they teamed up to protest unfair pricing. In England, this was a previously untapped demographic in the political sphere. Their highly visible support provided a powerful and constant visual reminder of Caroline's widespread popularity. Their omnipresence buoyed her spirits, and caused her enemies to worry similar violence to the French Revolution could erupt.

On July 15, Caroline officially hired Cobbett to write her

public statements. These included a letter ostensibly written to Prinny but publicly shared in *The Times*, which reads partly as follows:

> **From the very threshold of your Majesty's mansion the mother of your child was pursued by spies, conspirators and traitors. . . . You wrested me from my child . . . and even in my sorrows pursued me with unrelenting persecution . . . .**

Cobbett's words firmly aligned Caroline's public persona with the radical cause. She surrounded herself with more radical voices such as Dr. Samuel Parr, a pamphleteer she'd known since 1814. Like Cobbett, he sought her out to offer his assistance. They were kindred spirits, as seventy-four-year-old Parr had a similar informal nature and fondness for freaking out the establishment as she did.* Parr, a curate, was appointed her senior chaplain, and through him, she met Reverend Robert Fellowes, who became another writer for her public responses.

Brougham was horrified by these additions to Team Caroline, and at the new radical underpinning of her entourage. Prinny and others in high society were surprised and dismayed to find that intellectuals like these chose to align themselves with her.

In August, Cobbett wrote a letter on Caroline's behalf called *Letter from the Queen to the King*, which he ensured was leaked to all the newspapers to be published a day before the trial commenced. The highly emotional letter recounts her decision to leave the country and the pain she felt after Charlotte's death:

* He also apparently wore a poorly fitting wig, similar to Caroline's own preferred hairstyle.

*Thus bereft of the society of my child, or reduced to the necessity of embittering her life by struggles to preserve that society, I resolved on a temporary absence, in the hope that time might restore me to her in happier days. Those days, alas! Were never to come. To mothers—and those mothers who have been suddenly bereft of the best and most affectionate and only daughters—it belongs to estimate my sufferings and my wrongs.*

*Such mothers will judge of my affliction upon hearing of the death of my child, and upon my calling to recollection the last look, the last words, and all the affective circumstances of our separation. Such mothers will see the depth of my sorrows. Every being with a heart of humanity in its bosom, will drop a tear of sympathy with me. And will not the world, then, learn with indignation, that this event, calculated to soften the hardest heart, was the signal for new conspiracies, and indefatigable efforts for the destruction of this afflicted mother? Your Majesty has torn my child from me; you had deprived me of the power of being at hand, to succour her; you had taken from me the possibility of hearing of her last prayers for her mother; you saw me, bereft, forlorn, and broken-hearted; and this was the moment you chose for redoubling your persecutions.*

The letter caused a huge sensation among the public, as a public condemnation by a Queen about a King had never before been viewed. Cobbett's daughter Anne worried he would be sent to prison for seditious writing, but this was never an option. The Six Acts were ostensibly stifling what could be published, but the sheer amount of material published in 1820 left the government unable to monitor it all. Additionally, the government knew that to arrest Cobbett would only set ablaze the already fiery mob. And the government's entire attention was currently set on the upcoming trial.

The government had access to the green bag papers,

containing two years' worth of investigations into Caroline's conduct. Caroline's team had just two weeks to prepare, without knowing who would be called as witnesses and what they would say.

What *was* known is that numerous witnesses were traveling from Milan to London. These witnesses should have been greeted in Dover by government officials, including a translator, who would lead them to their London accommodations. But mix-ups in the travel arrangements found the Italian witnesses arriving without anyone there to greet them. Lower-class English people were often suspicious of lower-class foreigners, and the general pro-Caroline atmosphere brought two strikes against these confused and stranded Italian witnesses.

The people of Dover were fervent Caroline supporters* and had been following the trial updates in newspapers. Everyone knew that witnesses were coming over from Italy to testify against Caroline. Dover residents had already been vigilantly waiting for the Italians to arrive, and when they came ashore, the residents (mostly women) attacked them with sticks and punches. Giuseppe Restelli, one of Caroline's fired servants, was badly beaten, and all were shaken from the experience. To the English mob, nationalism combined with anti-Italian xenophobia, and this affair was christened the Dover Massacre.

Stories of the "massacre" spread quickly, particularly into Italy and France, where the next batches of witnesses were preparing to depart. News spread that Restelli was beaten to death, the other witnesses were in jail, and Caroline was usurping the throne. Understandably, they were reluctant to travel to England.

The Italian witnesses became an iconic new addition to the satirical prints being circulated to a public waiting with bated

---

* Remember, they'd been the first to pull her carriage instead of horses.

breath for the latest updates. While Caroline and other public figures were also parodied, Prinny took this satire personally, writing to his friend the Lord High Chancellor demanding that "If the law as it now stands has not the power to protect the Sovereign against the licentious abominations of this description, it is high time that the law should be amended." Or, in other words, "wah wah, boohoo, I'm being made fun of and I don't like it." Knowing how much Prinny hated being mocked only made the cartoons more enjoyable to the public.

The most popular anti-Prinny satire was a poem called *The Queen's Matrimonial Ladder* by William Hone. Prints were sold along with a toy wooden ladder.

In the weeks leading up to the trial, public opinion remained firmly on Caroline's side. Graffiti was etched throughout the city reading *The Queen for ever, the King in the river.** Newsboys were out on every street corner selling pamphlets and broadsheets blasting Prinny and his ministers or comparing Prinny to Henry VIII (who cruelly rid himself of four of his six wives through execution or annulment) and the Roman Emperor Nero (who allegedly set Rome on fire to clear space for him to build a new luxury palace). Percy Bysshe Shelley's *Swellfoot the Tyrant*, completed in August, was so seditious that only seven copies were printed before it was suppressed by the government. It was never performed. The Six Acts could not be enforced, but Prinny's thin skin meant that he had the government suppress the most insulting publications about him.

Sir Matthew Cholmeley wrote:

> *No man could go through the streets of London without having his eyes insulted by the most offensive placards and comparisons*

---

* Which presumably rhymes when spoken in an early nineteenth-century London accent.

*of an odious kind between the highest personage and the greatest of tyrants!*

Along with images of Prinny, Caroline, and the Italian witnesses, satiric images inevitably also included a portrayal of the infamous green bags. These green bags went 1820-viral, to the extent that after this point, lawyers used bags of a different color since the green bag was so intrinsically tied to this affair.

The people of London wanted to act on their intense fandom for Caroline. Rallies were held for her. A shipwright named John Gast arranged a meeting outside city limits* for other mechanical artisans, which led to the creation of a written address to present to Caroline. Copies of this were left in nearby taverns and pubs for other supporters to sign: within two weeks, these acquired 29,786 signatures of support. This was 15 percent of the population of the outer borough of London at the time. Supporters traveled to London from other cities to be nearer to the drama and their injured heroine.

In early August, Caroline moved to Brandenburg House, a mansion on the Thames at Hammersmith. The residents of Hammersmith were overjoyed to hear she was coming to live there. With Pergami back in Italy, she hired Lord Henry Hood† as her new chamberlain, taking on his wife Lady Jane Hood as her personal attendant. She came to rely on both; Caroline, agitated and anxious about the trial, was often seen walking the grounds of Brandenburgh House on the outskirts of the city with them and others. As concerned as she was, there was little she was personally being called upon to do. Brougham and her other advisers were busy persuading

* The Lord Mayor would not permit such a meeting to be held in London.

† Who had potentially been one of her lovers back in the Blackheath era.

public opinion to ensure it remained on her side, knowing this was one of their most powerful weapons.

Brougham spread word of the injustices she faced not only around England but into Scotland as well. This was an unusual strategy, as Scotland (despite joining the United Kingdom in the 1801 Act of Union) was politically separate from England, and the Scottish were generally against the English monarchy (which included both Prinny and Caroline). Brougham banked on building support there, and wrote letters to the *Edinburgh Review* and his Edinburgh University alumni friends to support Caroline.

As Caroline's PR operation continued to rile up the public, the disgruntled lords made their way to London for the trial. Usually on holiday this time of year, many were annoyed by the mandatory attendance. Absent members would be fined unless their absence was excused due to age (those over seventy were not required), sickness, bereavement, or absence from the country on government service. This excluded 109 of the 367 peers, including some who claimed to have had other excuses to avoid being present due to their personal history with Caroline: Malmesbury pleaded age and sickness, Lord Byron was out of the country,* and failed freelance spy Lord Sligo couldn't fake a reason but just didn't show up.

Even with these men absent, the House of Lords was not equipped for the full membership to attend at once, not to mention having to fit in Caroline and her entourage, along with reporters, translators for the Italian witnesses, and the witnesses themselves. Architect Sir John Soane was directed to alter the chamber to accommodate everyone; given the time constraints, he oversaw the addition of two temporary balconies supported on iron struts.

---

* He wrote to a friend that he thought Caroline would be found innocent. "I wish she may," he wrote. "She was always very civil to me."

By now there were sixty-one Italian witnesses staying in London, all housed in dormitories in Cotton Garden, Westminster. The witnesses continued to be main characters in the ongoing public interest in the trial, with rumors spreading that they were being fed by cooks originally sent to London to prepare food for the now-postponed coronation.

As the trial date approached, Caroline's health concerns* led her to move closer to Westminster to reduce her commute. She chose to stay with a friend in St. James's Square, next door to Lord Castlereagh, leader of the House of Commons. This selection of location was likely intentional, meaning he would be constantly surrounded by the pro-Caroline mob. The mob faithfully followed her to this new address, filling the square to such an extent that it was difficult for her carriage to come and go. Castlereagh eventually chose to temporarily relocate, to stay safe from the mob that hated him. With his exit, Caroline reigned supreme over the whole neighborhood.

The trial had yet to begin, but she had decidedly won in the court of public opinion.

* She was "still weak from an illness that had arisen from a disorder of the bowels."

CHAPTER TWENTY-TWO

# THE TRIAL*

## *NOT REALLY A TRIAL

Before sunrise on Thursday, August 17, 1820, two rows of heavy wooden barriers were erected near the Houses of Parliament to hold back the mob. By 7:00 a.m., nearly every law-enforcement-adjacent man* was positioned along Caroline's predicted route from St. James's Place to the House of Lords. At 9:30 a.m., further troops took up positions close to the House of Lords, and gunboats patrolled up and down the Thames.

Whig politician (and Lord Byron's bestie) John Cam Hobhouse noted: "there was no sympathy between [the representatives] and the people!"

Coincidentally, the trial was set to begin the week of the one-year anniversary of the Peterloo Massacre. Commemorative processions were also taking place that week, with the memory of that tragedy fresh in many people's minds.

An estimated ten thousand to twenty thousand people filled the streets from the House of Lords barricades to Caroline's residence hours before the trial began. They were there to support Caroline, ogle at her and the arriving lords and

* Including magistrates, Bow Street runners, beadles, watchmen, constables, and any other kind of law-enforcement.

royals, and otherwise pay witness to a moment in history. Many carried banners and placards, with a high proportion of the supporters being women. With the streets overrun, people climbed onto rooftops and the tops of carriages.* Radical activist Samuel Waddington walked around with a green bag on a long pole. Along with the notorious green bags, the color white† had been chosen to represent Caroline's innocence. Men wore white cockades‡ in their hats, and women wore white dresses with white sashes.

Back at her residence in St. James's Place, Caroline appeared at an upper window shortly after 9:00 a.m. to roars of appreciation from the crowd below. When she tried to leave, the crowd chanted, "The Queen! The Queen!" until she re-emerged for an encore.

She had been using a plain carriage in recent weeks, so as to emphasize her role as the People's Princess. But today, she needed to remind them all she was also their Queen. She arranged for a grand state carriage drawn by six large bay horses. Artist Robert Blake prepared a print, published by Thomas Kelly, illustrating Caroline's departure that morning. The print shows both sides of the street and around the corner completely filled with supporters, barely making space for Caroline's procession.

In contrast to her white-clad supporters, Caroline chose to wear black in mourning for her sister-in-law Princess Frederica, who had recently died. Of course, the ensemble included one of her trademark hats, in black, with black feathers.

"Her Majesty's appearance was commanding and digni-

---

* Entrepreneurial-minded carriage owners were said to charge a shilling a person for the privilege of sitting on top.

† Caroline herself had not been known for wearing white. She preferred brightly colored dresses, usually red.

‡ A button made of ribbons that resembles a rosette.

fied," reported *The Times.* "She repeatedly bowed to the people, who rent the air with their acclamations: her countenance, though pale and seemingly careworn . . . had yet an expression of great dignity and fortitude."

When her procession passed Prinny's home, Carlton House, the guards presented their arms as a sign of respect. The crowd loved it.

Back at the House of Lords, the arriving peers were alternately cheered or booed by the crowd, depending on their past history with Caroline. But these weren't the main characters of the day.

As Caroline approached, the crowd erupted in cheers of "God save Queen Caroline!" which devolved into general huzzahs, then into roars and screams. The crowd surged forward, knocking down the wooden fence as they swarmed their heroine.

Caroline was escorted inside by guards, while outside, the barriers were hastily reinstalled. As she entered the hall, Caroline was heard to say, "I am sorry indeed that the people make so much noise."

She had been provided with a dressing room, where she removed her feathered hat, replacing it with a white veil wrapped around her head and shoulders. She entered the chambers, clearly moved by the enthusiasm of the crowd, and took her seat to the right of the throne "with an air of indifference." The formidable Lady Hamilton stood behind her.

The first order of business was roll call, as the names of lords unable to attend were announced, along with their excuses. Lord Byron sent regrets, despite Caroline's efforts to lobby him to leave Italy and come support her.* Prinny's

* Byron refused to return to England due to his ongoing feud with Brougham, claiming that should he come to England, his first task would be challenge him to a duel.

brother Prince Augustus sent regrets, claiming he could not attend due to his blood relation to both Caroline and Prinny. Her other brother Prince Frederick expressed his annoyance at this, considering he was also blood-related to Caroline, not to mention in mourning for his wife, yet still had shown up.

Prinny chose not to attend.

The trial then began with a reading of the Bill of Pains and Penalties, followed by an opening statement by the prosecution. And then Caroline's team strutted in, presumably in slow motion like the *Law & Order* opening credits, all dressed in the white wigs and long gowns of English lawyers. Brougham set the tone with his opening statement, which displayed the star quality that he was (for now) using to support Caroline. His speech was so moving that *The Times* printed it in full the next day, praising Brougham's "fervid eloquence, powerful reasoning, intense thought and glowing language." Brougham's Whig friends predicted the bill would be thrown out by the end of the week.

On the second day of the trial, Caroline (who had been up late the previous night strategizing) was seen to fall asleep at points, inspiring the rhyme:

Her conduct at present no censure affords
She sins not with peasants but sleeps with the Lords.

The trial continued on, and London was alight with gossip about Caroline's guilt or innocence. Brougham played both sides, joking to his society friends that Caroline was "pure in-no-sense." Meanwhile, Caroline spit out the best one-liner when she claimed she only committed adultery once, "and that was with Mrs. Fitzherbert's husband."

With the matter of Caroline's guilt still in question, most women from high society refused to visit her lest this taint their own reputations. Aside from the loyal Hamilton, the only other notable women to publicly align themselves with Caroline were her frenemy Jersey's daughter-in-law Sarah Villiers* and Mary Berry's significant other, Anne Damer.

On August 19, the prosecution raised the accusation of adultery against Caroline. Knowing this was to come, the mob filled the streets again both to support Caroline and to try and catch a glimpse of the scandalous heroine. However, Caroline chose to remain home for this part of the trial.

As a thunderstorm raged outside, the lords heard about Caroline's alleged behavior with Pergami: the imprints of two bodies in her bed in Naples, their shared tent onboard a ship in the Mediterranean, claims that Pergami had been present when she bathed. The trial adjourned for the weekend, giving the public days to feast upon verbatim reports in the newspapers of all these salacious details. Sunday newspapers were already popular, and this weekend's edition was even more so.

On August 20, the prosecution's case resumed, though this speech (and speaker) did not go over as well as Brougham's. To be fair, the prosecution didn't have much of a case as Caroline and Pergami's relationship was not treasonable, due to his nationality, and not adulterous, due to her separation from Prinny. It was felt that the prosecutor's speech, compared to Brougham's polished finesse, was "ill-delivered and wretchedly put together."†

On August 21, the Italian witnesses took center stage. The wildly unpopular group had been subjects of vicious pamphlets and cartoons ever since their ignominious arrival in

* A Regency-era society hostess known for living on her own terms and who clearly didn't take after her mother-in-law.

† In the opinion of British army officer Henry Edward Fox, who was in attendance.

Dover. They were often illustrated alongside the green bags: the Italian witnesses may be shown popping out of the bags, or the bags were shown to contain rotten grain alongside the Italians. Anti-Italian songs rang out in the streets, where it was widely accepted that they had all been bribed to perjure themselves against Caroline*.

Caroline was visibly anxious upon her arrival, clenching and unclenching her hands as she waited to see who would show up. She and Brougham hadn't been told in advance who the witnesses would be, or what evidence they would be facing. When she saw twenty-eight-year-old Teodoro Majocci, Caroline "sprang up with the rapidity of lightning, advanced two or three steps, put her left arm akimbo, and threw her veil *violently* back with her right," as described by Fox. "She looked at him steadily for about two or three seconds during a dead silence; she then exclaimed in a loud, angry tone, 'Theodore!' and rushed out of the House (followed by Lady Anne Hamilton)."

There was some disagreement among witnesses at what she had yelled before leaving. It may have been the man's name, Teodoro. Some heard her say *traditore*—the Italian word for traitor. Whatever the cause, her actions were widely discussed. Did she flee out of guilt? Anger? As a result of her ongoing medical symptoms?

The latter seems most likely, as Caroline needed medical attention that night, being "copiously bled" by her physicians. When she returned to the House of Lords the next day, she looked unwell:† pale, listless, low energy. Brougham and his cocounsel advised her to stay away from the trial, perhaps for her own health, or perhaps because she had become a dis-

---

* Which, to be fair, they had been.

† Perhaps from the "copious bleeding"?

traction to their case. Caroline, true to herself as ever, did not heed their advice. She had sworn to be present in Parliament every day so that her presence might shame the witnesses against perjuring themselves. But, after the upsetting appearance of Teodoro, she chose to spend part of each day in a room adjacent to the House, playing backgammon with Wood. This was not due to shame, nor embarrassment at seeing the characters of her past; rather, she had a deep sense of propriety. She did not feel it dignified to be present as more lies were spoken about her.

Majocci testified again the next day, seemingly honest and straightforward. He was overshadowed by his translator, Marchese Spineto, who tended to use dramatic hand gestures and full-body acting to represent what was being described.

But Majocci soon supplanted the green bags as the trending meme of the trial. Brougham cross-examined him using legal skills that would fit in a Shonda Rhimes legal TV show, and absolutely decimated Majocci. He asked a series of specific questions about Majocci's tale, and Majocci repeated "Non mi ricordo" ("I don't recall") over eighty times. This was his response to questions about anything other than the facts he had recited during his initial testimony. Brougham further was able to establish that Majocci had not told anyone his anti-Caroline information until paid to do so by the Milan Commission, putting his honesty into question. The testimony ended with Majocci breaking down in tears, unable to recall if he had been paid for his testimony or not.

When news of this saga hit the streets, *Non mi ricordo* merchandise went viral, along with numerous cartoons of Majocci saying his now-iconic catchphrase.

The next day, Caroline arrived for the trial in a new outfit. In place of her usual white veil, she wore a light blue scarf with "a gay border" on her shoulders, and a peach-blossom satin hat with a huge white feather. The trial had started going in her direction, and she was dressing for this new optimistic mood. *The Times* reported daily on her various outfits, and the women of the mob continued to cheer for her from the streets, from the rooftops, and from close quarters—rushing past the guards to shout their support as the Queen passed by in her carriage.

The next most notable witness was Louise Demont, Caroline's former maid and secretary, who had been fired for her role in stealing Caroline's money. The young, pretty Demont made for a sympathetic witness, and her testimony backed up much of what Majocci and others had claimed about Caroline's behavior around Pergami. But under cross-examination, she was prodded into saying the French version of *Non mi ricordo: Je ne me rappelle pas.* Most damning against her were letters she had written after being fired, flattering Caroline and begging to be reinstated.

Other witnesses, en route from Milan, were told not to come. The case for the prosecution was concluded. Brougham applied to adjourn before presenting the defense case, which was granted, with instructions to reconvene on October 3.

CHAPTER TWENTY-THREE

# THE DEFENSE RESTS

Caroline's team had three weeks to prepare a case to dismantle the prosecution's two years' worth of investigations. Brougham's cocounsel, Thomas Denman, went to the spa town of Cheltenham to recover from exhaustion and jaundice. Even there, a pro-Caroline mob was present and rowdy as ever. Denman tried to quiet them by delivering a speech, which only served to inspire the mob to start smashing windows of nearby houses, yelling "Queen! Queen!"

As her team worked late into the night, Caroline—still suffering from her various ongoing symptoms, as well as the perpetual state of anxiety she'd been living with since the trial began—went for walks with Willikin and Hamilton.

She was forbidden to correspond with Pergami lest it taint their case, but her counsel was in constant communication with him. They were unsure if his presence in London would help or hinder the case. Pergami revealed that he had been offered large sums of money to testify against Caroline. Ever the golden retriever boyfriend, he refused the money and instead threatened to beat up the would-be briber. He also made a solemn vow that he had never had sexual intercourse with Caroline.* Ultimately Caroline's team decided it was best for

* A statement that could be true, and that also leaves room for other intimate acts to have occurred between them.

him to stay away. His soothing presence may prove a balm for Caroline's nerves, but the appearance of the six-foot-tall mustachioed Italian could tip the mob into a more violent frenzy.

The mob had already reached new heights of energetic mayhem during the three-week recess. Anne Cobbett wrote, "Nobody seems to *think* of anything but the Queen, and nobody seems to *expect* anything but a revolution."

Caroline didn't set out to be the figurehead of a revolution. But she allowed herself to be viewed in this manner to ensure the public continued supporting her. Public opinion, she intuitively trusted, was crucial for her victory in the trial.

Thousands of supporters made pilgrimages to Caroline's residence at Brandenburg House, including numerous newly mobilized women's groups. *The Times* published a list of seventy-eight organizations that had presented her with gifts and addresses. These included a "splendid dress" from the lace makers of Loughborough and a bonnet from the straw hat weavers of the Midlands. Caroline's responses to these gifts, written by Cobbett or other staff members, reassured them of her radical opinions about the government.

Many of these groups came dressed in Caroline white, such as the Married Females of the Parish of Marylebone, who arrived "covered with feathers and white cockades, escorted by the mob." The Married Ladies of Southwark and Westminster arrived at her home on September 19 to congratulate her on the end of the prosecution's case, having walked over fourteen miles. The women's support horrified men, including the editors of the *Morning Post* who described them as "shameless females, who tearing off the veil of modesty with unprecedented audacity, insulted the King."

This was the first time in British history that so many women had moved defiantly into the public sphere, advocating for a feminist revolution. Working-class women had been on the frontlines for decades, agitating for radical organizations and strikes. But never before had they been joined by middle-class women, whose political work had previously been focused on missionary or charity work.

Caroline's status as a wronged woman inspired them all to fight for her, which meant banding together against the status quo. Anne Cobbett was thrilled to see the system was being shaken up by a woman. She wrote:

> *It is not of little credit to our sex that all the reformers, radicals, Jacobins &c. &c. have ever been able to perform in the work of years to shake the present system has almost failed, but been completed by a woman! at last. An Old Woman will not now be thought so foolish a thing. Papa says that for the future Husbands must be content to be henpecked, and he has given Mama notice that she may begin to exert her Sovereign authority forthwith.*

Caroline was a symbol of radicalism, of feminism, of a new kind of monarchy, of a new world order. The Peterloo Massacre had produced a sense of solidarity among the working classes, and Caroline's trial added to this by providing inspiration for women to organize and assert themselves politically. Side by side, lower class men and women were now a force to be reckoned with.

News of the trial was inescapable through broadsheets, newspapers, and gossip. Essayist William Hazlitt later recalled that the trial "stuck its roots into the heart of the nation; it took possession of every house or cottage in the kingdom; man, woman, and child took part in it, as if it had been their own concern . . . it spread like wildfire over the kingdom."

As evidence, the prolific diarist Anne Lister recorded on September 1: "dawdled away this morning from eleven to twelve upstairs reading the newspaper about the [Queen's] trial." Four days later, she admitted to staying up past eleven at night talking about the trial.

From Ravenna, Northern Italy, Lord Byron wrote on September 23, "Nobody here believes a word of the evidence against the Queen: the very mob cry shame against their countrymen."

Support of Caroline's case was present in the public and private spheres, as evidenced by a sex worker who warned soldiers at the Crown alehouse that if they saluted Prinny, "you shall not come to bed to me. I am for Caroline. I am a whore and if she has had a whore's stroke is that any reason she is not to be Queen?"

Men also made the trip to visit her, with new groups arriving hourly every day. These were not just people from London: She received letters of support from Bristol, Nottingham, Edinburgh, Manchester, Glasgow, and more. In total, more than eight hundred petitions were received from men's and women's groups, with nearly one million signatures of support. One such group began fundraising to purchase a new set of china dishes to replace the set Prinny had refused to let Caroline bring with her when she left England.

Pro-Caroline merchandise became widely available. One such item was a handkerchief printed with a portrait of the youthful Caroline, inscribed *Her Most Gracious Majesty, Queen Caroline of England*. This souvenir was then stitched in the middle of a patchwork quilt, currently at the National Museum of Wales at St. Fagans. This handcrafted object illustrates the passionate, visceral love so many held for Caroline, despite the unflattering portrayals Prinny attempted to foist upon his subjects.

Crowds gathered to watch the groups heading to deliver their addresses at Brandenburg House. One of the biggest spectacles of this kind was when a group of seamen arrived via boat to meet with her. The navy at this time was seen (especially in opposition to the army) as the pinnacle of British heroism and manliness. And Caroline, a longtime fan of men in uniform, must have particularly appreciated these visitors.

The overall vibe for these three weeks veered toward anarchy. The *Manchester Observer* stated that the trial "has enabled all who dislike the present system, to league together for its destruction."

Those known to support Caroline became popular celebrities to the mob while Prinny's governmental officers were jeered, sent death threats, and forced to hide in their offices to save their homes from broken windows. Prinny hid out at his Windsor cottage, safe from the mob.

Even as the mob action was reaching its peak, many were aware that their passion was not actually about Caroline or the trial. The discontent of the masses from decades of economic hardship while Prinny and the government lived large resulted in a powerful group of radicals, using Caroline as an excuse for them to voice their general disapproval of the status quo. And yet, the widespread nature of public protests moved many, even some who had never before engaged in politics, to take to the streets.

Newspapers in every major city were selling out with stories (made up or not) about the main characters in this reality show: Caroline, Prinny, Brougham, and others new to the scene like Demont, Majocci, and the green bags. While public sentiment continued to be mostly pro-Caroline, caricatures and verse-poems against Caroline appeared for the first time during this three-week break. The details of her alleged liaisons with Pergami had, to some, stained her previous reputation as an angelic wronged woman.

The trial resumed on October 3, a bright and sunny day. The three weeks' preparation time paid off, as a newly rested and prepared Brougham delivered yet another persuasive opening statement. He artfully unwound each part of the prosecution's case while calling upon their sympathy for Caroline. He reminded them of all the cruel acts Prinny had subjected her to: separating her from Charlotte, excluding her from Charlotte's wedding, sharing news of Charlotte's death indirectly, instead of in person. His speech, which went into the second day (and which was printed in newspapers), connected Prinny to his notorious predecessor Henry VIII, who he claimed had also gotten rid of an unwanted wife with the perjured testimony of untrustworthy Italians.*

Brougham spoke for the full day, and then another six hours the following day, concluding his remarks with the following statement:

> My lords, I pray your lordships to pause. You are standing upon the brink of a precipice . . . Save the country, my lords, from the horror of this catastrophe—save yourselves from this situation—rescue that country, of which you are the ornament, but in which you could flourish no longer, when severed from the people, than the blossom when cut off from the root and the stem of the tree.
>
> Save that country, that you may continue to adorn it—save the Crown, which is in jeopardy—the aristocracy which is shaken—the altar itself. . . . I do here pour forth my supplications at the throne of mercy, that that mercy may be poured down upon the people, in a larger measure than the merits of its rulers may deserve, and that your hearts may be turned to justice.

It was Brougham at his finest. Lord Erskine was so moved, he ran from the room in tears. Charles Greville described

* The wife in this instance was Henry VIII's first wife, Katherine of Aragon.

the speech as the "most magnificent display of argument and oratory that had been heard in years." Brougham's cocounsel Denman wrote that this was "one of the most powerful orations that ever proceeded from human lips." Caroline's other solicitor William Vizard wrote to Brougham's brother James, "your brother has today concluded one of the most magnificent speeches ever made in this or any other country." At Brooks's gentleman's club, bookies placed good odds that the bill would be thrown out based on the strength of Brougham's performance.

As Caroline's defense went on, the mob outside continued riotously. On October 11, a mass procession took place as groups in carriages headed to Brandenburg House to deliver yet more addresses of support to the Queen. The procession began with forty-one carriages carrying women from the parish of St. Abbot's in Kensington, all dressed in Caroline white, with Caroline's medals hanging from necklaces. Caroline greeted them, dressed in her now trademark black silk and velvet. She remained standing through the day, warmly greeting all her visitors and gratefully receiving their addresses.

In London, Covent Garden theater was presenting William Shakespeare's *Cymbeline.* The crowd responded with roars to any lines that made them think of Caroline and the trial, such as any mention of a servant turning on her employer (as Demont had turned against Caroline) or a line about a "false Italian." The biggest cheers came near the end of the play, at a line about "The princess of this country."

While most of Brougham's witnesses were noble British people, he also called some Italian servants to the stand. One witness intimated that the Milan Commission had been bribing witnesses to speak out against Caroline and named Giuseppi Restelli, Caroline's former head of stables and a previous prosecution witness, as being involved in this bribery.

Brougham demanded to bring Restelli back out to answer this; disastrously for the prosecution, Restelli had already returned to Italy. At this, Charles Grey, 2nd Earl Grey (leader of the Whigs in the House of Lords), stood to declare if Restelli could not be cross-examined, the entire bill should be abandoned. Grey's support meant that all the Whig-affiliated lords were now firmly on Caroline's side. Brougham pivoted his case to outline how this whole trial was the result of a Tory conspiracy against Caroline.

When Brougham rested his case, public sentiment was that Caroline would emerge victorious. With the Whigs decidedly behind her, Caroline was welcomed back into society, with the Duke and Duchess of Bedford lending her use of their boxes at Covent Garden and Drury Lane theaters.

The vote on the Bill of Pains and Penalties was held on November 6. One hundred twenty-three of the lords voted for, and 95 against. This was not enough of a majority for the bill to pass. A statement from Caroline was read, in which she said that if they dropped it, she would not reveal intimate secrets about Prinny. If the bill passed and went on to the House of Lords, she would make these public revelations.

On November 10, a second vote was held, which passed 108 to 99.

Liverpool declared that with the country in such a frenzy, and with the vote so close, the bill would not progress. Caroline was acquitted.

She learned the news from her side room, playing backgammon. Caroline declared herself "Regina still, in spite of them!" She wept all the way back to Brandenburg House.

Caroline's victory was celebrated by a crowd that soon encompassed all of central London. City businesses shut down for the day as the population took to the streets to celebrate what they felt was their victory along with hers. Anne Cobbett wrote, "This is the triumph of the people, and they do enjoy it . . . her triumph is ours."

And indeed, the mob's unrelenting support had certainly been as crucial as Brougham's memorable speeches. Without them, perhaps Liverpool would have continued to pursue the bill. But, knowing how close the kingdom was to full-on revolution, he chose to let the case rest.

That night, the city was again lit up with more candles than when London celebrated Wellington's victory over Napoleon at Waterloo, all to celebrate the Queen's victory.* Cannons and guns were fired in celebration, and the mob went full-on *Purge* with looting and rioting well into the night. Effigies of the traitorous Demont and Majocci were burned. Caroline was celebrated, as were Brougham and Denman. Charlotte's widower, The Leo, ordered his house lit up in honor of his mother-in-law.

The festivities were not limited to London. As word spread of her victory, similar celebrations were held throughout England, Scotland, and Ireland. Edinburgh was in an uproar, with celebratory fireworks set off from St. Giles Cathedral. In the town of Royton, celebrations for Caroline were combined with those for the recent revolutions in Spain, Portugal, and Naples; toasts were raised to more revolutions "till the whole civilised world has adopted representative governments on the principle of Universal Suffrage." Throughout Lancashire, the county that had borne witness to the Peterloo Massacre, joyous festivities were held in towns and villages. Bonfires burned, church bells rang, and magistrates cowered at home in fear of the crowds.

Throughout the kingdom, offices of newspapers who had

* Maybe because this time, the mob smashed the windows of any house found not to have lit candles in their windows.

dared to present anti-Caroline points of view were torched. In London, *The Times* (which had always been on Caroline's side) was celebrated. They declared this a triumph of public opinion; unlike the execution of Marie Antoinette, this time Britain's people had saved their Queen. And unlike in France, the government neutered the mob's chaos by giving them this victory.

Caroline's team released a message to the nation thanking them for their support and reiterating her innocence. But inside Brandenburg House, Caroline was exhausted both physically and emotionally. She wrote to Campbell:

> *This business has been more cared for as a political affair, than as the cause of a poor forlorn woman. [But no matter!] I ought to be grateful; and I reflect on these proceedings with astonishment . . . That I should have been saved out of the Philistines' hands is truly a miracle considering the power of my enemies and their chiefs.*

She signed off noting how she felt:

> *Very unwell, fatigued, and [exhausted]; I wonder my head is not quite bewildered with all I have suffered—and it is not all over yet with me. That cruel personage will never let me have peace so long as I stay in this country; his rancor is boundless against me.*

Caroline had been chosen as a symbol for a cause she did not necessarily support. She was fifty-two years old, ill, and tired. Radical allies like Wood had hopes for her to continue on as a political figure, but she no longer had the energy for nor interest in continuing to play that role. She had come to England to face off against Prinny, and had won. Now she yearned to rest.

A Thanksgiving service in Caroline's honor was arranged by Wood at St. Paul's Cathedral on November 29. Brougham later wrote that "it was with great difficulty that we could get her [to the service]." Caroline was tired of playing this public role, but she relented to provide her fans with one more public appearance.

A procession from Brandenburg House to St. Paul's was attended by the usual huge crowd. Caroline rode in a state carriage led by six chestnut horses, with 140 men in horseback in attendance. One estimate was that over fifty thousand people witnessed the procession. Many of those processing carried banners, the first of which read "The Queen's Guard—the People."

As had been the case with her processions to the trial, women stood on rooftops to watch her pass, and everyone wore white ribbons. Caroline herself was resplendent in a white silk pelisse trimmed in white fur, a white turban with a white veil on her head. She was greeted by Wood and members of the city council. Sixty women clad all in white preceded her into St. Paul's for the service. She was the people's champion, the People's Princess, seemingly adored by all just as she had hoped back in Braunschweig when she first met Malmesbury. But Caroline, Queen of Great Britain and Ireland and Queen of Hanover, was longing to retire to her quiet life back in Italy.

CHAPTER TWENTY-FOUR

# NOT INVITED TO THE PARTY

The aftermath of this legal decision was similar to the 2021 hearing that dissolved Britney Spears's conservatorship. If you don't recall that story, movements on an international scale, both online and in person, rallied to *Free Britney*. Months later, she had a legal victory. And then her supporters weren't sure what to do next. Spears was posting videos of her twirling on Instagram, her conservators continued on with their usual work, and life seemed to continue on mostly as it had before.

Similarly, after Caroline's acquittal, the mob was unclear on their next steps. Caroline quickly found that nothing had really changed. She demanded her rights as Queen: a crown, an increased annuity, a royal residence, and restoration of her name in the liturgy. Prinny, furious at her legal victory, did everything he could to stand in her way. He needn't have tried so hard, as the slow-motion decision-making abilities of Parliament bureaucracy stalled things all on their own. She was told that no decision on her annuity could be made until the House of Commons reconvened in January, meaning she couldn't financially afford to return to Italy and Pergami until then.

So, she resumed correspondence with him, much to the

annoyance of her lawyers, not just because the letters could be used against her if they were seized, but also because of the cost of sending mail across the Alps during the winter months.

And much like the media turned on Spears after her legal victory, the popular press had a new newspaper to contend with: the staunchly anti-Caroline Sunday paper *John Bull.* The publisher, an enterprising dirtbag named Theodore Hook, claimed the paper stood for "the Truth, and King and Constitution." Much like how twenty-first century English tabloids offered tidbits provided anonymously by courtiers, Hook's paper supplied anti-Caroline rhetoric from Prinny's friends.

In particular, *John Bull* singled out the ladies known to visit with Caroline, shaming and mocking them. Brougham's wife, Marianne, it claimed, had been pregnant before their marriage. Rumors of Anne Damer's lesbianism were revived. The paper also claimed Caroline had a problem with alcohol, nicknaming her home "Brandyburg House." Damer and Villiers continued to visit, but most other Whig women avoided her so as to stay out of *John Bull.*

The paper's success was a testament to a change in public sentiment. Up to ten thousand copies a week were sold, causing Prinny to remark that "neither he nor his ministers nor his parliament nor his courts of justice all together had done so much good as *John Bull.*" Other satirical attacks were printed in the form of cartoons of her and Pergami in a variety of sexual situations, reminding the public of the accusations against her despite her acquittal.

Caroline turned to her usual hobbies to keep spirits high, including hosting parties for whoever might attend. She warmly greeted all who came to call, including her son-in-law, The Leo, who she was able to meet for the first time.

She pestered Liverpool with her ongoing complaint that she had not been provided with a royal residence, but he brushed her off. When Parliament met again following the Christmas holidays, the Whigs put forward a motion to restore her name to the liturgy; this was defeated 310 to 209. On January 31, Caroline delivered a message to Parliament stating that she would not accept a payout unless the liturgy issue was resolved to her satisfaction. Liverpool ignored her request, and made sure she knew they would provide her with £50,000, or $7 million today per year if she would leave the country.

On March 3, against the advice of Brougham and Cobbett, Caroline accepted the payout. She wanted to return to Italy, and Pergami, and the quiet life in which her illness was not so frequently triggered. By taking this payment, she abruptly lost her political power; she was no longer seen as the People's Princess. Caroline no longer needed their support, and the mob moved on to protest other outrages.

Prinny had spies watching her increasingly erratic behavior. In March, a mysterious Italian man known only as Baron Bisquetti arrived; some wondered if this was Pergami in disguise, but whoever it was vanished after a brief stay. Caroline's household staff was mostly foreigners, including Italians. She stated, "those that she had with Her were well known for their fidelity . . . and that she could place her life in their hands."

Caroline prepared for her move back to Italy. She wrote of wanting to "recruit her health by an excursion on the continent," as she had been suffering from "an extreme state of anxiety." She hired a carpenter to make fifty packing cases for her, each to bear a tin plate reading *Her Majesty the Queen of England*.

Prinny was making his own plans at this time to hold his long-delayed coronation. He hoped to be on par with the extravagant affair Napoleon had staged when he named himself Emperor. Caroline was specifically not invited to attend. But, in need of funds to get to Italy, she threatened to crash the coronation if she were not provided money from the government to cover her travel expenses. When none was offered, she stuck with the plan.

She wrote to Prinny, asking what dress he would like her to wear to his coronation. Liverpool responded on his behalf with a firm statement that she was not invited. Specifically, he wrote to her that it was Prinny's "Royal Pleasure that the Queen shall not attend."

Caroline and her friends and advisers set about deciding her next move, as Prinny's spies kept an eye on her plans. One rumor was that Caroline was leveraging her friendship with Wood and other city officials to plan her own coronation, in which she would be named Queen of the city.

Caroline invited her team over for a dinner party at Cambridge House, her latest leased home in the city. The guest list included Villiers, Denman and his wife, Brougham and his wife, and London's Lord Mayor. Altogether, there were twenty women and thirty men, mostly Whigs, all of whom knew their presence would be reported unflatteringly in *John Bull.* If any of these guests tried to dissuade her from crashing Prinny's coronation, which surely someone must have, she was still determined to follow through with Operation Coronation Crash.

Her longtime servant, John Hieronymous, noted that this stubbornness had always been part of her personality. He wrote that he "had been with her seven years and never knew of one instance of her Majesty altering her resolution when once she had made up her mind even if it would have cost her her life."

With Prinny's coronation in one month, Caroline had a dress made for her big moment. Knowing she would be riding in a yellow state carriage, she chose a complementary purple muslin dress with a silver brocade petticoat and a purple scarf. Her trademark hat was huge and feathered, as always. She arranged for matching ensembles for her attendants, Lady Hamilton and Lady Hood, with whom she would ride to the coronation, along with her friend Captain Hesse* and Willikin.

On June 25, she submitted a formal application to be crowned Queen. This worked its way through the bureaucracy, and finally, on July 12, the Privy Council determined that, in fact, this was indeed Prinny's decision alone. His response, unsurprisingly, was still no. On July 15, Caroline wrote to the Archbishop of Canterbury, requesting she be crowned one day after Prinny. This request was denied. In a surprise twist, Prinny's friend, (and longtime Caroline enemy) the Duke of Wellington, sent along his invitation so she would be permitted inside. Caroline did not intend to use this; she would enter the Abbey as Queen, not as an ordinary ticket holder.

And so, on coronation day, July 19, she and her entourage made their way to Westminster Abbey to cause a scene.

---

* The soldier who had maybe been both her lover as well as Princess Charlotte's lover.

CHAPTER TWENTY-FIVE

# Final Days

The streets were again filled, though the mood was celebratory and not violent. By this time, most of Caroline's upper-class support had cooled. But the lower- and working-classes continued to support her. As she made her way to Westminster Abbey, some called out her former catchphrase, "The Queen forever!" but the mood was mixed with her supporters and those now against her. Others, like Brougham, joined the crowd out of curiosity to see what would happen.

Caroline stepped out of her carriage at Westminster Abbey on the arm of Lord Hood. They approached the West Cloister entrance, the one used today for tourists to enter the Abbey. The guards had been given strict instructions to keep her out at any cost. As such, the doorkeeper wouldn't let her pass. Cobbett recorded that "she was actually thrusted back by the *hands of a common prize-fighter.*"* She then walked to the East Cloister door, near where the gift shop is now housed. This doorkeeper also refused to let her inside.

Caroline called for her carriage. As she was driven around to the next doorway, some in the crowd cheered, while others called, "Shame!" Midway there, Caroline changed her plans.

---

* Cobbett was not there in the doorway. Some sources suggest that Prinny had hired prizefighters to guard the doors against Caroline, but that is not confirmed.

She was driven instead across the road and down to nearby Westminster Hall, where invited guests were assembling.

One of these was Miss Elizabeth Robertson, who described the scene as follows:

> We were electrified by a thundering knock at the Hall door, and a voice without loudly said, 'The Queen—open!' A hundred red pages ran to the door, which the porter opened a little, and from where I sat I had a glimpse of her, leaning on Lord [Hood], followed by Lady [Hood] and Lady Anne Hamilton, standing behind the door on her ten toes, with the crossed bayonets of the sentry under her chin . . . [Caroline] was raging and storming and vociferating, 'Let me pass; I am your Queen, I am Queen of Britain.'
>
> The Deputy Lord High Chamberlain then arrived and "with a voice that made all the Hall ring, cried, 'Do your duty, shut the Hall door,' and immediately the red pages slapped it in her face.

Caroline would not be stopped. She headed in her carriage back to Westminster Abbey to try the door at Poets' Corner. There, Sir Robert Harry Inglis* was waiting for her. He recorded their conversation as follows:

"Madam," he said, "it is my duty to inform your Majesty that there is no place for your Majesty in the royal box, or with the royal family."

Caroline replied, "I am sorry for it."

Inglis then accompanied her back to her carriage. As she left, some in the crowd shouted, "Shame!" "Go away!" or "Go back to Pergami!"

Five hours later, Prinny arrived for his ostentatious five-

* He was an ultra Conservative politician, not a prizefighter.

hour coronation ceremony to great cheers from the crowd outside. Their complaints about the cost of living and Prinny's overspending were forgotten in the face of this opulent event. The coronation cost £243,000,* and it was apparent. Prinny entered through the Great West Door (the huge one where Princess Diana, for instance, entered to walk down the aisle for her wedding), wearing a £24,000† velvet robe with a twenty-seven-foot-long train decorated with gold stars,‡ and an enormous Spanish hat mounted with ostrich feathers. Caroline may have made feathers her trademark, but ostrich feathers were also long the symbol of being Prince of Wales. Prinny's hat was removed and replaced by his royal crown, indicating his promotion from Prince to King.

Caroline, in her own feathered hat, returned to Brandenburg House, where she remained alone in her bedroom for four hours. When she finally emerged to join her friends, Hamilton noted:

> Her Majesty put on the semblance of unusual gaiety, but the friends who were around her observed that though she laboured hard to deceive them, she only deceived herself, for while she laughed, the tears rolled down her face—tears of anguish so acute that she seemed to dread the usual approach of rest.

Before heading to bed at three o'clock in the morning, Caroline called for "a tumbler of water and some magnesia, putting in such a quantity of the latter that it was literally a tumbler of paste, to which she superadded a few drops of laudanum." Clearly, her stomach issue had flared up from

---

* Over $34 million in 2025 amounts.

† Over $3 million today.

‡ Later purchased by Madame Tussaud to adorn her Prinny waxwork.

the excitement of the day, and she needed the pain relief of opiates, which she had been relying on more heavily of late.* Hamilton and Wood both tried to prevent her from consuming this strange paste-like concoction, but Caroline used a spoon and swallowed it all.†

A few days later, she hosted a party where Denman saw her "dancing, laughing and romping, with spirits frightfully overstrained." She was working on a new scheme to build upon support Brougham had helped her garner in Edinburgh and elsewhere in Scotland; she hoped to visit there to help fan these flames.

However, Caroline was by now behaving erratically, perhaps from overreliance on laudanum. She became paranoid, firing Lord and Lady Hood for imagined slights against her (though the couple remained living with her). To replace them as chamberlain and mistress of the wardrobe, she hired commoners named Mr. and Mrs. Wood,‡ perhaps because of the affection she had for their young child. Yet, the Hoods remained by her side, accompanying her on July 30 to Drury Lane Theatre, which presented, as were many theaters in town, a re-creation of Prinny's coronation (without an appearance by a Caroline stand-in).

Caroline was noticeably ill on the return home from this outing, becoming "very sick and had much pain in her bowels." Dr. Holland came to see her. "Do you think I am poi-

* The side effects of laudanum, as noted previously, would likely have exacerbated her preexisting constipation, causing her more harm in the long run.

† Of the ingredients to be worried about here, don't discount water. Water in London in this time was not safe to drink. It may have been drawn from the polluted River Thames, from a polluted well, or from contaminated rain barrels. Hopefully Caroline at least boiled this before she drank it.

‡ Seemingly no relationship to Alderman Matthew Wood or his son Reverend John Wood, both of whom continued to visit with Caroline.

soned?" Caroline asked, perhaps in her usual dry joking manner or perhaps in a foggy state, asking a legitimate question. After all, back in her Pesaro days, there had been fears of poisoning.

Her condition was so dire that Holland summoned Dr. Richard Ainslie and Dr. Warren, two of Prinny's physicians. The three conferred and agreed that Caroline's condition was terminal. Perhaps at her request, they bled her. They broke the news to her that she was dying and recommended she destroy any papers she didn't want to be viewed following her death.

Hamilton wrote that Caroline "astonished them all by the greatness of her mind; for her Majesty did not betray the slightest agitation, but immediately and coolly answered, 'Oh yes, I understand you; it shall be done.'"

And so Caroline stayed up through the night, burning letters and papers along with her maid Mariette Bron. She summoned Hieronymus, ordering him to burn more documents in a kitchen fire, including her memoirs. She then sorted some trinkets, wrapping each in papers for different friends, and went to bed.

The next day, August 2, she summoned Brougham, Denman, and two other lawyers to make her will. As per Denman:

> We . . . were received with the most unselfish kindness. The Queen was lying on a sofa-bed without curtains; she sat up in it, her head bound with a silk handkerchief, the face flushed, the eyes remarkably bright. She spoke cheerfully, though sensible of her danger.

She instructed that she wanted to be buried in Braunschweig and for her tomb to read only "Here lies Caroline of Brunswick, the injured Queen of England." She named Willikin her residuary legatee. Pergami's daughter Vittorine was to inherit the Villa Vittoria.

Hamilton and the Hoods remained steadfast by Caroline's side. After hearing the finished will read out loud to her, Caroline "put her hand out of bed and signed her name . . . in the steadiest manner possible. In doing so she said with great firmness—'I am going to die, Mr. Brougham, but it does not signify.' Brougham said, 'Your Majesty's physicians are quite of a different opinion?' 'Ah,' she replied, 'I know better than them. I tell you I shall die, but I don't mind it.'"

In unrelenting pain, Caroline fell into a delirious state in which she called out and wailed to see Willikin. Unbeknownst to her, Willikin himself was weeping nearby, forbidden to visit her by the doctors. The only other names Caroline uttered were those of her other beloved foster children: Vittorine Pergami and the young Wood boy. Hamilton wrote that Caroline's cries "could be heard in all the adjacent rooms."

Caroline wished to take communion, but no clergyman arrived. She told her lady's maid, Mariette Bron, to let her sister, Louise Demont, know that Caroline forgave her for her negative testimony. Bron was able to briefly cheer Caroline with news that she and Hieronymus were now engaged. Caroline, delighted, joined their hands on the couch upon which she lay.

At 10:25 p.m. on August 7, Dr. Holland closed her eyelids and declared, "All is over."

Queen Caroline was dead, age fifty-three.

CHAPTER TWENTY-SIX

# A CROWN FOR A QUEEN

Caroline's death was announced in *The Times* on August 8 as follows:

> The tragedy of the persecutions and death of a QUEEN is at length brought to its awful close; and thousands—we may say millions—of eyes will be suffused in tears when they shall read in this column that CAROLINE OF BRUNSWICK is no more . . . She died as she had lived, a Christian heroine and a martyr . . .

Publisher James Catnach rushed to print a memorial broadsheet that included a rhyme called *A Lament for Caroline, Rose of England*, as well as the following obituary:

> We have the heart-rending task of announcing to our readers that Caroline, our beloved Queen is no more. She died at 10 o'clock Tuesday night, to the inexpressible grief of the whole British nation . . . From the moment of her illness she entertained no hopes of recovery but observed to those around her that she

> **had undergone many Trials and Troubles, but this would be the last. When the melancholy tidings arrived in town the most poignant grief was visible in every countenance.**

Prinny was en route to Ireland when Caroline's illness progressed and was in Dublin when news of her death reached him on August 12.* He seemed somewhat affected by the news, walking quietly around his cabin for most of the night. By morning, he was back on his bullshit, drinking too much whisky and singing "many joyous songs." He conveyed a message that he saw no need for national mourning, but allowed a compromise calling for mourning within the royal court for the minimum period of three weeks.

Even in death, Caroline was making things awkward for the government. While Liverpool was fine sending her body to Braunschweig for burial, he refused her demand to install a plate on her coffin that would read *Here lies Caroline of Brunswick, the injured Queen of England.* Her executors, however, saw to it that this plate was engraved. The night before her funeral, they removed the tasteful Latin plate Lord Chamberlain's officials had already installed, replacing it with a plaque bearing her requested phrase.

It was lightly raining the morning of August 14 when Caroline's funerary procession headed out from Brandenburg House. Three mourning coaches led the procession, one of which carried a ceremonial crown on a black-and-gold-embroidered cushion. Behind this was the hearse, drawn by eight black horses, then seven more mourning coaches bearing members of her household, including Willikin. More carriages of supporters brought up the rear, includ-

* Coincidentally, his fifty-ninth birthday.

ing Brougham and Wood, making a procession of sixteen coaches total.

The funerary route had also been a challenge for Liverpool. Like the rerouting of Spencer Perceval's procession due to a fear of riots, Liverpool was wary of pro-Caroline uprisings, which led to his decision to avoid a traditional procession through the city. He knew that, though public opinion about Caroline was mixed among the middle and upper classes, she was still fiercely supported by the working class and by women, who constituted a large proportion of the city (and had already proven themselves capable of public demonstrations of their adoration for her).

Liverpool recommended the funeral procession avoid streets altogether, transporting her coffin down the Thames to the sea. This plan was vetoed by the admiralty, who knew how fond the seamen had been of her and might block the river with their boats.

So instead, a route was planned that would travel around London, specifically avoiding the locations where the most fervent Caroline supporters tended to congregate. For safety, this route was kept secret from the public. But that had never stopped the devoted pro-Caroline mob before. Learning that the government was trying to keep them from paying tribute to their Queen, the mob returned to its highest heights of pro-Caroline passion.

Crowds began to follow the official procession, both people in carriages and on foot. At Kensington Church, the road ahead was blocked by Caroline supporters, forcing the procession to stop outside of Cobbett's house (which was covered in black mourning cloth). Members of the mob began to dig up the street to prevent the procession from moving on, as the crowd began to chant, "Through the city! Through the city!"

The Life Guards, the most senior regiment of the British army, were dispatched to break up the scene, to which the mob cried, "No butchers! Kill the buggers!" And so it was decided that the procession would abandon plans to proceed up Kensington Church Street and, rather, would cut through Hyde Park to steer clear of the city.

At Hyde Park, the mob had shut the gates to prevent this detour and threw mud and stones at the Life Guards who tried to open it. The procession attempted to bypass them at Hyde Park Corner, but market carts had been placed to block that route for them. Park Lane was also barricaded, and soon enough, a brawl had begun between members of the mob and the Guards. The procession made its way into the park, but their exit to the northern route was blocked by more mob members at Cumberland Gate.

The situation escalated as the mob threw bricks at the Guards, who retaliated with their sabers and pistols. Several men were wounded, with two fatalities: carpenter Richard Honey and bricklayer George Francis.

Ultimately, the Chief Metropolitan Magistrate surrendered to the mob and, to prevent further bloodshed, allowed Caroline's procession to proceed through the city.*

The crowd now cheered "Victory!" as they proceeded into London. The procession left the city at five o'clock that evening, heading east.

Caroline's coffin was laid overnight at St. Peter's Church in Colchester. Wood arrived to pay his respects, smuggling the *Injured Queen of England* plate inside his coat. It fell out, causing Hamilton and Lady Hood to erupt into laughter, and a cabinetmaker swiftly affixed the plate to the coffin. When officer of arms Sir George Naylor learned of this, he called for the plate to be removed. Arguments over the plate continued

---

* This man, Sir Robert Baker, lost his job for this action.

until midnight when Naylor removed the *Injured Queen* plate and replaced the Latin one.

The next day, Caroline's coffin was loaded onto a vessel at Harwich, where the dock was filled with mourners both on foot and in the many boats crowding the harbor, their flags at half-mast. In his memoirs, Brougham described how moving he found this scene, particularly at the sight of Captain Manby, one of Caroline's alleged lovers, weeping on the pier. He then watched Caroline's crimson velvet-covered coffin slowly descend onto a ship to carry her back to Braunschweig.

Caroline's coffin landed at Stade on August 20 and was then taken to Braunschweig, where officials had been warned of potential riots and had taken precautions to bury her late at night to avoid protests. However, Caroline's instigating abilities did not end with her death, as a mob broke through the soldiers, badly crushing some of the mourners.

Caroline's nephew, the new Duke, ordered a hundred maidens to hold flowers and lighted candles and align themselves along the aisles of the cathedral. Caroline's coffin, with a ceremonial crown on top, was placed in the crypt near those of her brother, The Black Duke; her father, Karl Wilhelm Ferdinand; and her heroic ancestor, Henry the Lion. In the crypt, the Reverend Mr. Wolff delivered a prayer in German and the maidens gathered in a circle around her coffin, extinguishing their candles.

Caroline finally had her crown.

EPILOGUE

# Caroline's Legacy

Prinny's time as Regent, then King, left a legacy of buildings and other artwork that is still admired today. The Georgian and Regency Eras are known for the exquisite workmanship of furniture, architecture, art, and literature that he oversaw. Prinny himself is little remembered, and when he is, it is mostly for his weight and unpleasant personality.

In his 2020 book *The Time Traveller's Guide to Regency Britain*, Ian Mortimer wrote:

> [Prinny] is one of the laziest, most vain, spoilt, arrogant, self-indulgent, profligate, uncaring and conceited Englishmen ever to have lived. He is a lecherous, drunken boor; a glutton, a prig and a snob. He does have some positive virtues but they are so heavily outweighed by the negative aspects of his character that to give them priority would be disrespectful to anyone who is forced to put up with him.

His personality has made him mostly unremarkable in the annals of British monarchs, but many of the buildings he oversaw are still admired today. It was under his reign that Buckingham House became Buckingham Palace.* Many of

* Following the demolition of Carlton House, which he'd gone into debt several times over to remodel previously.

his gold pieces from the Carlton House era continue to be part of the royal collection, a testament to his aesthetic taste.

In a 2013 essay, David Graebar quoted Immanuel Wallerstein's habit of referencing the French Revolution of 1789 as the "'world revolution of 1789,' followed by the 'world revolution of 1848.'" The many London riots during Caroline's lifetime compounded through the years, leading to the public pressure that forced Parliament to declare the abolition of slavery (1833), of votes for all men and women over age thirty or those who owned property (1918), and then, votes for all women (1928). The famously white-clad suffragettes echoed the white-clad women supporting Caroline a century earlier. Their violent demonstrations, and those of women around the world, paved the way for more feminist movements such as the one that fought for no-fault divorce (1970 in the US, 2022 in the UK) that would have made her life a whole lot easier.

The ripples of change affected by people brought together by her cause have longer, even more invisible legacies. The working-class people of London and elsewhere, whose passionate legacy of protest and riots, are also not remembered as visually as Prinny. Walk down any older street in London, and you'll see their work in the cobblestones they laid, and the doorways they carved, but their spirited protests are invisible now. What is seen and remembered from this era are the splendid homes and beautiful furnishings purchased by the wealthy and passed on to their descendants.

In London's National Portrait Gallery, there is a large portrait of Caroline sharing a wall with one of Prinny and one of Princess Charlotte. This portrait is the 1804 work by Sir Thomas Lawrence, featuring Caroline in a red dress posing near a bust she had sculpted of her father's head and shoulders. Her steady gaze challenges the viewer, especially as the nearby portraits of Prinny and Princess Charlotte have their subjects looking off to the side. The power of this image is juxtaposed against a nearby family tree, explaining the convoluted succession from Queen Anne through Queen Victoria, which excludes both Caroline and Princess Charlotte. Yet it is through this invisibility that both women's lives profoundly affected world history.

To begin, we need to wrap up a few other people's storylines. Prinny reigned, unpopular to the end, until his death in 1830, ten years after Caroline's demise. His death was the result of gastrointestinal bleeding resulting from a ruptured blood vessel in his stomach. An autopsy later found a large tumor attached to his bladder, and his heart was enlarged with heavily calcified valves. Doctors consulted for this book theorize that his heavy drinking likely led to liver damage, which led to portal hypertension and ultimately, the bleeding that killed him. He was buried in St. George's Chapel at Windsor Castle, where Princess Charlotte had been interred. Prinny never remarried* and, therefore, fathered no legitimate heirs. He was succeeded to the throne by his younger brother, William, who became King William IV.

Though William fathered at least ten children, none were legitimate. The next oldest Prince, Edward, died prior to the birth of his legitimate daughter, who at age eighteen became Queen Victoria. Victoria was Caroline's first cousin once removed and Charlotte's first cousin.

Prince Leopold remained in England for a decade after Prinny's death. He had a brief relationship with a German actress named Caroline Bauer, who was said to strongly resemble the late Princess Charlotte. In 1831, he accepted the

* Though he was outlived by his first wife, Maria Fitzherbert, who lived seven years longer than he did.

newly created position of King of the Belgians, relocating to his new kingdom. He then married Louise of Orleans, twenty years his junior and the daughter of the French King. Together, they had four children.

When The Leo died in 1865, his son succeeded him as Leopold II of the Belgians. This Leopold is viewed today as one of history's worst war criminals for his personal hand in founding the Congo Free State. He never visited the Congo, but conceived of and oversaw forced labor, torture, murder, kidnapping, and the amputation of the hands of workers who did not reach their rubber harvesting quotas. He was the first person to be described as a "crime against humanity."* Today's Democratic Republic of Congo is still dealing with the repercussions of his rule.

Had Charlotte not died, perhaps The Leo would have refused the offer to rule Belgium. Perhaps Leopold II would never have been born, removing his odious effects on the Congo. If Prinny and Caroline had conceived another child, perhaps Victoria would never have reigned or have even been conceived, as there would have then been no need for the royal brothers' baby race. No Victorian era, no Victorian descendants ruling over most of Western Europe during World War I. Caroline's and Charlotte's early deaths provide numerous sliding door alternate histories to consider.

But what traces can we find of Caroline in this timeline? I visited her birthplace of Braunschweig, Germany, to see what evidence remains. Much of the city was destroyed in bombings in World War II and has been rebuilt. The front of Schloss Braunschweig, her family's palace, has been reconstructed in the city square. Two statues out front honor her father, Karl Wilhelm Ferdinand, and her brother Fried-

* In 1890, by George Washington Williams.

rich, The Black Duke. Both men are shown heroically on horseback, a reminder of their roles defending and protecting this city.

The reconstructed Schloss contains the Schlossmuseum, current custodians of several artifacts from Caroline's lifetime. One of the first objects you see is a bust of Caroline from 1821, the year of her death. The artist, Peter Turnerelli, also created a bust of Princess Charlotte shortly before her death. Perhaps Caroline spoke with him about his time with her daughter. The family resemblance between the two is strong when considering this bust and the portrait of Princess Charlotte in London's National Portrait Gallery. No wonder Prinny had such a visceral dislike of a daughter who was a copy-paste of his estranged wife.

A display case in the Schlossmuseum contains nineteenth-century prints of Caroline in a feathered hat as well as one of Pergami, handsome as ever. Next to these is an example of a coin minted in Braunschweig following the verdict of Caroline's second trial. It was touching to see that even as she faced so much difficulty in Britain, her homeland had continued to support her in this way.

Her only remaining family home in Braunschweig is Schloss Richmond, her mother's English-style summer palace. When I met my guide at this site, her first question was if I was surprised by its dimensions. It is startlingly small for a palace. It's just big enough for a large dining room, adjoining rooms for after-dinner chat, and bedrooms upstairs. Caroline's mother, Augusta, had the nearby landscape designed to resemble her childhood home in Richmond. Caroline, who spent time here, may have gazed out at the gardens and imagined herself in England. Maybe when she spent time in the gardens of Greenwich Park or Brandenburg House she would think how they resembled this place.

The interior of the Schloss has been maintained to resemble its original design. The dining room walls are decorated with artwork inspired by the ruins of Pompeii, recently uncovered and trendy at the time it was built. Caroline would have looked at these images, dreaming of a future in which she could visit Italy to see them for herself.

I felt Caroline's memory most strongly at Braunschweiger Dom, the grand medieval cathedral. During her lifetime, only the royal family attended services here; today it is home to a vibrant church community. Caroline's coffin is still in the same crypt where she was interred in 1821. When walking in, The Black Duke's memorial is the first thing you see. At the center of the room on an elevated platform, his coffin is draped in black fabric with two black flags at each side. His popularity has caused the church to cordon off the crypt except for guided tours, as too many visitors were plucking threads or tassels off his coffin.

To the left of this is Caroline's coffin. Seeing it in person was the first time I really felt her presence in this city. Her coffin is draped in red velvet, her favorite color to wear. Atop a red velvet pillow sits a ceremonial crown. This was the coffin being led through London that incited riots. The one that her friends tried and failed to install a plaque atop of, naming her *The Injured Queen of England*. She grew up anxious to leave Braunschweig and see the world. In her final moments, she chose to have her remains brought back here. The woman who once went by Caroline d'Este in honor of her ancestors would be glad to know her resting place is also adjacent to that of the heroic Henry the Lion.

Caroline's Lake Como retreat, the Villa d'Este, is now a luxury resort. Her smaller property, the Villa Vittoria, is now a boarding school. In the summers, students provide tours of the grounds for visiting tourists. Considering her passion for youth and mentoring children, she would probably appreciate this tribute.

Most of her London homes are no more. Carlton House, where she first lived with Prinny, was demolished in 1826 and replaced with homes known as Carlton House Terrace. Prinny's name and image are all over London. There is a bronze statue of him in Trafalgar Square. King's Cross Station is named after a short-lived statue that had been erected of him on the corner. Regent's Park, King Square, and King Square Gardens are all named for him. His Brighton pleasure palace, now known as the Royal Pavilion, can still be visited and contains many of his gold-plated belongings. But Caroline's memory is still alive in Brighton, where the Caroline of Brunswick Pub advertises itself as the city's "friendliest rock/alternative bar."

Caroline's longtime residence in Blackheath, Montague House, was torn down shortly after she left for Italy in 1816. Some sources claim this was due to structural issues; others claim that Prinny had it torn down out of spite. One brick wall is all that remains of this house in modern-day Greenwich Park. I set out one afternoon to track down this wall, and the bathtub apparently also left behind from the demolition. It's easy to find, as signposts direct visitors to "Queen Caroline's Bath." The tub, like the coffin, is the most real Caroline felt to me during my trip. Her remains were in the coffin, but her vivacious body was frequently in this 1.6-meter-deep tub. During her time, it was not exposed to the elements as it is now. She had it covered by an ornate summer house for privacy. Considering her reputation for bad hygiene, it feels correct for one of the only remaining objects from her life to be the bathtub she used faithfully every day. A plaque on the wall describes her as "the Princess of Wales, later to become QUEEN CAROLINE, wife of George IV." At least here, she's remembered as Queen.

The homes in Mayfair where Caroline stayed during her second trial* have been refurbished into hotels, luxury condos, and private homes. Her temporary home at Brandenburg House is no longer there, though she is the namesake of the Caroline Estate, a housing estate in this area, as well as to nearby Queen Caroline Street.

I found the most fitting tribute to Caroline by accident during my stay in London. I went to visit the Foundling Museum in Bloomsbury out of personal interest. This museum runs out of the building that housed generations of London's abandoned orphans, and provides a moving tribute to the reasons their parents left them there. As I walked closer to the building, I noticed that I was now in a neighborhood called Brunswick Square Park. There are many areas of Britain and in colonized parts of the world named Brunswick or Hanover, after the German territories of the eighteenth-century British monarchs. At first, I presumed this was one like that.

But then signage in the park itself revealed that, in fact, this area was named for Caroline herself. The park had opened around the time of her marriage to Prinny, when she arrived full of optimism for her life as Princess of Wales, and the city was already celebrating her. One remnant of the original landscape is an exceptionally large plane tree, known as the Brunswick Plane. This tree, still thriving, is thought to have been one of the original trees planted when the park was created. It is the second-oldest plane tree in London, and is one of London's ten great trees.

The square was designed to provide an airy countryside feel for the health of the foundling children raised in the nearby hospital. For over two centuries, generations of children grew up using this park for outdoor activities, which seems a perfect tribute to a woman who loved to care for

* Not technically a trial.

abandoned children. Today, it is a peaceful green space enjoyed by the public.

Caroline of Brunswick, when she's remembered at all, is often dismissed as an unsuitable consort to an unpopular King. What I found when researching this book and retracing her steps was evidence of a misunderstood woman who refused to compromise her principles or dull her personality to fit in. Like so many women in history, her legacy has been largely controlled by what others wrote about her. When Queen Victoria took the throne in 1837, she set about a lengthy quest to return the British monarchy to what it had been in the early days of George III and Queen Charlotte. With royals as role models of perfect family life, the parents of the nation had no room to remember the toxic relationship of Caroline and Prinny. As in *Bridgerton*, history was refashioned as though Princess Charlotte's mother was not worth mentioning.

Caroline's story may be largely forgotten, but her memory lived on among the working-class people who adored her. Thirty years after her death, a London crossing sweeper recalled, "She was a woman, she was. The yallers, that is the king's party was [against] her."

★ ★ ★ ★ ★

# ACKNOWLEDGMENTS

It has been a privilege and a pleasure to work with my editor, Eden Railsback. Thank you for taking a chance on me. This book, and Caroline, needed a ferocious champion just like you. I am also grateful to copy editor Cathy Joyce, senior production editor Stephanie Van de Vooren, and art director Mary Luna.

I'm eternally grateful to Amy Bishop-Wycisk, my equally ferocious agent. Thank you for picking me out of the slush and for believing in me and this project.

For the opportunity to visit sites related to Caroline's life in Braunschweig, I am grateful to the Braunschweig Tourism Bureau and to Ilse Geiler for providing me access to Schloss Richmond; Marc Bühner and Ms. Evensberg at Braunschweiger Dom for arranging and providing me with a tour, including to Caroline's crypt; and to Helga Berendsen at the Schlossmuseum for speaking with me about Caroline's family and Braunschweig history. Thanks also to Nicole Brüderle-Krug of the Richard Borek Foundation for allowing me use of photographs from her collection.

I wrote this book entirely from the Canadian prairies, and I'm so grateful to the Murray Library at the University of Saskatchewan and to Saskatoon Public Library (and the Saskatchewan Information Library Service Consortium) for either possessing or helping me acquire the books I needed to research. Speaking of the Saskatoon Public Library, thank you to my colleagues for making me laugh and for providing cookies, Timbits, and other treats to keep me going.

Special thanks to Lana Wood Johnson for a) loving Caroline as much as I did, right off the bat, b) suggesting I start a podcast, c) encouraging me to write this book, and d) helping me begin to understand the effect of Caroline's health on her story. Thank you to Allison Epstein for explaining the French Revolution and the Napoleonic Wars to me, repeatedly. I would also like to thank the many people who have spoken with me and helped with the development of this book: Georgina Boyle, Katie Carpenter, Leah Redmond Chang, Carolyn Harris, Jennifer Morag Henderson, Amanda Matta, Annalisa Nicholson, Mallory O'Meara, Shelley Puhak, Bridget Quinn, Annie Reed, and Kate Stephenson. Thank you to Emily Aspland for recommending I visit the Foundling Museum in London.

Many, many thanks to everyone on the Team B Slack for being there for me from the beginning!

Special thanks to my sister, Mary Foster, for helping facilitate my German research trip, translating, and ensuring I got on all the correct trains. Thanks to Karthika Devarajan and Isobel Hall for their advice on understanding the events leading to Princess Charlotte's death; your patients are all so lucky to have both of you on their side, rather than people like Charlotte's actual physicians. Thank you also to Amanda Li and Dagmar Moulton for insight into other olden days medical issues, and thank you to Vivien Hamilton for information about leeches, even when the diagrams grossed both of us out.

Thank you also to the various people on social media who have answered my random questions and helped point me toward helpful resources. Extra very special thanks to my podcast listeners, the Tits Out Brigade. Your support of me and the show means the world and has changed my life.

It turns out that writing a book has an effect on one's entire life, and the following people were crucial in my not losing my mind this past year: Gina Berry, Melanie Cole, Margaret Foster, Susan Foster (who also provided me with last-minute research books from her extensive collection), Jasmine Loewen, Marlene Ma, Caroline MacLeod, Lauren Meads, Ritchie Po, Candace Rutar, Theressa Slind, and Deborah Wong.

Extra special thanks to Hepburn Foster, whose purrs and conversation were the soundtrack for every letter of every word in this book. And a very special thank-you to my boyfriend, Joe Geary, who is nothing at all like Prinny.

# BIBLIOGRAPHY

## PART ONE:
## *Caroline Begins*

### CHAPTER ONE: *Once upon a Time*


*Caroline and Charlotte: Regency Scandals* by Alison Plowden (1989)

*An Injured Queen, Caroline of Brunswick volume 1* by Lewis Melville

"Leechcraft in Nineteenth-Century British Medicine" by K. Codell Carter, PhD (Journal of the Royal Society of Medicine, volume 94, January 2001)

*Princess Auguste: On a Tightrope Between Love and Abuse* by Riëtha Kühle (2021)

*Regency Sex Ed* by Alexandra Vasti (History News Network, October 2024)

*A Royal Affair: George III and His Scandalous Siblings* by Stella Tillyard (2010)

*The Unruly Queen: The Life of Queen Caroline* by Flora Fraser (1997)


### CHAPTER TWO: *We Need to Talk About Prinny*


Brighton Museums: History. https://brightonmuseums.org.uk/visit/royal-pavilion-garden/our-history/

*Caroline and Charlotte: Regency Scandals* by Alison Plowden (1989)

*George IV: King in Waiting* by Stella Tillyard (2019)

*In the Arms of Morpheus: The Tragic History of Laudanum, Morphine, and Patent Medicines* by Barbara Hodgson (2001)

*The King's Wife: George IV and Mrs. Fitzherbert* by Valerie Irvine (2005)

*Poetry and Popular Protest: Peterloo, Cato Street and the Queen Caroline Controversy* by John Gardner (2011)

*The Regency Revolution: Jane Austen, Napoleon, Lord Byron and the Making of the Modern World* by Robert Morrison (2019)

*Royal Mistresses and Bastards: Fact and Fiction 1714–1936* by Anthony J. Camp (2007)

*Scandal: The Sexual Politics of the British Constitution* by Anna Clark (2004)

*Style & Society: Dressing the Georgians* by Anna Reynolds (2023)

*The Time Traveller's Guide to Regency England* by Ian Mortimer (2020)

*The Unruly Queen: The Life of Queen Caroline* by Flora Fraser (1997)

### CHAPTER THREE: *Princess Lessons*

*Caroline and Charlotte: Regency Scandals* by Alison Plowden (1989)

*An Injured Queen, Caroline of Brunswick volume 1* by Lewis Melville (1912)

*Jane Austen's World* by Maggie Lane (1996)

*The Time Traveller's Guide to Regency England* by Ian Mortimer (2020)

*The Unruly Queen: The Life of Queen Caroline* by Flora Fraser (1997)

### CHAPTER FOUR: *"What an Odd Wedding"*

*Caroline and Charlotte: Regency Scandals* by Alison Plowden (1989)

*In These Times: Living in Britain Through Napoleon's Wars 1793–1815* by Jenny Uglow (2014)

*An Injured Queen, Caroline of Brunswick volume 1* by Lewis Melville (1912)

*Mad and Bad: Real Heroines of the Regency* by Bea Koch (2020)

*Poetry and Popular Protest: Peterloo, Cato Street and the Queen Caroline Controversy* by John Gardner (2011)

*Scandal: The Sexual Politics of the British Constitution* by Anna Clark (2004)

*Style & Society: Dressing the Georgians* by Anna Reynolds (2023)

*The Unruly Queen: The Life of Queen Caroline* by Flora Fraser (1997)

*The Wives of George IV: The Secret Bride and the Scorned Princess* by Catherine Curzon (2021)

### CHAPTER FIVE: *Blackheath*

*Caroline and Charlotte: Regency Scandals* by Alison Plowden (1989)

*Contraception: A History* by Robert Jütte (2008)

*A History of Contraception: From Antiquity to the Present Day* by Angus McLaren (1990)

*In the Arms of Morpheus: The Tragic History of Laudanum, Morphine, and Patent Medicines* by Barbara Hodgson (2001)

*An Injured Queen, Caroline of Brunswick volume 1* by Lewis Melville (1912)

*Royal Mistresses and Bastards: Fact and Fiction 1714–1936* by Anthony J. Camp (2007)

*Scandal: The Sexual Politics of the British Constitution* by Anna Clark (2004)

*Spencer Perceval: The Evangelical Prime Minister, 1762–1812* by Denis Gray (1963)

*The Time Traveller's Guide to Regency England* by Ian Mortimer (2020)

*The Unruly Queen: The Life of Queen Caroline* by Flora Fraser (1997)

## CHAPTER SIX: *Willikin*

*Caroline and Charlotte: Regency Scandals* by Alison Plowden (1989)

*An Injured Queen, Caroline of Brunswick volume 1* by Lewis Melville (1912)

*Royal Mistresses and Bastards: Fact and Fiction 1714–1936* by Anthony J. Camp (2007)

*The Unruly Queen: The Life of Queen Caroline* by Flora Fraser (1997)

## CHAPTER SEVEN: *The Not-So-Delicate Investigation*

*Caroline and Charlotte: Regency Scandals* by Alison Plowden (1989)

*An Injured Queen, Caroline of Brunswick volume 1* by Lewis Melville (1912)

*Jane Austen's World* by Maggie Lane (1996)

*Spencer Perceval: The Evangelical Prime Minister, 1762–1812* by Denis Gray (1963)

*The Spirit of the Book volume 1* by Thomas Ashe (1812)

*The Time Traveller's Guide to Regency England* by Ian Mortimer (2020)

*The Unruly Queen: The Life of Queen Caroline* by Flora Fraser (1997)

## CHAPTER EIGHT: *Family Reunion*

*Caroline and Charlotte: Regency Scandals* by Alison Plowden (1989)

*An Injured Queen, Caroline of Brunswick volume 1* by Lewis Melville (1912)

*Jane Austen's World* by Maggie Lane (1996)

*The Lives of the Kings & Queens of England*, edited by Antonia Fraser (1995)

*Mad and Bad: Real Heroines of the Regency* by Bea Koch (2020)

*The Time Travellers Guide to Regency England* by Ian Mortimer (2020)

*The Unruly Queen: The Life of Queen Caroline* by Flora Fraser (1997)

## CHAPTER NINE: *The Regency Era*

*Caroline and Charlotte: Regency Scandals* by Alison Plowden (1989)

*An Injured Queen, Caroline of Brunswick volume 1* by Lewis Melville (1912)

*Jane Austen, Selected Letters*, edited by Vivian Jones, (2004)

*Jane Austen: The World of Her Novels* by Deirdre Le Faye (2003)

*The Regency Revolution: Jane Austen, Napoleon, Lord Byron and the Making of the Modern World* by Robert Morrison (2019)

*Royal Mistresses and Bastards: Fact and Fiction 1714–1936* by Anthony J. Camp (2007)

*Secret Voices: A Year of Women's Diaries*, edited by Sarah Gristwood (2024)

*Spencer Perceval: The Evangelical Prime Minister*, 1762–1812 by Denis Gray (1963)

*In These Times: Living in Britain Through Napoleon's Wars 1793–1815* by Jenny Uglow (2014)

*The Time Traveller's Guide to Regency England* by Ian Mortimer (2020)

*The Unruly Queen: The Life of Queen Caroline* by Flora Fraser (1997)

## CHAPTER TEN: *The Royal Pariah*

*Caroline and Charlotte: Regency Scandals* by Alison Plowden (1989)

*An Injured Queen, Caroline of Brunswick volume 1* by Lewis Melville (1912)

*An Injured Queen, Caroline of Brunswick volume 2* by Lewis Melville (1912)

*The Regency Revolution: Jane Austen, Napoleon, Lord Byron and the Making of the Modern World* by Robert Morrison (2019)

*Lord Byron: The Complete Miscellaneous Prose*, edited by Andrew Nicholson (1991)

*The Unruly Queen: The Life of Queen Caroline* by Flora Fraser (1997)

## CHAPTER ELEVEN: *A Royal Escape*

*Caroline and Charlotte: Regency Scandals* by Alison Plowden (1989)

*An Injured Queen, Caroline of Brunswick volume 1* by Lewis Melville (1912)

*An Injured Queen, Caroline of Brunswick volume 2* by Lewis Melville (1912)

*Lord Byron: The Complete Miscellaneous Prose*, edited by Andrew Nicolson (1991)

*The Regency Revolution: Jane Austen, Napoleon, Lord Byron and the Making of the Modern World* by Robert Morrison (2019)

*The Unruly Queen: The Life of Queen Caroline* by Flora Fraser (1997)

## PART TWO: *Caroline Abroad*

### CHAPTER TWELVE: *No Fucks Given Era*

*The Hanoverian Dimension in British History, 1714–1837*, edited by Brendan Simms and Torsten Riotte (2003)

*An Injured Queen, Caroline of Brunswick volume 2* by Lewis Melville (1912)

*Radical Underworld: Prophets, Revolutionaries and Pornographers in London 1795–1840* by Iain McCalman (1988)

*Royal Mistresses and Bastards: Fact and Fiction 1714–1936* by Anthony J. Camp (2007)

*Secret Voices: A Year of Women's Diaries*, edited by Sarah Gristwood (2024)

*The Unruly Queen: The Life of Queen Caroline* by Flora Fraser (1997)

### CHAPTER THIRTEEN: *A Spy in the Villa d'Este*

*How Napoleon Plotted One of History's Greatest Prison Breaks* by Erin Blakemore (2023, History.com)

*An Injured Queen, Caroline of Brunswick volume 2* by Lewis Melville (1912)

*The Time Traveller's Guide to Regency England* by Ian Mortimer (2020)

*The Unruly Queen: The Life of Queen Caroline* by Flora Fraser (1997)

### CHAPTER FOURTEEN: *Eat, Pray, Fuck*

*Jane Austen: The World of Her Novels* by Deirdre Le Faye (2003)

*An Injured Queen, Caroline of Brunswick volume 2* by Lewis Melville (1912)

*The Unruly Queen: The Life of Queen Caroline* by Flora Fraser (1997)

### CHAPTER FIFTEEN: *Villa Cabrile*

*An Injured Queen, Caroline of Brunswick volume 2* by Lewis Melville (1912)

*The Unruly Queen: The Life of Queen Caroline* by Flora Fraser (1997)

### CHAPTER SIXTEEN: *The Triple Tragedy*

*An Injured Queen, Caroline of Brunswick volume 2* by Lewis Melville (1912)

"Leechcraft in Nineteenth-Century British Medicine" by K. Codell Carter PhD (Journal of the Royal Society of Medicine, volume 94, January 2001)

*Mad and Bad: Real Heroines of the Regency* by Bea Koch (2020)

*Royal Mistresses and Bastards: Fact and Fiction 1714–1936* by Anthony J. Camp (2007)

*The Unruly Queen: The Life of Queen Caroline* by Flora Fraser (1997)

### CHAPTER SEVENTEEN: *The Milan Commission*

*An Injured Queen, Caroline of Brunswick volume 2* by Lewis Melville (1912)

*The Unruly Queen: The Life of Queen Caroline* by Flora Fraser (1997)

### CHAPTER EIGHTEEN: *Caroline's Scheme*

*An Injured Queen, Caroline of Brunswick volume 2* by Lewis Melville (1912)

*Peterloo: The English Uprising* by Robert Poole (2019)

*Poetry and Popular Protest: Peterloo, Cato Street and the Queen Caroline Controversy* by John Gardner (2011)

*The Time Traveller's Guide to Regency England* by Ian Mortimer (2020)

*The Trial of Queen Caroline: The Scandalous Affair That Nearly Ended a Monarchy* by Jane Robins (2006)

*The Unruly Queen: The Life of Queen Caroline* by Flora Fraser (1997)

## PART THREE:
## *Queen Caroline*

### CHAPTER NINETEEN: *Caroline on the Move*

*An Injured Queen, Caroline of Brunswick volume 2* by Lewis Melville (1912)

*Peterloo: The English Uprising* by Robert Poole (2019)

*Queen Caroline* by Sir Edward Parry (1930)

*Radical Underworld: Prophets, Revolutionaries and Pornographers in London 1795–1840* by Iain McCalman (1988)

*Scandal: The Sexual Politics of the British Constitution* by Anna Clark (2004)

*The Unruly Queen: The Life of Queen Caroline* by Flora Fraser (1997)

### CHAPTER TWENTY: *Chaos in the Streets, a Queen in the Sheets*

*An Injured Queen, Caroline of Brunswick volume 2* by Lewis Melville (1912)

*Life in the Georgian Court* by Catherine Curzon (2016)

*Poetry and Popular Protest: Peterloo, Cato Street and the Queen Caroline Controversy* by John Gardner (2011)

*The Time Traveller's Guide to Regency England* by Ian Mortimer (2020)

*The Trial of Queen Caroline: The Scandalous Affair That Nearly Ended a Monarchy* by Jane Robins (2006)

*The Unruly Queen: The Life of Queen Caroline* by Flora Fraser (1997)

### CHAPTER TWENTY-ONE: *Court of Public Opinion*

*Poetry and Popular Protest: Peterloo, Cato Street and the Queen Caroline Controversy* by John Gardner (2011)

*A Queen on Trial: The Affair of Queen Caroline* by E. A. Smith (1993)

*Radical Underworld: Prophets, Revolutionaries and Pornographers in London 1795–1840* by Iain McCalman (1988)

*Royal Mistresses and Bastards: Fact and Fiction 1714–1936* by Anthony J. Camp (2007)

*The Time Traveller's Guide to Regency England* by Ian Mortimer (2020)

*The Trial of Queen Caroline: The Scandalous Affair That Nearly Ended a Monarchy* by Jane Robins (2006)

*The Unruly Queen: The Life of Queen Caroline* by Flora Fraser (1997)

### CHAPTER TWENTY-TWO: *The Trial* *Not Really a Trial*

*Mad and Bad: Real Heroines of the Regency* by Bea Koch (2020)

*Style & Society: Dressing the Georgians* by Anna Reynolds (2023)

*The Time Traveller's Guide to Regency England* by Ian Mortimer (2020)

*The Trial of Queen Caroline: The Scandalous Affair That Nearly Ended a Monarchy* by Jane Robins (2006)

*The Unruly Queen: The Life of Queen Caroline* by Flora Fraser (1997)

### CHAPTER TWENTY-THREE: *The Defense Rests*

Anne Lister's Diaries, West Yorkshire Archive Service, Calderdale, SH:7/ML/E/4

*An Injured Queen, Caroline of Brunswick volume 2* by Lewis Melville (1912)

*Peterloo: The English Uprising* by Robert Poole (2019)

*Poetry and Popular Protest: Peterloo, Cato Street and the Queen Caroline Controversy* by John Gardner (2011)

*Quilts 1700–2010* by Sue Pritchard (2010)

*Radical Underworld: Prophets, Revolutionaries and Pornographers in London 1795–1840* by Iain McCalman (1988)

*Scandal: The Sexual Politics of the British Constitution* by Anna Clark (2004)

*The Trial of Queen Caroline: The Scandalous Affair That Nearly Ended a Monarchy* by Jane Robins (2006)

*The Unruly Queen: The Life of Queen Caroline* by Flora Fraser (1997)

### CHAPTER TWENTY-FOUR: *Not Invited to the Party*

*Scandal: The Sexual Politics of the British Constitution* by Anna Clark (2004)

*The Trial of Queen Caroline: The Scandalous Affair That Nearly Ended a Monarchy* by Jane Robins (2006)

*The Unruly Queen: The Life of Queen Caroline* by Flora Fraser (1997)

### CHAPTER TWENTY-FIVE: *Final Days*

*Poetry and Popular Protest: Peterloo, Cato Street and the Queen Caroline Controversy* by John Gardner (2011)

*Scandal: The Sexual Politics of the British Constitution* by Anna Clark (2004)

*The Time Traveller's Guide to Regency England* by Ian Mortimer (2020)

*The Trial of Queen Caroline: The Scandalous Affair That Nearly Ended a Monarchy* by Jane Robins (2006)

*The Unruly Queen: The Life of Queen Caroline* by Flora Fraser (1997)

### CHAPTER TWENTY-SIX: *A Crown for a Queen*

*An Injured Queen, Caroline of Brunswick volume 2* by Lewis Melville (1912)

National Army Museum: "The Life Guards" https://www.nam.ac.uk/explore/life-guards

*The Trial of Queen Caroline: The Scandalous Affair That Nearly Ended a Monarchy* by Jane Robins (2006)

*The Unruly Queen: The Life of Queen Caroline* by Flora Fraser (1997)

## EPILOGUE:
## *Caroline's Legacy*

*Hope in the Dark* by Rebecca Solnit (2004)

*Jane Austen's World* by Maggie Lane (1996)

*The Lives of the Kings & Queens of England*, edited by Antonia Fraser (1995)

*Radical Underworld: Prophets, Revolutionaries and Pornographers in London 1795–1840* by Iain McCalman (1988)

*The Time Traveller's Guide to Regency England* by Ian Mortimer (2020)

# INDEX

**M**